Books by Robert G. Allen

Nothing Down
Creating Wealth
The Challenge

Nothing Down for the '90s

NEW REVISED EDITION

HOW TO BUY REAL ESTATE
WITH LITTLE OR NO MONEY DOWN

Robert G. Allen

SIMON AND SCHUSTER
New York London Toronto Sydney Tokyo Singapore

Simon and Schuster
Simon & Schuster Building
Rockefeller Center
1230 Avenue of the Americas
New York, New York 10020

Designed by Irving Perkins Associates
Manufactured in the United States of America

9 10

Library of Congress Cataloging-in-Publication Data
Allen, Robert G.
Nothing down for the 90's/Robert G. Allen.—New rev. ed.
p. cm.
Rev. ed. of Nothing down. New rev. ed. © 1984.
Includes index.
1. Real estate investment. I. Allen, Robert G. Nothing down. II. Title.
HD1382.5.A38 1990
332.63'24—dc20 90-10221
CIP

ISBN 0-671-72558-0

To my father, John L. Allen,
the greatest man I have ever known.

Contents

CONTENTS

Nothing Down for the '90s

INTRODUCTION

How Much Proof Do You Need?

You are holding in your hand the latest edition of the book that has sold more copies than any other real estate book in history. More people have used and profited from *Nothing Down* than from any other financial guide. And now it's your turn. You are going to learn the secrets that have helped thousands of Americans participate in the American dream—from buying a first home to getting started in real estate investing. Some have even become millionaires. They may have a head start but they would be the first to say, "It's never too late." So read on. I wrote this book for you. You are in the right place at the right time. Your someday is now.

Unless, of course, you let some "expert" talk you out of it.

When *Nothing Down* was first published, a chorus of "experts" said it was impossible to buy property with no money down. I remember one Realtor® in particular who challenged my thesis on a call-in radio show in Boston. "Mr. Allen," he said with a heavy Boston accent, "I'm a Realtor in the business for twenty-five years and I've yet to see a nothing-down deal."

I reminded him that millions of American veterans buy their first home using a popular government-sponsored, nothing-down program. He reluctantly agreed but countered that he had never seen any "normal" person use nothing-down techniques to make any serious money in real estate.

"What's your net worth?" I asked him.

"I don't think that's any of your business," he shot back.

"I think it is. If you're going to give financial advice, I think you owe it to the listeners to tell us how well you did during those many years while you were 'in the real estate business.' "

He finally admitted that he was worth less than a hundred thousand dollars. (I suspect it was a lot less.)

"Well," I said, "my seminar graduates and I have made millions of dollars doing what I describe in this book. The way I see it, people can either listen to you and end up where you are or listen to me and end up where I am."

With that he hung up.

That's the way it is with experts. They can tell you a thousand reasons why the bumblebee shouldn't be able to fly—but darn if it doesn't baffle 'em all. When *Nothing Down* was released in 1980, another book appeared with the ominous title, *The Coming Real Estate Crash* by Gray Emerson Cardiffe and John Wesley English. These "experts" foretold a calamitous decline in nationwide real estate prices in the 1980s. Citing voluminous statistics and detailed analysis, they predicted that:

—Housing demand would peak in the early 1980s
—The demand for land, and thus its price, would soon drop
—Foreign demand for U.S. real estate would decrease
—Lower inflation, rent regulation, and tax law changes would be disastrous for U.S. real estate prices
—Homeowners were in real danger, and
—Real estate investors should sell their property immediately!

Obviously my message was just the opposite. I predicted that:

—The cost of real estate would continue to increase in the future
—The dream of owning a home would become an impossibility for more and more Americans
—The demand for apartment buildings would increase along with rents

—The sooner you invested, the faster your investment would grow.

The 1980s are now behind us. All of these predictions have now become hindsight. And the *Nothing Down* strategy was right on the money! In most areas of the country, real estate prices increased substantially—some places they even doubled or tripled. Even in those few areas where prices were stagnant or declining—such as Texas—savvy investors were able to pick up fabulous properties at rock bottom prices.

But whether I predicted right and others predicted wrong is not really the point. Savvy investors like you should be able to make big money in any market—no matter which way prices are heading. You just change your tactics to fit the circumstances. If you plan on playing the real estate investment game for any length of time, your target area will go through natural price cycles—from stagnation to boom to bust and back again. You can learn to read the signs, select the proper strategy, and have fun making money in the real estate game—even when prices are dropping like a rock. (More about this in chapter 27: WealthStrategy 2000: The Fastest, Safest Way to Financial Freedom Before the Year 2000.) Just remember before you start, there will always be "experts" telling you it can't be done. And you can either listen to them or show them how right you are.

You may have seen one of the full page ads I ran in *The Wall Street Journal* and other major newspapers in the early eighties. It carried the following headline:

"Send me to any city in the United States. Take away my wallet. Give me $100 for living expenses. And in 72 hours I'll buy an excellent piece of real estate using none of my own money."

By making such a statement, I was trying to show dramatically that, in spite of the experts, I could prove how well these techniques work. It was a gutsy thing to do—even reading that ad now gives me a chill—but I was convinced it was the only way to gain popular acceptance of these ideas. You may remember what happened. In late 1980, I was challenged by the *Los Angeles Times* to live up to my claim. Although I knew I could do it, I didn't relish the thought of negotiating a creative transaction with an *L.A. Times* reporter by my side. On the morning of January 12, 1981, I met Martin Baron, the *L.A. Times* reporter, and together we flew from Los Angeles to San Francisco. When we arrived at the airport, I handed him my wallet and he handed me five crisp twenty-dollar bills. I was now virtually bankrupt with a seventy-two-hour ticking time bomb strapped to my back. If I couldn't pull it off, my reputation would be ruined. Shall we say I was motivated?

The next days were the most harrowing, discouraging, pressure-packed, fast-paced, nerve-wracking, and exciting days of my life. I had literally risked everything to prove a point. And for the first few hours I seriously wondered if I hadn't bitten off more than I could chew. After a slow start, my first offer was accepted approximately twenty-four hours after we landed in San Francisco. It was for a $158,000 condominium in the Diamond Heights section of the city. With that under my belt, and after breathing a huge sigh of relief, I proceeded to sign up six more properties: a condominium and five single-family residences. After fifty-seven hours, two restless nights, 400 miles of searching, countless telephone calls, dozens of written offers, and seven accepted deals, I was totally exhausted. I had accepted offers to buy $722,715 worth of property and I still had $20 left over! Not bad for a few days in San Francisco. I got my wallet back, said my goodbyes to the reporter, checked into a decent hotel by the airport, soaked in the tub for an hour, had a huge room-service celebration banquet, and collapsed for a well-deserved night's rest. Within days, I closed and took title to four of those seven properties.

A few days later, on February 1, 1981, the front page of the *Los Angeles Times* Business Section carried the following headline:

"Buying Home Without Cash: Boastful Investor Accepts Time Challenge—and Wins."

The long and detailed article chronicled the entire story from 6 A.M. Monday until 5:15 P.M. Wednesday. I had done it!

Little did I realize how well my gutsy challenge was going to pay off. The bold article was carried by dozens of newspapers in the *Times* syndicate, and within weeks the story was everywhere. (If you want a free transcript of the full, blow-by-blow story call 1-800-345-3648.) With such wonderful publicity, *Nothing Down,* already a bestseller, went on to sell over one million hardcover copies. Continuing to sell strongly throughout the entire decade of the eighties, it became the largest selling real estate book in history.

Yes, the strategies and techniques I describe in *Nothing Down* really work! But still the experts and skeptics couldn't be convinced. I remember a television show I went on in Houston. After explaining my story, the host said with a sneer, "Yeah, you proved *you* could do it. But I doubt one of our average viewers could do it."

That really ruffled my feathers. I found myself saying the following words, which stunned even me when I heard myself say them: "Anybody can do it. Send me to any unemployment line. Let me select someone who is broke, out of work, and discouraged. Let me teach him in two days' time the secrets of wealth. And in ninety days he'll be back on his feet, with $5,000 cash in the bank, never to set foot in an unemployment line again. . . ."

The host still wasn't convinced. (Skeptics never are.) But as I left the show I began to wonder. "What if I *could* go to any unemployment line . . ." The idea stewed for a year or so and resulted in my going to St. Louis in June 1984. There, the ex-mayor of St. Louis, a former FBI agent, monitored my every move as I selected three people from the unemployment lines of St. Louis and taught them my secrets for two full days. In ninety days one of the three people bought a property, fixed it up, and sold it again for a $5,000 cash profit—all starting with nothing down. (The entire story is told in my 1986 book, *The Challenge*. Call 1-800-345-3648 and I'll send you a free tape that tells more of the details.)

Once again I had proved that my strategies work. I have been challenged again and again by various people in the news media over the past ten years and always with the same result.

I was challenged by a San Diego television station to buy a property with nothing down. I flew in one morning in 1981, bought a condominium that afternoon, and flew home the same day.

I was challenged in Boston in 1982 on a Howard Ruff syndicated television show to take a member of his studio audience and prove that my strategies work. A few weeks later the young man I had picked bought a beautiful home in a Boston suburb with only minimal telephone coaching from me. Of course, it was purchased with no down payment.

In 1987 I was challenged by Regis Philbin in New York City to select a person from his studio audience. I picked a young black woman, flew her to San Diego to attend my intensive investment program, WealthTraining. In less than ninety days after her return to the Big Apple, she found and purchased a nice duplex apartment building. Even more gratifying to me than her financial success was the look on her face as she explained to Regis Philbin how she had done it. She radiated a sense of self-confidence that was worth far more than a million. She knew she could make her dreams come true.

That same year on the San Francisco morning talk show "People Are Talking," Ross and Ann, the two hosts, invited me to select a member of their studio audience. This time I chose Natalie, an attractive woman in her early twenties. She was so excited to be selected. For her it was like winning the lottery. Unfortunately, Natalie passed away unexpectedly a few weeks later of a rare brain aneurysm. It was a shocking reminder to me and my staff of how important it is to pursue your dreams constantly and strive to fulfill your destiny. The woman who was chosen to replace Natalie attended my WealthTraining program and bought a beautiful bargain property within the ninety-day limit. When she appeared on the show to tell her story, the audience was awed at her growth and maturity. Unlike too many women today, she was in control of her destiny.

After so many successful challenges, I can only ask the experts, skeptics, and critics, "How much proof do you need?" For me, the verdict is resounding and final. What you are about to learn is the most powerful set of wealth-building tools you will ever lay your hands on. It has been tested and thoroughly proven over more than a decade. It's a rocket ship loaded and ready to put you into the orbit of financial freedom. So have a seat. Strap on your seat belt. Your countdown has begun:

Five . . . four . . . three . . . two . . . one . . .

CHAPTER 1

You Can Still Make a Fortune in Real Estate!

November 9, 1989.

Will you ever forget that day?

That was the day the Berlin Wall fell. The day freedom finally broke through.

For decades the wall stood as the symbol of the struggle between capitalism and communism. When it collapsed, shouts of joy echoed round the world. Suddenly, freedoms forbidden to the people of Eastern Europe for decades were now accepted and even encouraged—the freedom to vote, to travel, to own property, to start a business. Truly incredible!

Like me, weren't you excited for them?

Then one day it hit me like a falling brick! Freedom was breaking through to millions in Eastern Europe, but it still hadn't dawned on millions in our own country! Very few Americans fully participate in the American Dream. Most are unaware of or afraid to pursue the incredible opportunities that exist all around them. Whole generations stand at the American banquet begging for scraps. It's more than tragedy. It's a travesty. The invisible walls of erroneous belief still hold too many of us hostage.

And I'm not talking about the homeless and underprivileged.

I'm talking about millions of average Americans needlessly trapped in dead-end jobs who have given up on their future. I'm talking about young couples in financial bondage. I'm talking about a generation of young people who don't understand that capitalism is about risk and reward. I'm talking about millions who ache to become financially independent but who hesitate because they are unsure of themselves and don't know where to begin. I'm talking about those who dream big and talk big but who don't take the first necessary step.

I've written this book to teach you how to break through the Berlin Wall in your own life. I want to help you tear down those old worn-out beliefs that have kept you imprisoned for entirely too long. It's time for you to break out! It's time for you to participate in the American Dream. I want to show you how to become financially free.

As you can see from the following chart, we've got some work ahead of us.

As the chart shows, about 20 percent of us rely on some form of charity or welfare to survive. But even those in the bottom fifth of the financial scale are still well-to-do by world standards. Recently a Los Angeles taxi driver with a heavy Russian accent reminded me that people on welfare in America live better than 90 percent of the whole Russian population. Just imagine the plight of a Polish couple who had to wait fifteen years to be eligible for a one bed-

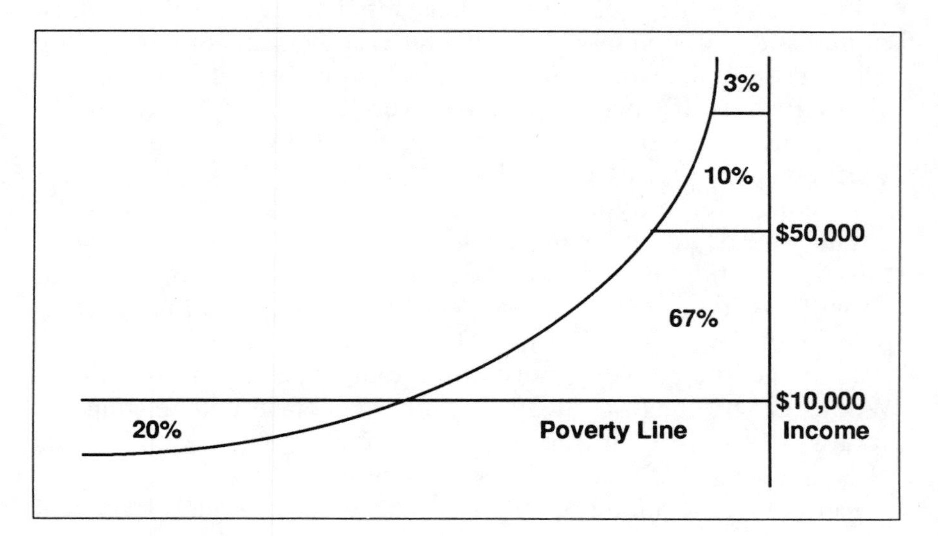

room apartment with a separate bathroom. That puts things in perspective.

As the chart also shows, two-thirds of Americans will live from paycheck to paycheck until the day they die. Many of them earn a nice living because both spouses work. But that's not financial freedom. Only about 10 percent of us achieve a measure of financial security. And only 3 percent break into the blue sky of true financial freedom.

Why do so few Americans ever reach financial freedom? Three reasons:

1. Most people don't believe it's possible or have given up trying.
2. Most people don't have a specific plan for achieving it.
3. Most people aren't willing to do something about it *now*.

I once saw a television commercial portraying an elderly gentleman standing on the docks in New York City. Behind him, in the harbor, a beautiful ocean liner is putting out to sea filled with rejoicing vacationers. The old gentleman looks directly into the television screen and says, referring to the departing ship: "When I had the money, I didn't have the time. Now, I have all of the time in the world, and I don't have the money."

But this would never happen to you, right?

It will unless you do something about it. If you don't, life just slips away. Where did your last ten years go? Poof! They're gone. Are you substantially better off than you were ten years ago? If you are, it's because you had a plan and acted on it. Thousands of Americans bought this book ten years ago and are financially free today! Where are you going to be in the next ten years? In a too-small apartment or in your dream mansion? It's entirely up to you.

You don't have to live from paycheck to paycheck for the rest of your life. You don't have to retire broke. You don't have to believe that "It takes money to make money" or that "The rich get richer and the poor get poorer" or even that "Money talks." You can "make it" financially. This I know for sure.

But let's face something right now. In order to make it financially, you're going to have to become a life-long investor. There just isn't any other way. The lottery isn't going to bail you out.

Forget about winning a million and concentrate on making it the good old-fashioned way.

So let's get right to the basics. I call it the Guns or Butter theory.

Guns or Butter?

In simple terms, the theory states that each of us has a limited amount of income (in case you hadn't noticed). We may spend our precious dollars for guns or butter, or a combination of both. By "guns" I mean investments such as stocks, bonds, precious gems, gold, land, or real estate, all of which you hope will grow in value. "Butter" refers to consumer goods such as stereos, televisions, fancy cars, and other "keeping-up-with-the-Joneses" items that depreciate and lose value over time. As you know, the more you spend on butter, the less you are able to spend on guns, and vice versa. Each decision requires a sacrifice. In fact, the word investment is just a fancy word for "sacrifice." You invest in things which either go up or go down in value. However, if you invest wisely today, your guns will generate enough money to buy you all the butter you could ever want. And conversely, if you put all your money into butter today, you won't have much to show for it tomorrow.

Are you a guns or butter spender? I remember a client who came to me with a tough decision. He and his wife received a $10,000 windfall and were agonizing about how to spend it. His wife wanted new carpets and drapes for their home. He wanted a new car. I convinced them to hold off for a bit longer—and to invest the windfall dollars in a small house a few miles from their own home. Three years later they had more than doubled their money. It was a small sacrifice. But it paid off big.

Each of us is faced with guns-or-butter decisions every day. Money spent is money invested. But remember, it takes *guns* money to make money. The *guns-minded* get richer and the *butter-minded* get poorer. Money spent on guns talks the loudest.

And when it comes to investments, real estate is your biggest and most powerful gun. Real estate has always been and will always be the safest way for the beginner to get started on the road to financial freedom. Just look at its track record since 1970. The median price of a new home in 1970 was $23,400; by 1976, the price for the same home was $44,200. By 1990, that same home cost almost $100,000!

If you are still renting while hoping prices will come down before you buy, you have a long wait. If you are a sophisticated real estate investor, you probably wish you had bought more real estate in 1970. And if your only investment for the future is a savings account, you're just treading water. And that's not good enough, is it?

But what about the future, you ask? Is the real estate game over?

Three things have got to happen for you to grow concerned about the future of real estate. You can start to worry when:

1. People become addicted to sleeping without a roof over their heads.
2. Young families stop making "tricycle motors." (Think about it.)
3. Someone invents a new way to manufacture vast quantities of cheap, vacant land near major cities.

Seriously, can you envision a time when Americans won't be buying and selling real estate? Can you envision a time when Americans won't want to be financially independent? Of course not. That's why I am so confident about real estate. As long as people need roofs and families grow kids, real estate is a sure bet —barring, of course, another Great Depression. In which case, we'll just keep on playing the game at lower prices, because even in a depression, people still need a roof over their heads and families still grow kids.

Yes, it's still possible for you to retire wealthy from your real estate investments. Thousands of my seminar graduates have done it. A retired couple in Arizona earned more in three years than they had earned in an entire lifetime. A young woman in California left a job that paid well because she was earning too much money and having too much fun investing in real estate. A man in Florida made a million dollars in less than three years. Thousands of courageous investors from coast to coast have decided to take matters into their own hands by buying their first piece of investment property. It works!

The Berlin Wall fell because the theories behind it didn't work.

If your financial life is not working as well as you would like, you had better check the theories upon which you are building your future. The theories in this book work marvelously. As you read these words, hundreds of people in hundreds of American cities are investing in choice investment properties using the principles outlined in this book.

Isn't it about time you got into the real estate game?

The question is, which kind of real estate is right for you?

CHAPTER 2

They're Not Making Any More Land

So real estate is the best investment. But what *is* real estate? Real estate is all around you. It's the home you live in. It's the building you work in. It's the factory or warehouse you see next to the freeway. It's the store where you shop. It's the playground where your children play. It's the field where your uncle plants his wheat crop. It's the mountain cabin where you spend your summer vacation.

Real estate is everywhere, because the common denominator of all real estate is land. And land is everywhere. And well-selected real estate always increases in value. Why? Because, as Mark Twain put it, "They ain't makin' any more land." But they are making more and more people every year to populate that land.

But certain kinds of real estate are a better investment than others. Land can be utilized in several different ways, and some kinds of property are increasing in value faster than others because of the way they're used. This story should illustrate my point.

Three wealthy old poker buffs were playing a very important game. The stakes were high. After several hours of playing, there came a hand in which all three of them had been dealt excellent cards. The antes increased, and finally each of them ran out of cash and began to gamble with the deeds to their various real estate holdings. The rancher from Montana began the last round of raises by pledging his entire 10,000-acre ranch, including all of his cattle and equipment. The oil baron from Oklahoma met the challenge by pledging his entire 2,000 acres of oil-producing wells with all of his oil derricks and equipment. The wealthy Texan ended the bidding by offering his seven acres of ground in Texas.

"Seven acres!" gasped the other two partners. "Here we have pledged thousands of acres, and you expect us to accept your measly *seven acres?*"

"Yup," replied the Texan. "My land is right in the middle of downtown Dallas."

Obviously, some ground is more valuable than other ground. And the shorter the supply, the higher the sales price and the higher the probability the property will increase in value.

There are four major categories of land use. *Undeveloped land* is located away from civilization centers and has no immediate development potential. It is the kind of ground that is only good for holding the earth together.

Recreational ground has little use except for limited recreational value. Unless you are a seasonal investor, stay away from recreational property.

The same goes for *agricultural land*. You can tell how much the farmer is making from his land investment by the number of farmers who are selling out. As the story goes, one farmer went to his bank and withdrew $100 in $1 bills. He then stood in front of the bank and sold each $1 bill for 75 cents. When someone asked him why he was doing it, he replied, "Well, it sure beats farming."

The fourth type of land utilization is *urban/suburban*. Urban/suburban land is more valuable because it is near population centers and because of the various uses to which it can be put. It can be sold as individual building lots for homes. It can have apartment buildings built on it, or factories or warehouses. And it can house various commercial businesses such as retail stores or office complexes. This is the kind of property you should invest in. With this kind of land the factors of supply and demand will be working in your favor.

For the beginning investor, the safest investment is in income property. This may include rental homes, apartment buildings, office buildings, shopping centers, retail and wholesale buildings, hotels, motels, rest homes, warehouses, and industrial parks. Of the properties listed above, rental homes and apartment buildings offer the least risk and require the least amount of expertise.

A great deal of money can be made by finding older properties or poorly maintained properties, adding a coat of cosmetic paint, giving the property a general face lift, and reselling the property on the market for a much higher price than you purchased it for. This type of investing is called the "fixer-upper." The quickest money is made in this kind of real estate, but it takes a dedicated individual who knows something about fixing up buildings. Personally, this is not my cup of tea. I can barely tell which is the right end of a hammer.

The type of investment that is universally beneficial—whether or not you have the special training and personality to fix up run-down real estate—is choosing well-constructed properties in a growing area. The long-run appreciation from such an investment may be slow, but it will be steady and predictable. And it does not require a lot of supervision or work to bring such a building up to rentable standards. Don't be frightened away from investing in real estate because you don't understand a thing about repairs. Just buy solid property and hang on to it.

Several general principles will guide you as you invest in real estate. First, become very familiar with your own local real estate by studying properties on the market. Learn all about your particular city, its growth patterns, its depressed areas, where the path of growth is likely to extend. The more you know, the more prepared you will be to invest. And the more prepared you are to invest, the more confident you will become in your ability to spot a good opportunity. How do you find this information? Talk to real estate agents, pick an area of town, and drive through the neighborhoods noting all of the "For Sale" signs . . . and stop and ask questions. Check with your city or county planning departments, which will be more than happy to tell an interested citizen about real estate areas. Use your common sense and always ask questions. Is this area growing or declining? How fast will the city grow and in which directions? Would I like to live here myself?

A good opportunity always goes to the investor who knows how to locate a good investment (something that only comes through practice) and who has the courage to act quickly.

Second, stay away from raw land—at least at first. This does not mean that land in predevelopment stages is a bad investment; it simply means that predeveloped land has some basic disadvantages that increase the risk for the beginning investor—it takes a greater degree of sophistication to invest in raw land. One big disadvantage: Land does not generate a cash flow. Mortgage payments must be made out of the investor's pocket. That's why it's called an "alligator" investment—it eats up an investor's capital through monthly payments, but it does not produce any cash flow. The beginning investor soon runs out of money to feed his alligator a daily diet of principal, interest, and taxes. When you don't feed an alligator, it becomes very hungry and it eats you alive; many a property has been foreclosed because the owner couldn't keep the payments current.

Third, the safest kind of investment for the beginner is an income-producing property. Income-producing property is the kind of real estate that is rented out to a tenant: an apartment building, rental home, commercial retail space, office building, or industrial/warehouse building. The tenant pays rent that should be adequate to make your mortgage payment, pay operating expenses, and produce a small cash flow as a return on your investment. As a beginner you should concentrate on buying small houses (for rental) and small apartment buildings. Your first purchases of income-producing property will give you the knowledge, experience, and confidence you need to venture into other areas. However, I have found in my experience that the easiest and safest dollars can be made by concentrating one's efforts in homes and apartment buildings. I like to invest my money in a sure thing. I know that business and commercial properties are dependent upon a healthy economy and sound business management for success. This last requires sophisticated knowledge and experience. On the other hand, homes and apartment buildings will always be in demand, regardless of what the economy may do. Housing is a basic need. People must live somewhere; they have no choice. It might as well be on your property.

Fourth, as often as you can, you should try to buy your properties with as much leverage as possible, in other words, with little or no money down. This book was written to tell you how.

Fifth, since well-selected real estate income properties are steadily increasing in value, the sooner you buy, the sooner you will reach your financial goals.

It all sounds so easy, you say. If it is so easy to become wealthy through real estate investing, then why isn't everybody doing it? I think I would be safe in saying that most Americans now realize that real estate investment is one of the surest and safest ways to financial freedom. There is, therefore, only one explanation why so few Americans fail to reach financial independence. So few are willing to pay the price. So few are willing to take the risks. So few are willing to set their sights high and start climbing. Only a small number of those who read this book will actually buy any real estate, even though they may agree with the concept. And the difference between the failures and the successes is the subject of our next chapter. Goals.

CHAPTER 3

Why Financial Goals Don't Work

Most people choose real estate because it's the fastest, safest way to financial freedom. And who doesn't want financial freedom? If you make enough money, the world is yours! Right?

That's one of the reasons a lot of people go to work each day. In the back of their minds they say, "If I work and save long enough, I can retire and do what I really love." Some yearn for a faster way. They play the lottery. Or get caught up in some get-rich-quick scenario. Or turn to legitimate investments such as stocks or real estate. The underlying assumption is always the same: First make some money, then you'll be able to do what you love—pursue your passion. It's the American way. In fact, it's so ingrained in the American psyche, we could almost call it the Great American Formula:

Money = Happiness, Fulfillment, and the Freedom to Pursue Your Passion.

So what's the first step in making money? All success books preach the same thing: You must set a goal. Make it specific. Write it down. Visualize it. Read it every day. Magnetize your subconcious mind with single-minded, money-making determination. Simple.

Well, if it's so simple, why aren't more people financially independent? Is it because so few set financial goals? Or is it a faulty goal-setting technique? Perhaps they need to visualize the money better—smell it, see it stacked in neat bundles as high as a house, make the image clearer. Maybe they need to set a goal to read their goals more regularly. Or to cut their goals up into bite-sized pieces. What's the answer?

Many years ago, before I understood why goals don't work, I was teaching a seminar in Dallas on the power of goal setting. A woman came up to me afterward with a puzzled look on her face. "Mr. Allen. I'm a full-time real estate investor. I get up in the morning excited. I love to make deals. I have so much fun making money, I hate to go to bed at night. And yet, I've never written down a financial goal in my life. What am I doing wrong?"

I was stumped for a moment. She didn't fit into my picture of the successful person (since all successful people have financial goals, right?). I stammered something about how much more successful she would be if she did set goals. She nodded wisely. And I shrugged off the whole incident.

About this time, a good friend and fellow real estate investor told me that he was going to liquidate his small portfolio of properties and concentrate on his painting. I said, "But Sam, if you stick with real estate for five more years, you can retire and be free to paint for the rest of your life." His answer was mildly unsettling. "Bob, I've discovered I don't like real estate. But I love to paint." I walked away shaking my head at this soon-to-be-a-poor-and-starving artist. But a year later he was doing rather well financially. And loving every minute of it.

And then, one day these seemingly unrelated incidents coalesced into one gigantic Aha! It happened while I was watching a golf tournament on TV featuring Jack Nicklaus, Lee Trevino, Fuzzy Zoeller, and Arnold Palmer. As these four great golfers were asked why they golfed, I suddenly knew why they were so successful: "I love the game of golf." "I love the competition." "I love to try to beat the best players in the world." "I love the people you meet in the game of golf." "Challenge is important to me." "I could play golf every day, all day long." "I'm one of the luckiest guys in the world. There are very few of us who get to do what we love and make a lot of money doing it."

That was it! These guys weren't playing for money! They were playing because they loved to play. Sure, maybe in the beginning money was a part of it—maybe a big part—but money was never the primary motivator. First and foremost, they were passionate about the game of golf. I doubt any one of them had a written financial goal: "I want to become a millionaire playing golf before my thirty-fifth birthday." What's more, I bet the golfers who play just for money rarely make it to the leader board. It's not that their financial goals don't work. But they've got the formula backwards! Remember the Great American Formula?

Money = Happiness, Fulfillment, and the Freedom to Pursue Your Passion.

In truth, that formula should be just exactly the opposite.

Pursuing Your Passion = Fulfillment and Leads to Financial Freedom.

When you're doing what you love to do, the money comes naturally. Maybe not at first, but eventually—if you stick with it. Do you think Bob Hope started out with a goal: "I want to become a millionaire by making people laugh, then I'll retire to do what I really want"? I doubt it. He just did what he did best. And the money came. Slowly at first, but then in truckloads. Now that he's extraordinarily wealthy, why doesn't he retire? When you're living your dream, why would you want to retire?

Do you think Tina Turner sings just so she can make a lot of money and then retire? Of course not. She loves to entertain. The money is just a by-product. Even during the tough times in her career, I doubt she ever considered real estate as a way to make it. She always knew she was born to sing.

What about the presidents of the Fortune 500? They each make about a million dollars a year. Why do they do so well financially? Because they're greedy? Of course not. They love the game of business. And the money is just how they keep score.

I read a study in which the employees and executives of a major company were asked what they would do if they won a million dollars in a lottery. Eighty percent of the rank-and-file employees responded that they would immediately quit their jobs. Asked the same question, only 20 percent of the executives said they would quit. Why would 80 percent stay even though they were now financially independent? Because they find a lot of happiness and fulfillment in their day-to-day activities. They love what they're doing. They're not leaders because they make so much money. They make so much money because they love to lead.

If Bill Cosby won the state lottery, would he retire from show business? Would Barbra Streisand quit singing? Would Magic Johnson quit playing basketball? If Lee Iacocca won the biggest lottery in the world, would he quit making cars? I doubt it.

What would you do if you won the lottery?

Imagine what you would do if you won ten million dollars. Would this make you happy? Sure. (Whoever said money doesn't bring happiness doesn't know where to shop!) What would you spend it on? A larger house in a better neighborhood? And a nicer car? Pay off those debts? Buy some new clothes? Give a little away to your favorite charitable cause? Blow a few thousand for the heck of it? Sock some away for a rainy day? And, of course, you'd quit your job and do what you love to do, right?

Seriously, how would you spend your time if you didn't have to worry about money? Want to know a secret? Most people never bother to ask themselves that question. They just assume that if they win that ten-million-dollar jackpot, then they'll be happy forever.

But wait! Is that what really happens? After all, the lottery doesn't pay you ten million in one big chunk. The money is spread out over twenty years—$500,000 a year. Still, that's a lot of money. But what about taxes? O.K. So knock off 40 percent for state and federal taxes. That still leaves you with $300,000 a year after taxes, $25,000 a month. You didn't use to make that much in an entire year! Now, you can retire and live like royalty.

Or can you? Now that you're rich, you automatically acquire wealthy habits. Instead of the $39 Timex, you're going to want a $10,000 Rolex. Instead of a $10,000 Toyota, you're going to die for that $80,000 Mercedes. Instead of the $100,000 tract house, you just won't be satisfied until you're in a million-dollar mansion. Your standard of living goes through the roof—absorbing all of the extra money—and before you know it, you feel broke again. And what are you going to do in twenty years when the money runs out? Obviously, you're going to have to make more money in order to stay happy.

But wait! *That's the trap!* More money isn't going to make you happy. (Not that any of us wouldn't want that kind of misery. "Oh well," you say to yourself, "I always knew that money couldn't buy lasting happiness, but I just wanted to find out for myself.") But it's not the money that you want, really. It's the ability to earn your financial freedom doing something that you love to do. Something that makes your life worth living each day. Instead of looking for happiness in some future goal of financial freedom (like almost all Americans), you want to find something that fulfills you every step of the way. Obviously, there's more to your success than writing down your goals and dabbling in real estate.

People who achieve success and maintain it, whether it be in real estate investing or show business, have something that gives power to their goals—something I call "purpose." In my opinion, without purpose, goals aren't worth the paper they are written on. In fact, without purpose, goals ruin a perfectly good piece of blank paper.

So what is purpose?

Purpose is knowing what you want and doing it because it expresses who you really are. Billy Graham, Julio Iglesias, Michael Jordan—they are "on purpose." They are living the life they were born to live. It's hard to imagine them doing anything else. They don't need goals to motivate themselves. They would do it anyway. And if they do set goals, it's just to keep score.

I've spent a lot of my time studying highly effective people, including graduates of my WealthTraining™,* and I find four threads that run through all of their conversations:

1. *Passion:* They love what they do. If they weren't making so much money, they would be tempted to do it for free.
2. *Values:* Their daily activities are extremely important to them.

* WealthTraining is a hands-on, intensive, year-long course of study to teach you how to master the basics of wealth and real estate investing. It is taught in major cities nationwide. For more information call toll free 1-800-345-DOIT.

3. *Talent:* They are good at what they do. Call it talent, ability, skill, a special gift. Although they may have to work at it, they have got what it takes to be one of the best.
4. *Destiny:* They have a sense that they are doing what they were born to do—making their own unique contribution. It's almost a spiritual thing. They're fulfilling their destiny.

Is purpose only found in the lives of geniuses? Absolutely not. I believe every person has a unique purpose. And that includes you. You have unique talents, abilities, interests, and values that only *you* can bring into greatness. You have a destiny that only *you* can fulfill.

So how do you tap into this sense of purpose? Actually, there are at least three distinct steps.

Step One: Ask Yourself the Purpose Questions

What do I love to do? What am I good at? What is important to me? What was I born to do? Complete the following Purpose Finder exercise to help you find out. List the top seven answers to each of the four questions. I've given you some additional clues to get you started. Don't be too serious. Enjoy yourself. When you've finished, rank each of the items in each list in order of importance assuming you only have five years to live. I encourage you to spend at least one uninterrupted half hour completing this exercise.

Purpose Finder Exercise

WHAT DO I LOVE TO DO?
Additional clues:

What has given me the most satisfaction in the past?
What excites me about life?
What activities give me the most satisfaction and inner peace?
What are my hobbies?

WHAT AM I GOOD AT?
Additional clues:

What have other people told me I'm good at?
What have I excelled at in the past? (e.g., sports, entertaining, relationships, communicating, problem solving, persuading, leading)?

What have I been happiest doing?
What is my secret ambition?

RANK ACTIVITY

1. ______________________
2. ______________________
3. ______________________
4. ______________________
5. ______________________
6. ______________________
7. ______________________

What are some of my strengths?
What have I been successful at ?

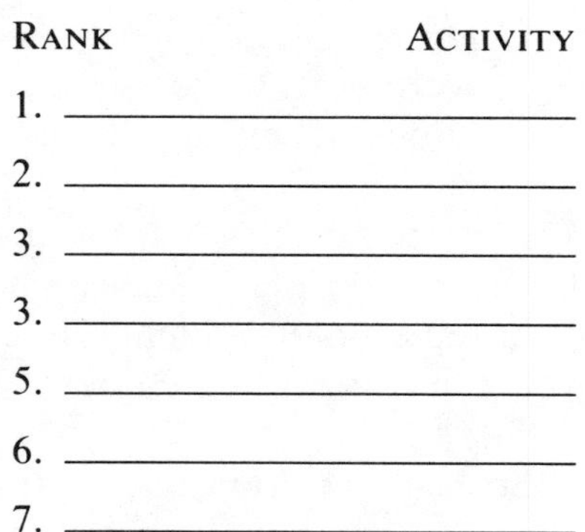

RANK ACTIVITY

1. ______________________
2. ______________________
3. ______________________
3. ______________________
5. ______________________
6. ______________________
7. ______________________

WHAT IS IMPORTANT TO ME?
Additional clues:

What would I commit myself to if money were not an object?
If I only had five years to live, what would I absolutely have to accomplish for my life to have been meaningful?
What do I stand for?
What won't I stand for?
What has caused me to make great sacrifices in the past?
What would I be willing to risk my life for?

RANK ACTIVITY

1. ______________________
2. ______________________
3. ______________________
4. ______________________
5. ______________________
6. ______________________
7. ______________________

WHAT WAS I BORN TO DO:?
Additional clues:

What is my unique mission in life?
What can I do that will make a difference?
What specifically does God want me to do?
What can I contribute?
What is my niche?
What unique opportunities have been placed in my path?

RANK ACTIVITY

1. ______________________
2. ______________________
3. ______________________
4. ______________________
5. ______________________
6. ______________________
7. ______________________

Step Two: Prepare a Purpose Statement

Using the information on your Purpose Finder Exercise, try to discover what thread runs through your life that connects you to your life's energy. What activities make you come alive? What values guide your daily decisions? Most people complete this exercise and are amazed at what they discover. Try to see patterns in your answers. See how many of the top priorities in one quadrant are similar to those found in other quadrants. These are good clues. Use this information to construct a Purpose Statement, a short description of the priorities which guide your life and give it meaning. (See page 40.)

Don't let this intimidate you. You're not trying to discover the meaning of life—just what motivates you at this time in your life. You will revise your Purpose Statement periodically as your life unfolds. I once heard a radio interview with Dr. Benjamin Spock. The interviewer couldn't understand why the famous pediatrician and best-selling author was now involved in anti-nuclear demonstrations. Dr. Spock explained, "I became a pediatrician because I loved children. I became an author because I wanted to teach parents how to raise more healthy children. And now I fight against nuclear weapons because I hate the thought of what war does to children." Although his life has taken many turns, his purpose was always the same: helping children. Same tune, different lyrics. If Dr. Spock wrote a purpose statement it would probably read something like this: "I was born to heal people, especially children. My purpose is to use my talents and skills to help children all over the world."

By the way, my own Purpose Statement used to be a page long. I finally honed it to one sentence: "My purpose is to live and teach the principles of real wealth."

This one sentence says it all for me. I love to teach. I love to write. And I love to create new ways to help people live life to the fullest. Real estate just happens to be the specific vehicle I use. These things are really important to me. It is where my talents lie. The principles of real wealth are ideas which I feel I have been born to teach. And one of those principles is Purpose.

Purpose Statement

____
____
____
____
____
____
____
____
____
____
____
____
____
____
____
____
____
____
____

So what does all this have to do with a book on real estate? Actually there are several reasons it's necessary to link purpose to your real estate activities. You may be one of those fortunate souls who has the real estate "knack," who is a "natural" for this kind of business in the same way that Jack Nicholson is a natural actor or that Beethoven was a natural composer. If so, your investment career may not bring you fame but will certainly bring you more fulfillment and financial success. To determine this, ask yourself the following questions:

—Do I like real estate? Or am I choosing real estate just because I want to be rich?

—Do I enjoy taking risks?
—Do I like to negotiate?
—If real estate made me wealthy, what would I want to do if and when I retired?
—If I were wealthy, would I still do real estate?
—Do I like the challenge of doing deals?
—Am I an entrepreneur?
—Does the thought of being an investor give me a surge of excitement?
—Is business important to me?
—Will real estate help me express who I really am?
—Is real estate my equivalent of an artist's canvas?
—Am I good at creative problem solving?
—Do I have a drive to grow my real estate business bigger and bigger?
—Is real estate in my blood?
—Would I be "on purpose" as a real estate investor?

If real estate is a big part of your purpose, then the odds of your success go up dramatically. You see, purpose is like your favorite dessert. Have you ever noticed that no matter how full you are, your favorite dessert always makes room for itself? You always find time for the things you really want to do, no matter how busy you are. When you are "on purpose," nothing stops you. When you aren't, any distraction, problem, obstacle, disappointment, or negative thought or feeling can divert you.

So what if you weren't "born" to be a passionate real estate investor? What if you just want to make some fast, safe money to pursue some other dream or passion? Moreover, what if you don't want to be financially free at all but just want some extra financial security? That's O.K., too, as long as you link your intentions to a sufficiently motivating reason.

Step Three: Link Your Intentions to a Compelling Reason

There is an old saying that I will paraphrase: "If the 'why' is important enough, then no 'how' is too difficult."

In other words, very few of us would hang-glide off the Empire

State Building for ten thousand dollars. But if it meant saving our children, we would be the first in line.

The "how" of real estate investing is simple to understand but not easy to implement. It takes commitment, dedication, time, and effort. If your only reason for starting is because you want to get rich, then you don't have a compelling enough "why." You need some reason that motivates you to go through the "gravel digging" until you uncover a real estate nugget. Lee Trevino sometimes hits a thousand balls a day on the practice tee in preparation for a major tournament. He couldn't do it unless he had a major reason. What is your major reason for wanting to be financially free? The more specific the reason, the more compelling the drive and the more probable the success.

I asked a woman at a recent WealthTraining seminar why she was there. She explained that she had a handicapped son who required substantial government assistance. This assistance was scheduled to run out in a few short years. At that time, she "had to be a millionaire" just to be able to take care of him. In other words, her reason for investing is so compelling that she will be motivated to do whatever it takes to make it. When she is dealing with a banker, seller, or Realtor, her commitment is going to radiate from every cell in her body. This will translate into more opportunities and closed transactions.

The following five steps will help you link your goals with the power to realize them:

1. Find Out Where You Are

If you don't know where you are, how do you expect to get where you want to go? Sit down and prepare a realistic financial statement. You will find a blank copy of an excellent financial file on the next pages. You should fill it out.

I know you're tempted to skip over this step. *You can't*. It is essential to this process. As you prepare your financial statement, remember to list all of your assets whether you think they are valuable or not.

Then, take inventory of your inner strengths and values. Your Purpose Finder Exercise and Purpose Statement will clarify this

Confidential Check List and Survey of Investment Objectives

PERSONAL AND FAMILY DATA

Name__________ Date__________

Mailing Address__________ Phone__________

Employer/Position__________ Phone__________

Spouse's Employer__________ Phone__________

	Age	Date of Birth	Health	Occupation	Social Security No.
Client					
Spouse					
Children					
Other Dependents					

	Firm	Phone
Attorney		
Banker		
C.P.A.		
Insurance Broker		
Property Manager		
Other Financial Adviser		

When was your present will executed?__________ Spouse's?__________

Do you have a trust arrangement? ☐ Yes ☐ No Type__________ Trustee __________

INCOME AND TAXATION

	Self	Spouse	Total
Current Annual Taxable Income			
From salary, fees, bonuses, etc.	$	$	$
From interest	$	$	$
From dividends	$	$	$
From real estate	$	$	$
From capital gains (½)	$	$	$
Other (trusts, etc.)	$	$	$
Total taxable income	$	$	$

Expected future income?__________ When? __________

What income increases or decreases do you expect?__________

Do you receive additional non-taxable income?__________

Do you have a regular savings or investment program now? ☐ Yes ☐ No

Present monthly savings $__________ Could comfortably save $__________ monthly.

TAX RETURN SUMMARY (LAST 4 YEARS)

	19___	19___	19___	19___
Adjusted gross income	$	$	$	$
Taxable income	$	$	$	$
Federal taxes paid	$	$	$	$
State ( ) taxes paid	$	$	$	$
Exemptions claimed				

How many exemptions this year?___________ Estimated personal deductions $ ____________________
Do you have any personal carry-over losses from last year?____________________
Factors affecting future income ____________________

Comments ____________________

ASSETS AND LIABILITIES (EXCEPT INSURANCE)

Lender and Loan Number

REAL ESTATE

Type of Property and Location	How Acquired	Title Held In Name Of	Date Acquired	Adjusted Basis	Market Value	Amount of Mortgages	Present Equity	Monthly Cash Flow Before Taxes
				$	$	$	$	$
						TOTAL	$	$

SECURITIES (Listed and Unlisted)

Company and Type of Security	Registered In Name Of	Date Acquired	Cost Basis	Market Value	Margin or Loans	Present Equity	Annual Cash Flow Before Taxes
			$	$	$	$	$
					TOTAL	$	$

BUSINESS INTERESTS

Name of Company	Form of Organization	Date of Organization	Number of Employees	Percent Ownership	Client's Current Net Value	Client's Annual Net Income
					$	$
				TOTAL	$	$

EMPLOYEE BENEFITS

Type of Plan Company	Tax Qualified?	Retirement Age	Retirement Benefits	Voluntary Contributions	Current Value	Death Benefit Now
Pension			$	$	$	$
Profit Sharing						
Savings						
Tax Sheltered Annuity						

LIFE AND HEALTH INSURANCE

LIFE INSURANCE

Company	Type	Date Acquired	Insured	Owner	Beneficiary	Face Amount	Cash Value	Loans	Annual Premium
						$	$	$	$
					TOTAL	$	$	$	$

MEDICAL AND DISABILITY INSURANCE

Type	Cancelled? Yes	No	Insurer	Insured	Periodic Benefit	Maximum Benefit	Exclusion	Annual Premium
Disability Income								$
Disability Income								
Hospitalization								
Major Medical								
Business Overhead								

FINANCIAL STATEMENT

ASSETS

cash and checking	$
savings accounts	
real estate owned	
securities	
notes receivable	
bonds – face value	
furniture & personal	
automobiles	
life ins. cash value	
net worth business	
net lease value	
boats, trailers	
alimony	
deposits on real estate	
pension & annuity value	
other	
TOTAL ASSETS	$

LIABILITIES

mortgages	$
notes payable	
loans on life ins.	
debts, unsecured	
installment purchases	
property tax reserves	
income tax reserves	
long-term leases	
TOTAL LIABILITIES	$

NET WORTH $

INVESTMENT OBJECTIVES

What priority do you assign to the following investment objectives?

___ Additional current monthly income of $________________.
___ Capital growth/Inflation hedge. ☐ Short Term ☐ Long Term
___ Tax shelter for ☐ Income ☐ Capital gain ☐ ________________.
___ Professional management for ☐ Property ☐ Securities ☐ Trust
___ Safety of investment.
___ Maintain minimum cash reserve of $________________.
___ Diversification of investment program.
___ Provision for family in event of premature death or disability.
___ Other

At what age do you anticipate full retirement? ________________
What do you consider to be a minimum retirement income (Today's dollars) $________________
What do you consider to be a comfortable retirement income (Today's dollars) $________________
Comments (Education funds, etc.): ________________

COMMENTS

____

BUDGETING - create your own wealth for pyramiding

Gross Income - including interest, dividends, rents $________
Less deductions - Federal ________ F.I.C.A. ________
State ________ Others ________ (________)
$________

Spendable Income

		BUDGET	SPENT
1. Savings for investment = at least 10% of gross income			
2. Committed expenses:	a. Charitable		
	b. Housing		
	c. House maintenance		
	d. Utilities		
	e. Life insurance		
	f. Automotive		
	g. Medical		
	h. Others:		
3. Manageable expenses:	a. Food		
	b. Clothing		
	c. Personal expenses		
	d. Appliances		
	e. Furnishings		
	f. Building and grounds		
	g. Entertainment		
	h. Others:		

Total Expenses $________
Spendable less expenses $________

If there is income remaining apply to your savings. If there is a deficiency of income find ways to alter your expenses or increase income. Do not decrease savings!

step for you. Look at your past experience. What qualities do you possess that are necessary to success?

You should also take inventory of the barriers that will slow you down from reaching your objective. Is your desire sufficient? Are you financially prepared? Will your family support you? Do you have enough knowledge? Is there a local mentor who can coach you through the rough spots? Can you find five to ten hours a week to devote to this process?

Now that you better understand where you are, it's time to sharpen your focus.

2. Focus on a Specific Intention

Rather than using the word "goal," I am going to replace it with the word "intention." An intention is actually different from a goal. Most people set goals based upon external motivation or whim. They see a billboard picture of a new car and their "greed glands" fire up. "I want that car and I won't be happy until I get it!" That's a goal. A goal is wanting to become a doctor or lawyer because it will please your parents. An intention is when your own "inner voice" tells you to become an architect. A goal is often fueled by fear. "Real estate prices are jumping upward. I better get in and make some money before it's too late." An intention is fueled by a sense of purpose. "I've always wanted to be a real estate investor. I would love the personal freedom it could provide."

Here are some other differences between goals and intentions:

GOALS	INTENTIONS
External Motivation	Internal Motivation
Whim, Fancies, Appetites	Deep Needs, Desires
Happiness in End Result	Journey is the Reward
Future Oriented	Now Oriented
Unnatural	Second Nature
Dissatisfaction	Fulfillment
Imitation	Uniqueness
Mediocrity	Excellence

A goal is "I want to be a millionaire by January 1, 2000." An intention is "Within five years, I want to start a program to dramatically raise the self-esteem of children in my city."

But even this is not specific enough. You can't build a house from rough sketches. You need a blueprint—a specific game plan.

3. Formulate a Specific Game Plan

Your game plan outlines the specific steps you must take to make your intention come to life. Try this on for size:

Purpose: I have always felt a need to own my own business.

Intention: I will be a full-time real estate investor within two years.

Game Plan: I will remain in my job and spend five hours a week for the next six months learning, studying, and going to seminars to acquire the basics of real estate investing. Then I'll buy one property in the following six months. I will remain a part-time successful investor until I can afford to do it full time. I intend to make the leap to full-time status when I have accumulated a "safety net" of at least six months of cash and become experienced enough to earn at least twice my current salary from my investment activities. This should happen in the next twenty-four months. Within five years, I intend to own properties with accumulated equities exceeding one million dollars. Then I will broaden my focus to include the following additional intentions:

—Teaching kids about the importance of the free market system
—Increasing support for my church organization
—Finding reasonable approaches to saving the environment
—Writing a book
—Pursuing my talent for singing.

Got the idea? Let's try another one.

Purpose: I have always wanted to work with underprivileged children.

Intention: I intend to start a safe house for young teenagers on drugs.

Game Plan: I will establish myself with a solid financial base through my current occupation. At the same time, I will learn how to master the basics of real estate investment by study and experience. I will buy my first investment property within one year. With the profits generated from this property, I will start my youth program. I will approach "at risk" youth and encourage them to work with me as I invest, fix-up, and manage my growing investment portfolio. Within two years, I intend to buy one property to use as a group home. The profits generated from investing will be used to expand the program. Within five years, I will be "saving" 100 youths per year from the horrors of drugs and alcohol, and training them how to go back into the community to repeat this process with other youths. Within ten years, I intend to create an education program to be taught in schools citywide that shows young people a legitimate way to "make it" in America besides selling drugs. From this educational program, at least 1,000 youths per year will be involved in summer work programs.

Here's another one:

Purpose: I feel a deep responsibility to provide financial security for my family.

Intention: Within one year I will embark on a specific real estate investment program.

Game Plan: I will build my investment program on the sound financial foundation of adequate insurance, emergency preparedness, savings, credit protection, and company retirement benefits. Then I will protect my career by becoming an increasingly productive team player. In my spare time, I will acquire information and experience about small real estate investments. Within one year I will buy my first property and will add at least one property per year to this portfolio for the next ten years. This portfolio will appreciate in value as well as provide added cash flow. I will involve my family in the details of the program so that they can learn by doing. Give a man a fish and you feed him for a day. Teach a man to fish and you feed him for a lifetime.

Get the idea?

The key to a good game plan is to be specific with dates, time frames, and activities. The more specific the better. With this in mind, let's play around with some numbers just for fun. During the 1970s the average rate of appreciation on most rental properties was approximately 10 percent per year. *At that rate of appreciation, a well-selected property would have doubled in value in just over seven years!* Obviously, not all real estate appreciates in value. In the 1980s, some areas of the country boomed while others busted. What's so exciting about real estate is you can make a fortune no matter which way prices go. But let's make some general assumptions. Whether you're buying and holding for appreciation, renovating run-down properties or concentrating on super bargain foreclosures, it's not unrealistic to earn 25 percent to 100 percent on your investment. Depending on where you live, you can organize your buying strategy to create opportunities that will cause your entire real estate portfolio to "average" a 10 percent growth rate per year. To be safe, you shouldn't expect more than a 5 percent growth rate—and you should be prepared if prices head south as they did in Seattle in the late 1960s and Houston in the late 1980s. Just to show you what a 10 percent appreciation can do to your real estate portfolio, I have included the chart on p. 51.

For example, suppose you buy a $100,000 building today.* Within seven to ten years, if conditions have been favorable, that building will be worth approximately $200,000. The mortgage will be paid down to $75,000. Your profit will have been over $100,000.

This chart was created to teach you an important concept: The compounding effect of relatively low real estate price increases over time. You can see by playing with the numbers on the chart that there are infinite ways to creating a fortune. You just need to decide firmly how wealthy you want to become. However, there are drawbacks to the chart, since an investor doesn't just walk into the market and buy $1 million worth of real estate at a time and wait for ten or fifteen years to become wealthy. The normal process is to buy properties in increments—to eat the elephant bite by bite rather than at one sitting. This fact necessitates the use of another chart, which I call the Gross Equity Accumulation Schedule. This more closely approaches the actual real-life situation of the average investor, i.e., the purchase of individual properties slowly with building equities.

* With the median home price in America over $100,000, it's hard to imagine prices less, but there are still many areas of the country where properties sell for $50,000 or less.

GROSS EQUITY APPRECIATION SCHEDULE

Gross Value of Real Estate \ Net Equity Columns	$250,000	$500,000	$750,000	$1,000,000	$1,250,000	$1,500,000	$1,750,000	$2,000,000	$10,000,000
$2,000,000	1.3	2.4	3.4	4.3	5.1	5.9	6.6	7.3	18.8
$1,750,000	1.4	2.7	3.8	4.8	5.7	6.5	7.3	8.0	20.0
$1,500,000	1.7	3.1	4.3	5.4	6.4	7.3	8.2	8.9	21.4
$1,250,000	2.0	3.6	5.0	6.2	7.3	8.3	9.2	10.1	23.1
$1,000,000	2.4	4.3	5.87	7.3	8.6	9.7	10.7	11.6	25.2
$750,000	3.1	5.4	7.3	8.9	10.3	11.6	12.7	13.7	28.0
$500,000	4.3	7.3	9.7	11.6	13.2	14.6	15.8	16.9	32.0
$250,000	7.3	11.6	14.6	16.9	18.8	20.5	21.9	23.1	39.0

Assumptions:
- Property values increase by 10% per year
- All of your purchases are nothing down
- Equity build-up is not counted in equity
- Figures are rounded to highest tenth

This chart provides you with a quick and easy way to find out how much you can be worth in a prescribed time period. How does it work? Say that you want to have a net equity of $1,000,000 in 5–1/2 years. Find $1,000,000 in the Net Equity column; now follow the column up until you find something close to 5–1/2 years — 5.4. Now go across to the Gross Value of Real Estate column; you'll have to buy $1,500,000 worth of property to reach your goal. What if you now have $250,000 worth of property? Find $1,000,000 in the Net Equity column and the $250,000 point in the Gross Value of Real Estate column. The point at which the two intersect is the number of years it will take your property to appreciate to a $1,000,000 net equity — 16.9 years. Make sure you note the assumptions listed at the bottom of the chart.

Let me explain how this chart works. Let's assume that you want to generate a steady cash flow of $50,000 per year for the rest of your life. We'll also assume that this $50,000 income represents a return on your investment in ten years from now. If you could conservatively invest your money to yield 10 percent, then your $50,000 income would represent your yield on a $500,000 net worth ($500,000 × .10 = $50,000). What you will need to have ten years from now, therefore, is a net worth of $500,000, which can be invested to yield you 10 percent. The next question is "How can I attain a net worth of $500,000 in ten years?" This takes you to the Gross Equity Accumulation Schedule. Look for a net worth of

GROSS EQUITY ACCUMULATION SCHEDULE

Annual Accumulation	$250,000	$500,000	$750,000	$1,000,000	$1,250,000	$1,500,000	$1,750,000	$2,000,000
$300,000	3.5	5	6	7	8	8.5	9	9.5
$250,000	4	5.5	6.5	7.5	8.5	9	10	10.5
$200,000	4.5	6	7.5	8.5	9.5	10	11	11.5
$150,000	5	7	8.5	9.5	10.5	11.5	12.2	13
$100,000	6	8.5	10	11.5	12.5	13.5	14.5	15
$75,000	7	10	11.5	13	14	15	16	17
$50,000	8.5	11.5	13.5	15	16.5	17.5	18.5	19.5
$40,000	9.5	12.5	14.5	16.5	18	19	20	21

Net Equity Columns

Assumptions:
- Property values increase by 10% per year
- All of your purchases are nothing down
- Equity build-up is not counted in equity
- Figures are rounded to highest one half

$500,000 in the "Net Equity" columns in the table. Then follow the column upward until you find the number of years until your intended retirement date—in this case ten years. Then follow the column horizontally to the left to find the yearly purchase quota—in this case $75,000. This tells you that in order for you to accumulate a net worth of $500,000 within ten years, it will be necessary for you to purchase at least $75,000 worth of real estate each year for the next ten years. This should be held and not sold. If property values increase at an average rate of at least 10 percent per year for the next ten years, the $500,000 goal is feasible and realistic.

If you want to get fancy, you can use both the preceding charts to make a prediction on your future net worth. But the important concept to grasp here is that the building of a fortune is accomplished steadily, gradually, one step at a time. For some the purchase of even one property each year for ten years seems as formidable as climbing Everest. You must realize that every little step counts—one single-family home adds to your quota as does a large apartment building. Some years you will not be able to find anything. And the very next month, you could locate an excellent property to satisfy two or three years' quotas. I found that during one six-month period I could not locate anything that fit into my investment guidelines. Then, one week I located a "don't wanter" who had five smaller homes to sell in one transaction. And I was able to negotiate a *nothing-down* purchase! It's either feast or famine.

As your confidence and your experience increase, you'll learn that you can pyramid your investments. Make sure that you buy solid real estate in good neighborhoods in growing areas. You should begin by purchasing small homes and apartment buildings until you get the hang of it (and so you don't get stung by risking your investment capital in unknown areas). You must choose each property carefully—with legal protection, assurance from professionals, and some conservative long-range objectives for creative appreciation and cash flow. As you learn to master the techniques, you will eventually purchase larger apartment buildings, small office buildings, and land for subdivisions. Give yourself time. Most of all, give yourself optimism.

Whatever your dream is, take time to fill out the Commitment form at the end of this chapter. Don't pass up this opportunity to commit yourself in writing—and have your spouse witness it with his or her signature so he or she can be part of the process. This step could well be the most important thing you do to obtain financial independence.

With a completed Commitment form to focus your attention like a laser beam, you're ready for the next step.

4. Flood Your Imagination with Vision

In addition to a specific regimen of physical training, every Olympic athlete also incorporates a scientifically designed program of visualization. It is impossible to achieve world-class status without it. Why?

Over seventy years ago the French scientist Emil Coué uttered a statement which is a clue to why visualization is essential to long-term success: *"When the will comes in conflict with the imagination, the imagination always carries the day."*

In other words, no matter how determined you say you are, if your imagination is not in harmony, you are doomed to failure. To say this in a more positive way: If your deepest needs, values and internal beliefs agree with your direction, then you are more likely to succeed.

Have you ever sabotaged yourself? Ever come close to victory only to slide back into the jaws of defeat? When you are fighting yourself, you can't win. Suppose you desire financial success but a part of you thinks that rich people are "all bad." It's going to be a tough fight all the way to the bank. What if some part of you feels that you don't deserve to be wealthy. That's obviously going to slow you down.

There is a way to rechannel your imagination so that all of you is aiming in the right direction. I call it Neurobics™. Neurobics is a specialized way of visualizing. Obviously, there is not space here to share with you the complete program, but here, in general, is the way it works.

I recommend that you spend five minutes a day quietly visualizing your future. Imagine you are in a movie theater watching a film of your successful future. See yourself up there on the screen as the principal actor. Notice how you behave now that you have achieved what you set out to achieve. Notice how happy you look. Notice how you walk and talk and interact with the other people in the film. Notice the material benefits of success. Tinker with the imagined scene by adding color, moving images, adjusting the size of the screen and sharpness of the images as well as the sound. Adjust the imagined scene until it feels right to you—until it reflects the most real representation of your successful future. Then, move out of your seat in the theater, step into the body of the "future you" on the screen, and notice what it feels like to have achieved your dream. Look through your future eyes and notice, from this perspective, how others react to you. Notice the surrounding trappings of success. Concentrate on how it feels to have "made it."

Step back out of the screen and take your seat once again in the theater. Then scan the various steps in your game plan that brought you to your ultimate success. Notice exactly how you "made it" in such a way that all parts of you were in agreement. Notice what it's like to close on each property in your game plan from the last back to the first. Especially notice how you developed as an individual. Notice how you transcended each of the major obstacles in your path. Imagine how you overcame each fear.

Then return back to the present, bringing with you the insights of your journey into the future. Each day you can focus on a different aspect of that future. For instance, you might create in your mind a "mastermind" council or board of directors to advise you. This imaginary board might consist of your heros past and present. At each barrier, you could convene your internal mastermind team to counsel you.

That should be enough to get you started. Once your purpose, intention and game plan are in place and you have begun a regular Neurobics regimen, there is only one final step.

5. Force Yourself to Take at Least One Small Step a Day Toward Achieving Your Purpose

Don't let a day go by without doing something—no matter how small. I call this my "bottom line" for the day. A bottom line is saying to yourself, "When this day is done, no matter what else I accomplish, I must at least do this:__________(fill in)__________.

So to review:

—Determine your purpose
—Establish a specific intention
—Develop your game plan
—Practice your Neurobics
—Put your game plan into action by accomplishing at least one daily bottom line.

My purpose, and the purpose of this book, is to teach you the principles of real wealth through investing in real estate. Once you have mastered these principles, make me a promise that you will buy at least one piece of real estate a year—skipping a year or even two if there really is no reasonable investment no matter how hard you look, but making up for it by buying two or more properties in a year when opportunities are plentiful, so that you average at least one purchase per year. That's a challenge! You will be amazed at how fast your real estate garden will grow. And don't be worried by the fact that you don't have a lot of money to invest. You bought this book because you didn't have a lot of cash in the bank. Few people do. But you can still reach your investment goals. Keep reading, and you will learn how to do it with little or none of your own money.

Commitment

I, ______________________, hereby acknowledge the following:

PURPOSE STATEMENT

My destiny is to weave the following principles, values, and talents into the fabric of my daily life:

____

____

____

____

____

____

____

____

____

____

____

____

____

____

____

____

SPECIFIC INTENTION

Drawing upon the strength of my purpose, I intend to focus my efforts on the following specific intention:

GAME PLAN

I will pursue my specific intention by following the following game plan. I acknowledge that the game plan may change as circumstances change. I will be open to flexibility and intuition as my intention becomes clearer and clearer.

ADDITIONAL INTENTIONS

Upon achieving my primary intention, I may choose to focus more effort on achieving the following additional intentions:

1. ______
2. ______

3. ____

4. ____

5. ____

Signed this ______________________________day of ___19____

____

____

Witnessed by:

____

If you'd like a commitment certificate suitable for framing, just call me at 1-800-345-3648 and I'll be glad to send you one.

CHAPTER 4

Finding the Bargain: Once-in-a-Lifetime Deals Come Along Every Other Day If You Know What You're Looking For

Finding the right property for your limited investment dollars is like panning for gold: It takes a lot of sifting through gravel before any glitter is found.

And there are many properties that *appear,* like fool's gold, to be a rich find. Only close inspection will let you know for sure that you've located a real bargain. For this reason I try to maintain a very neutral, aloof attitude whenever I go looking for properties. If I get too emotionally involved in any investment decision, I may find myself swayed by too much nonfinancial detail.

One of the first assignments for students in my WealthTraining course is to find a property they think has potential, analyze it as best they can, and make an offer to the owner. We start them right out digging for information in the classified section of the newspaper. It isn't long before an excited student runs up with something they think is a golden opportunity.

"Bob, I think I've really found a winner!"

"Have you done your analysis yet?"

"Not really. But his ad sounds real desperate. He must be a don't wanter." ("Don't wanter" is our jargon for someone who, pardon the English, don't want his property. It means a highly flexible seller.)

"You can't get excited until you've finished your homework."

"Well, I can just smell the money." (Everything smells like money to a beginning investor who hasn't yet learned to sift the real stuff from the fool's gold).

Three major elements need to be considered before you can find what you're looking for—a property that's worth your gold: (1) location analysis, (2) market analysis, (3) seller analysis. Let's cover these one at a time.

Location is the first critical element. The three cardinal rules in buying real estate are: (1) Location. (2) Location. (3) Location. Don't be blinded by attractive terms. If the property is in a bad location, no amount of good terms can make up for the price you'll eventually have to pay in bad tenants, measly rents, and poor resale profits. You don't make profits by throwing your precious money and time and effort down the rathole of a poor location. I have owned property in a bad location before, and it wasn't long before I became the biggest don't wanter in town. My location attracted the worst tenants and commanded the lowest rents. Expenses were higher because of these tenants, and added to the expenses were my purchases of antacids for my unsettled stomach.

How do you analyze location?

Take a look around. Is the neighborhood deteriorating or improving? A drive down the street should answer this question easily enough. You don't have to be an expert to recognize slummy buildings, uncut lawns, and debris in the street.

A cardinal rule in buying property is to buy the worst property in the best neighborhood, *not* the best property in the worst neighborhood. If you buy the worst property in the best neighborhood, at least you have the chance to upgrade the property to match the standards of the neighborhood, and your property value will increase.

In a bad area, your property will only decline in value along with the rest of the neighborhood. Remember, you're buying a neighborhood, not just a property. Choose carefully.

If you're still in doubt about the neighborhood, there are several people who can give you some good insight about your prospective buy. First, ask the city's planning department what is planned for the area you're considering. The planning staff will be glad to answer any and all of your questions; just let them know you want the answers to be blunt. Or call a local property management firm, and ask one of its account managers to discuss the pros and cons of the area.

Another source of help is a local real estate agent. And if you still don't think you know enough about the area, start knocking on doors in the neighborhood. Ask some of the apartment owners what they think about their investment. You might get some good insight. Or ask the tenants themselves. They know better than anyone what the neighborhood's really like.

Another way to analyze location is to size up the competition. If you are buying a home as an investment, determine whether the neighborhood rentals are high enough to support your mortgage payment. If you are considering buying an apartment or commercial building, do a thorough study of competitive rents in the area; determine if there is room for increase. You'll also learn from this how your location compares with others in town.

Nearby amenities are another clue to a good location. Apartments and homes need to be close to shopping centers, churches, schools, and other services. If you're considering a commercial building, determine if there is adequate traffic flow or proximity to working establishments.

Generally speaking, the value of properties conforms to what I call the concentric circle theory. For example, let's assume you're analyzing an apartment building that is rented to single students who are attending your local university. The closer the apartment to campus, the higher the rents and the higher the sale prices. By the same token, the vacancy rates will be lower, and you will probably have less tenant turnover. The same theory applies to homes. How close are they to places of employment, shopping centers, and churches?

The diagram on page 62 illustrates the concentric circle theory. Section A buildings would command the highest rent, Section D the lowest.

Generally, I try to avoid properties in the D area unless it is for quick turnover. I try as much as possible to buy properties in A, close to the center of demand. Thus, my rents are higher and my property values increase faster.

The second major element to consider is the market. I usually don't start to get excited about any particular property until I determine that it can be purchased for below market price. *This implies that I first know what the market is!*

How can you know the market? First of all, keep track of every sale you hear about. Keep a record of the sale price and terms of the property; classify the information under type of unit, special amenities, price per unit, and available terms. Sometimes you'll get only sketchy information in a casual conversation; call the new owner and ask him what you need to know.

When you are in the market for single-family homes, you must know the approximate selling price of a 1,250-square-foot home with three bedrooms and one and a half baths. The best source for this information is a local real estate agent. Ask him about his present listings and the listings he has recently sold. The form on page 64 should be of great value to you in compiling any comparable sales information you should happen to find.

If you want to know the market values of homes or buildings in a specific neighborhood, stop and ask a property owner. We all keep our ear to the ground and we have a fairly good idea what our own property is worth by comparing it to what our neighbors sold

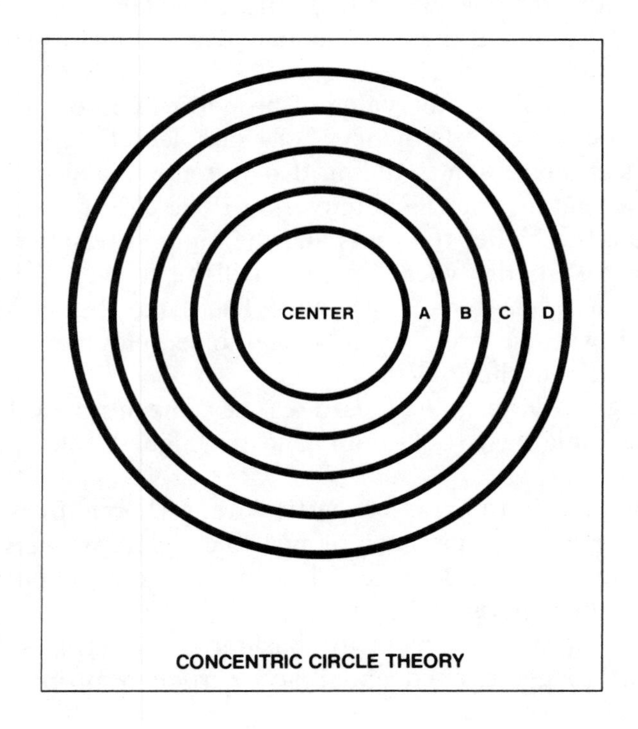

CONCENTRIC CIRCLE THEORY

their property for. Just ask around. In a few short minutes you'll know approximate values.

If you still aren't sure what kind of a deal you're getting, hire an appraiser. He can give you a professional opinion. Use any information you have already gathered to help you judge the validity of the appraiser's estimate. In the end, you're responsible for your decision, and you should use all the input you can get.

Identifying the owner as a *don't wanter* is the third major element in finding a good buy. A don't wanter is a seller who is willing to be flexible in his price or terms. Someone who is desperate to sell his property is usually flexible and willing to negotiate. Consider this classic example:

Information Sheet on El Dumpo Apartments

Property description: Ten-unit apartment building located at __________ approximately 50 miles northwest of __________ and 250 miles southwest of __________. The property is fully furnished and totally vacant.

Financial details: Price $45,000

Loans: $23,000, payable at $285.20 per month, including interest at 8½ percent per annum. Can be assumed. No qualifying.

Equity: $22,000

Special information: This is a newly acquired property. While it was still in escrow, the owner received a job offer in another state that he couldn't refuse. He cannot manage the property because of the distance problem. This property is listed at 33 percent under market value due to the vacancy situation. This is a good opportunity for an individual with initiative and ability to solve problems. Local officials are expecting a construction boom and a massive housing shortage in the area in the near future due to extensive geothermal exploration and construction of an alunite-processing plant near the city.

Will take and close: The owner will exchange his equity in this property for land, paper, construction equipment, or personal property. There are no geographic limitations. In other words, make me an offer. I won't refuse.

Sweeteners: In order to make a deal the seller will lease back the property at $285.20 per month until the occupancy reaches at least

COMPARATIVE MARKET ANALYSIS FORM

Subject Property Address ______________________________ Date ____________________

Information on other properties which are located in the same general area and have the same approximate value as the subject property:

FOR SALE NOW	Bed-rooms	Baths	Den	Sq.Ft.	Mtgs.	Price	Days on Mkt.	Terms

SOLD PAST 12 MONTHS	Bed-rooms	Baths	Den	Sq.Ft.	Mtgs.	Price	Days on Mkt.	Terms

EXPIRED PAST 12 MONTHS	Bed-rooms	Baths	Den	Sq.Ft.	Mtgs.	Price	Days on Mkt.	Terms

Realtors can be of great help in finding sold and expired information.

60 percent or for one year, whichever comes first. And he will also provide for a resident manager on the property on or before the possession date.

Do you get the picture? This is an actual example of a few years ago. *This owner is a don't wanter!* He can become one of your most valuable assets. Let's look more closely at this fascinating creature.

CHAPTER 5

The Don't-Wanter Seller: You Pick the Price and the Terms

What is a don't wanter?

A don't wanter is a person who will do anything to get rid of his property. Like the person in the previous example, he will take a personal note secured against nothing but your signature. He will take your stereo or your recreation lot in southern Nevada. He will take your Ford pickup. He will take anything, because he needs to act now. He wants out!

This is the kind of seller you need to do business with. He won't care if your MasterCard account is overdrawn, because he won't even check your credit. He's irrational. He is flexible. Don't wanters are on their knees every night praying for deliverance, and you could be the answer to their prayers.

How many don't wanters are there? Even in extremely tight sellers' markets there are still plenty of don't wanters. Perhaps 5 percent of all sellers are willing to be flexible enough to be called don't wanters. Most neophyte investors get discouraged early because they haven't learned that 95 percent of the sellers are not flexible. They need to be dealing with the 5 percent who are don't wanters.

One word of caution. Sometimes a don't wanter is a don't wanter for a very legitimate reason. Sometimes the problems that go with a property aren't easily solved. If you are not careful in analyzing what has made the seller a don't wanter, you could buy the property and end up being a don't wanter for the very same reasons!

But often a don't wanter's problems aren't as serious as he perceives them. They're only serious to the owner's situation, and you may be able to overcome them quite easily.

What makes someone a don't wanter?

Management problems lead the list of reasons why people want to sell their property. Some people cannot deal with tenants on a daily basis; they bought the property hoping to make a profit and didn't anticipate management problems.

The first multiple unit I purchased was a seven-unit building located in a fairly decent part of town on a busy street. The building was a converted home and had seven furnished apartments. Since the original structure was at least fifty years old, the plumbing was just beginning to cause weekly problems.

It took only a couple of months for me to realize that the good terms I'd received when I bought the building were the only good thing about the property. One morning at about 1:30 I was awakened by a telephone call from an upset tenant. She whispered, "Mr. Allen, I think you'd better get over here right away. The tenants in number seven are having an orgy." I rushed over immediately to find a drunken party in full progress. Since this was the third time this had happened, I called the police and went home.

All that summer I received similar complaints once or twice a week. "Mr. Allen, Ben in number three is running a heroin operation. He's smoking marijuana right now. I think that you should do something before he harms one of us."

"Mr. Allen, the unwed mother in number seven is having a brawl with her friends on the lawn."

"Mr. Allen, the girl in number six moved out in the middle of the night without paying her rent for the last two months."

"Mr. Allen, someone broke into our apartment last night and stole our television set." (As it turned out, Ben in number three, my resident manager, who *was* running a heroin operation, was arrested two days later with the television set in his possession. He was stealing from the tenants to help buy heroin.)

"Mr. Allen, I'm moving out of here unless you ask the people in number seven to leave immediately."

The last straw was when I cosigned with my trustworthy Ben of number three on a $200 loan to help him buy a pickup truck. Of course, I had no idea that he had been stealing things from other tenants. When the police caught him with the stolen TV set they gave him two alternatives: leave town before the sun set, or go to jail. And so he left town that night. In my truck! Every month when I made out that $22 check to pay for the small loan I had cosigned on, I remembered the seven-unit building, and I swore I would never get involved in another situation like that. I was a don't wanter.

Early that fall I put the building on the market for exactly the same price I had paid for it eighteen months earlier. I was suffering from a severe advanced case of don't wanteritis. I wanted to get rid of my property at all costs. Luckily I found someone to buy the building and cash out my equity.

But this decision was irrational. Rather than selling, I should have solved the real problem, which was the management of the property. I did not know how to manage. I would have been much better off to keep the property and turn the management over to a professional management company. This same property which I so hastily bought for $69,000 and resold for $69,000 a short while later sold again, one year after I sold it, for $85,000. It then sold again for $106,000. And again for $125,000. And now it is on the market again. What's the new asking price? $150,000! And someone will come along and pay it. A don't wanter is very often shortsighted and concentrates only on his immediate problem. If I had realized my problem and solved it without selling, I would have made $80,000!

Other management problems include:

—Vacancy problems (Your tenants move into a competitor's apartment.)
—Tenant problems (Your tenants refuse to pay the rent.)
—Anticipated future expenses (Old water heaters need replacing.)
—Distance factor (The owner is an absentee landlord living in a neighboring state; whenever there is a problem, he has to travel to solve it.)

—Time problems (The owner is an extremely busy man; his wife tells him it is either his family or his apartment building.)

There is a very simple solution to the management problem. Every city has access to professional management, and the services are listed in the Yellow Pages under "Professional Property Management." For a fee—usually around 10 percent of the gross income—the professionals will take responsibility for the maintenance, collect the rents, handle minor and major problems, evict bad tenants, advertise the building, and handle bookkeeping. In short, they do everything. If you are short on time, the management-company route may be just what you are looking for. Just make sure to watch over the management company.

Financial headaches can turn any owner into a don't wanter. Maybe he's been hit with a tax bill he wasn't expecting, maybe he has discovered another, better investment and needs cash to make the move, or maybe he's in trouble—needs to reduce indebtedness, pay a note that is coming due, or save himself from foreclosure. With experience you'll be able to recognize this symptom of "don't wanteritis." This kind of owner will usually negotiate willingly just to move his property quickly.

The first twelve-unit building I purchased was owned by an attorney. He had recently bought his partners out by placing a heavy wraparound mortgage on the building. The time required to manage the property, coupled with the unit's $300 monthly negative cash flow, made him a serious don't wanter. My required down payment was less than $4,500 with a $135,000 mortgage. I promptly did some minor repairs and cosmetic work, raised the rents, and turned the property into a positive cash flow. The reason I was able to get such a good deal was that I understood the attorney's problem, which was largely financial. He simply couldn't continue to feed his monthly alligator and still make ends meet with his family obligations. He was a perfect example of a don't wanter.

A third reason an owner becomes a don't wanter is that his property is suffering from physical problems—the building doesn't meet fire codes, the plumbing is deteriorating, or the parking lot is too small. Other physical problems are:

—The competition next door (All the units next to yours have been installing new swimming pools to attract new tenants, and it's working—they're attracting your tenants.)
—Age of the building (Structural elements or appliances may need replacing at great expense to the owner.)
—Location (The neighborhood is going to the dogs, and you're the only turkey left.)
—Functional obsolescence (Appraisers use this term to describe the particular faults of a building that will not be easily corrected: high ceilings, lack of electrical outlets, or small units, for example.)

Buyer beware. Physical problems are the most serious that confront owners. When you solve the problem of the don't wanter by buying his dilapidating building, you may end up making his incurable problem *your* incurable problem.

Individual owners have all sorts of personal problems, either real or imaginary, which cause them to want to sell their property. Foremost among these are:

—Retirement (The seller decides he has worked long enough; it's about time he sold his rental units and lived in the manner that he always wanted to get accustomed to.)
—Health (Some owners who have actively managed their own real estate portfolios may suddenly find that their health is so bad that they can't leave the house; one such owner refused to relinquish management of her lifetime investment, and she ran the business out of her home. Unfortunately, the units rapidly became the slum area of town because of lack of attention, and her children were forced to take over management themselves to avoid catastrophe. They became don't wanters when they saw the units' state of disrepair.)
—Social activities and status improvement (Some owners would rather have the money than the investments; they sell to buy a better life-style for themselves.)
—Transfers (When a property owner is transferred to a new location, he must dispose of all his holdings unless he plans to manage them from a distance; this gives a buyer the opportunity to buy the property at distressed prices.)

I have discovered more good buys as the result of dissatisfied partners in partnerships than as the result of any other kind of problem. In such a situation, the property isn't bad—the partnership is bad. The partners disagree about how funds should be spent or dispersed as dividends; one partner wants to sell, while the other partner can't because of tax problems. A don't-wanter partner will do almost anything to get out of a bad relationship.

Several years ago I was involved in the sale of a beautiful twelve-unit apartment building in an excellent location. The two partners had decided to sell; each of them wanted to keep the building, but neither could tolerate the other. Neither of them would allow the other partner to buy him out for fear of being cheated. They put the property on the market, and I was there immediately with an offer they accepted. They knew that the property was worth more than the price we agreed on, but each of them realized they could go on no longer. They sold for a price that was $30,000 under market, but they solved their problem.

Every fisherman has his "big fish that got away" story, and I have my "great deal that fell through" story. A partnership of seven brothers and sisters were left with a conglomeration of over forty apartment units in one small Midwestern town. They were living in different cities all over the West and had no way to manage the property effectively. They jointly decided that they would not sell the property to any family member for fear of what the future might bring. In addition, none of them wanted to be responsible for any litigation should anything happen to one of their tenants. They had sold the buildings once before, but the buyer had gone belly up in another enterprise and could not keep the units; the brothers and sisters reluctantly proceeded to try to sell the units again. They were serious don't wanters. The symptoms were all there: They were willing to sell for 30 percent below the appraised price, willing to subordinate their interest to a second trust deed secured by other property, willing to deliver free and clear title to their property, willing to close immediately, and willing to sell with 10 percent down and carry the rest on excellent terms with 7 percent interest. They were willing to do almost anything to get rid of the property. They knew that the property was worth more than the eventual sales price, but that was of little consequence—they were don't wanters; they didn't want the property.

Because of my heavy time commitments and because of a very

conservative banker, I wasn't able to secure a loan for the down payment and the money necessary for repairs to bring the units up to rentable condition. I calculate that my banker cost me tens of thousands of dollars in lost profit. (That is why he is no longer my banker.)

Another similar don't-wanter problem results when an owner dies and the property is divided among his heirs.

Heirs usually don't know the real value of the property they have inherited, and since it is just a gift anyway, they are sometimes inclined to give good prices for property they don't know what to do with. Many heirs also end up owning a piece of a larger property which, in order to simplify things, they sell at a reduced price for cash.

Keep your eyes open for good property that is being sold because of partnership problems—a family that can't agree on terms, a group who have become heirs to an estate, or property splits caused by a divorce. It's probably not a good idea to go into partnership yourself in an already poor situation, but you can often make an offer and take the disputed property off their hands—at a good price!

Whenever you get involved with a don't wanter, you must be sure that the problems you are buying are solvable; otherwise, you'll end up being a don't wanter for the very same piece of property and the very same reason.

When you recognize why the owner is a don't wanter, ask yourself, "Is this problem real or imaginary?" If the problem is real, consider whether it can be solved by a new owner. Realize that certain problems are not solvable. Sometimes the neighborhood is bad, sometimes the building has deteriorated too far. Use your best judgment, and don't take on someone else's incurable problems.

Now you know how to *recognize* a bargain. How do you go about *finding* one?

The first source, of course, is a real estate agent. I consider real estate agents so important that I have discussed them in detail in chapter 8. But what are other sources?

The classified-ad section of your local newspaper lists all of the don't wanters in town. *Isn't the newspaper just a collection of "cries for help"?* People are paying good money to let you know they want to sell. Most of the people advertising won't have what you need, but I can guarantee you that at least one out of twenty has a good piece of property and wants to sell it badly enough that he will lower his price drastically for your all-cash offer! Try it. Respond to every ad in the paper one night, and make verbal all-cash offers at least 20 percent below the advertised price on every property. Even if you have no cash, you will have satisfied yourself that such bargains do exist. You can then do some serious searching and secure enough money to take advantage of the best buys. *I guarantee you'll run out of cash before you run out of good properties to buy!*

The newspaper is your cheapest and most productive tool for finding properties for sale. Use it wisely and often. You might even consider running an ad yourself. Try something like this:

> I buy properties.
> Will pay fair price with small down.
> Quick closings. Call Bob, 555-2001

You probably won't have a lot of response, but when someone *does* call, you'll know the caller is genuinely interested and you'll be able to close if you want to. Run the ad in the "Real Estate Wanted" section of your newspaper. Yours won't be the only ad there, so write creative copy that will attract callers. It takes only one transaction to repay all of your advertising costs.

Pay attention to "For Sale by Owner" signs. When you see one, make a habit of stopping and asking the owner about the details of the sale. Don't be afraid to stop; the fact that the property has a sign on it is an indication that the owner welcomes passersby to stop and inquire. Walk in, inspect the property, and ask every question you can think of. It's the best free education available. When the property sells and the sign comes down, stop again and ask the new owner about the terms and conditions of the purchase. And, of course, if you should happen to find a bargain, buy it yourself!

Another good source is to establish a *listing farm*. Real estate agents choose one area of town they feel they can service well, and they contact every property owner in that area. They tell the owners that they are specializing in properties in that particular area, and they offer to help property owners either buy or sell property. The real estate agent will then visit each owner occasionally to learn about recent sales in the area and to discover any imminent plans to sell.

The listing farm is a very successful technique for real estate agents, and it could be useful to the real estate buyer as well. You can call it your "buying farm." Find a neighborhood you're interested in, and circulate a flyer similar to this one:

> Property owners! I buy real estate. If you are planning to sell in the near future, call me before you list with a real estate agent. I just might be able to save you a commission and the anxiety of waiting for the right buyer to come along. Call Bob at 555-2001.

You can find a wealth of information in your local county courthouse. Look at legal notices filed on the bulletin board. They will list individuals and companies that have had judgments rendered against them, that have had properties foreclosed, or that are behind on their payments. The same location should list individuals who are seriously delinquent in payment of property taxes. All of these people are don't wanters; most would welcome your help.

Another good source of don't wanters is the divorce file. Look for recent divorces. You can examine the complete files, which give information about property jointly owned (and probably available for sale).

Compile a list of recent divorce filings and addresses of the parties involved. Then try sending each individual a letter that reads something like this:

> Dear ____________: I understand that you have had some recent changes in your life and that you may need to sell some of your property. I buy real estate and will be more than happy to make an offer on your property. If you are interested, please call at your earliest convenience.
>
> Sincerely, Bob Allen, 555-2001

You will also be able to obtain at the courthouse the addresses of individuals who own property in your buying farm. You may want to send each of them a letter expressing your interest in buying his property. If you want to see what a property looks like on the official plats of the county, tell the county recorder. Be sure to ask questions; it's the only way you learn.

Still another good way to find bargains is to search the commercial record, a publication that lists all of the divorces, judgments, bankruptcies, foreclosures, deaths, and probates for the benefit of attorneys and title companies. The commercial record costs as little as $100 annually and can be a very valuable listing of don't wanters. Ask your attorney if he knows about such a publication. Check into the possibility of getting used copies from your attorney or title company. Most public libraries have copies for use.

Talk to as many attorneys and accountants as you can. The first person a seller talks to about selling his property is usually his accountant or lawyer. And be sure to let all your friends and acquaintances know you're interested—one might give you a good lead. Some people distribute printed cards that say:

I Buy Real Estate.
Call Bob, 555-2001

If you are really creative, try T-shirts and bumper stickers. Or contact your local apartment owners' association for a list of all apartment owners in your city. Contact them all, one by one, and explore the possibilities. Some people even try billboards.

Those of you who have teenage children might try involving them in the search for your real estate. It's a great training for adulthood, and they could get really excited if you paid them a couple hundred dollars for every super buy they located. I have used students between semesters or in the summer months to act as finders for me in locating real estate. These college students learn quickly and can make excellent money while they help you reach your financial goals. If you are extremely busy in your present job, this might be just what you need.

There are hundreds of ways to find out where property is for sale. Just remember that only a small percentage of the property on the market will be right for you. Don't get discouraged; don't get overanxious; your money will run out before the opportunity does.

Keep looking. Keep prospecting. Spend a few minutes a day on a regular schedule, and you're bound to discover a vein of pure gold if you just keep at it!

CHAPTER 6

Financial Analysis: The Numbers Tell an Important Story

Once you've located a property with promise, your next step is to conduct a financial analysis. Let's examine an income-producing piece of real estate to see how it operates. It's really not that difficult. The figures I use may not be representative of your particular area, but the principles I use should apply anywhere.

Our example, a five-unit apartment building, is well located in a growing city; the rental situation is excellent because the building is in good condition. Each has two bedrooms and one and three-quarter baths and is rented for $600 a month. The renter pays the electric and gas bills.

How do you determine if the investment is a good one? To help with our analysis, consult the form on page 78. This shows the annual property operating data, so you can determine from it your cash-flow situation. The top one-third provides space for all of the important data you will need to learn about the property. The purchase price is $200,000 and there is an existing loan of $150,000 with monthly payments of $1,363. (All figures are rounded to the nearest dollar.) The seller is extremely motivated and wants a quick sale. He realizes that the value of his property is close to $240,000, but he needs out and settles for a price of $200,000, which is about 20 percent below market. At this price the seller's equity (the difference between the sales price and the existing loan) is $50,000. The seller has even agreed to sell the building to us with a down payment of only $20,000. This will result in a new loan of $180,000. Payments over a twenty-five-year period with an interest rate of 10.5 percent will be $1,700 a month. In the illustration on page 79, the seller's situation is illustrated at left; our new situation is on the right.

This type of sale is referred to as a Uniform Real Estate Contract, a Land Sales Contract, a Wraparound Mortgage, or "seller carries the financing," depending on which area of the country you are in. The seller receives monthly payments of $1,700 from us (the buyer) on the new loan; with this, he makes the monthly payment of $1,363 on the existing loan of $150,000. The difference of $337 a month belongs to the seller as a repayment of the $50,000 equity, which he does not receive in cash at the time of the sale. The seller has an advantage, because we make payments to him based on a 10.5 percent interest rate, while he has to pay only 10 percent on his loan. This spread in interest rate sometimes prompts a seller to accept a lower down payment with a contract sale, especially if the spread is great. Under certain circumstances he will also receive substantial tax benefits (installment sale) if he does not receive his equity in cash. These two benefits often help the buyer who doesn't have a lot of cash to invest. Our seller has agreed to accept a small down payment ($20,000) and to have the rest of his equity paid to him over a twenty-five-year period.

We have also found out that the property has an assessed value for tax purposes as follows:

Land	$ 8,000	20 percent of value
Improvements	$32,000	80 percent of value
Total	$40,000	100 percent of value

You can obtain this information, which is important for computing individual tax return consequences, by looking at the county tax notice the seller should have in his files. If the seller doesn't have the information, call the county tax assessor and ask for the assessed value of the property. He'll give you a projection for the coming year's taxes. You will notice that the assessed value is different from the actual value of the property. Each state has a

Annual Property Operating Data

SAMPLE

Purpose ______________________
Name: Ridgeview Apartments
Location: 1005 Apartment Row
Type of Property: 5 units

Date: August 18

Price	$	200,000
Loans	$	150,000
Equity	$	50,000

Assessed/Appraised Values

Land	$ 8,000	20 %
Improvement	$ 32,000	80 %
Personal Property	$	%
Total	$ 40,000	100 %

Adjusted Basis as of ____________ $ ____________

	Balance	Payment	Period	Interest	Term
Existing	$ 150,000	1,363	mo.	10 %	25 yrs.
1st	$			%	
2nd	$			%	
3rd	$			%	
Potential					
1st	$ 180,000	1,700	mo.	10.5 %	25 yrs.
2nd	$			%	

		%	2	3	Comments
1	GROSS SCHEDULED RENTAL INCOME			36 000	5 x 600 x 12
2	Plus: Other Income			600	
3	TOTAL GROSS INCOME			36 600	
4	Less: Vacancy and Credit Losses	5%		1 830	
5	GROSS OPERATING INCOME			34 770	
6	Less: Operating Expenses				
7	Accounting and Legal		750		
8	Advertising, Licenses and Permits		695		
9	Property Insurance		1 000		
10	Property Management	7%	2 434		
11	Payroll - Resident Management 125/mo.		1 500		
12	Other				
13	Taxes - Workmen's Compensation				
14	Personal Property Taxes				
15	Real Estate Taxes		2 000		
16	Repairs and Maintenance	5%	1 738		
17	Services - Elevator				
18	Janitorial				
19	Lawn				
20	Pool				
21	Rubbish				
22	Other				
23	Supplies approx.	1%	350		
24	Utilities - Electricity		2 000		
25	Gas and Oil				
26	Sewer and Water				
27	Telephone				
28	Other				
29	Miscellaneous	4%	1 400		
30					
31	TOTAL OPERATING EXPENSES	40		13 867	
32	NET OPERATING INCOME			20 903	
33	Less: Total Annual Debt Service			20 400	1,700 x 12
34	CASG FLOW BEFORE TAXES			503	

The statements and figures presented herein, while not guaranteed, are secured from sources we believe authoritative.

Prepared by ______________________

Nothing Down Seminar Manual

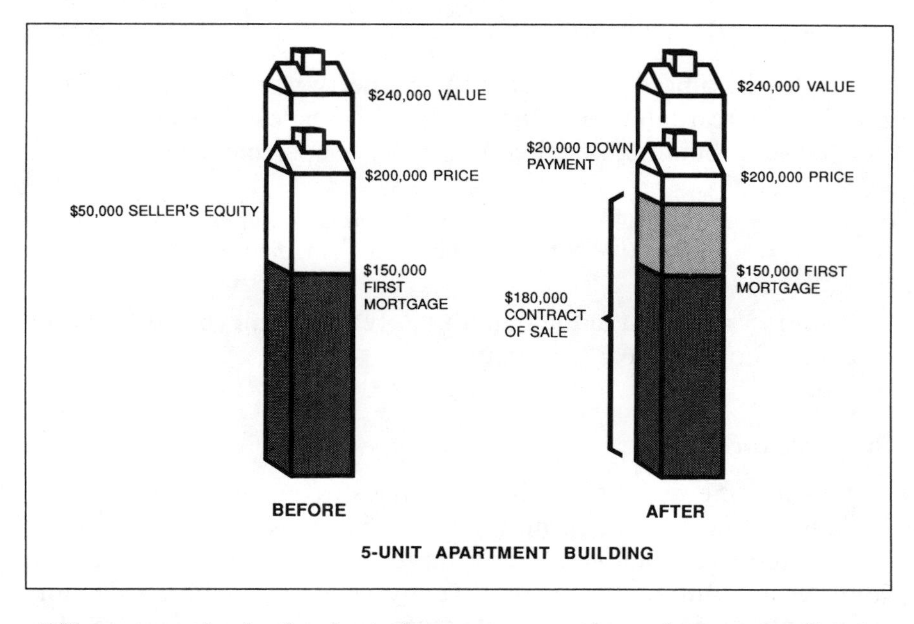

different method of calculating property taxes, but generally the county assessor determines an assessed value for each property, which is sometimes four to five times less than the appraised market value. This assessed value is the figure that is used to calculate the county taxes.

After you have obtained from the seller the information for the first one-third of the form, gather information for the income and expenses analysis (lines 1 through 34). This information is vital and *must* be verified whenever possible. The seller usually doesn't have readily available financial data on the operation of his building. He may estimate, projecting figures far from reality. He might not be lying (although this could be the case), but the tendency is to project high rents and low expenses, and neither figure is accurate. After all, he wants to portray a positive situation to the buyer. Therefore, be wary of the seller's figures; double-check *everything* yourself. If possible, try to obtain the seller's income tax records. The tax records will probably be closer to the truth; the seller will tend to report the lowest income and the highest expenses. The seller may balk at showing you these records, but it doesn't hurt to ask.

Let's examine each of the items in the Annual Property Operating Data form on page 78 to see how each is calculated:

1. Gross Scheduled Rental Income.

This is the amount of income the property would generate if the building were rented all year with no vacancies. In our example our five-unit building is rented for $600 per apartment.

$ 600 × 5 = $ 3,000 monthly income
$3,000 × 12 = $36,000 yearly income

If every apartment in the building were rented all year, you could expect to collect $36,000 in rents.

2. Other Income.

This income may be vending machines (from soft drink, candy, or laundry machines), furniture rental, pet fees, rental of parking spaces (covered or uncovered), or forfeited deposits. In our example, the building has a small candy-vending machine that generates about $50 a month net profit. Yearly income from this source is $600.

3. Total Gross Income.

List here the total of all money collected from the operation of the building—add lines 1 and 2.

4. Less Vacancy and Credit Losses.

Unless you are in an extremely tight rental market, your building will always have some vacancy. Even if the seller tells you that he hasn't had a vacancy in three years, you should impute a 3–5 percent vacancy rate on the gross scheduled income to account for lost days in rent between tenants or lost income when one of the tenants moves out in the middle of the night without paying the rent. It is almost impossible to have 100 percent rent collection, so plan accordingly.

There may be some markets where overbuilding of apartments has occurred. In this case, you should call up your local rental agency or several professional property management companies (listed in the Yellow Pages of the phone book under "Real Estate

Rental Services'' and ''Property Management Firms''). These people are experts in the field and will be able to give you valuable and free information concerning current rental rates and current vacancy rates in various areas of your city. You can also do your own rental and vacancy study by asking other area resident managers some pertinent questions about their rental projects. But seek professional advice early so that you cut your risk and increase your safety.

5. Gross Operating Income.

After vacancy and credit losses are subtracted from the gross income, you know the total amount of income this property should generate in a year's time.

6. Operating Expenses.

Subtract all of the expenses you will incur during the year from the gross operating income. These operating expenses include:

Accounting and legal
Advertising, licenses, and permits
Property insurance
Property management
Payroll and resident management
Taxes
Repairs and maintenance
Services
Supplies
Utilities

7. Accounting and Legal.

Make an estimate here based on your own situation. In our example, we have included $750 for an accountant to balance our books at the end of the year and for some minor legal work. It could be higher but I doubt it would be much lower.

8. Advertising, Licenses, and Permits.

This expense will vary from state to state and will depend on the various laws and rental markets. We have made provision here for about 2 percent of the gross scheduled income to be used for these purposes.

9. Property Insurance.

The seller may let you assume the existing insurance on the property. It would be wiser, however, to have your own insurance agent make a bid; the seller may have underinsured the property, and the building may not be fully protected. It pays to have several insurance bids; you will be amazed at the difference in rates. Bids are free, so you have nothing to lose.

10. Property Management.

If you plan to manage the property yourself, you will not have to include any fee here for outside professional management services. Although fees for such service vary from state to state, they range from 5 to 10 percent of the gross operating income. If you own many units, your rates can be negotiated even lower.

A professional management firm takes care of everything that has to do with operating the property, including the collection of rents, payments for expenses, and mortgage payments. If requested, the firm will send you a check each month with an accounting of all expenses and income. You never have to worry about plugged toilets or leaking roofs; your management company will take care of everything and will call you only for major decisions, if that's what you want. In addition, they have paid maintenance men on the staff or have connections for the lowest rates in town. They can even purchase supplies at wholesale prices.

Now, that's the good news. The bad news is that not all management companies are as competent as I describe. I encourage you to do some in-depth checking before you decide on your company and to monitor their service monthly until you feel that they are honest, trustworthy, capable, and professional. Whatever you do, don't walk away from your property after you have turned it over to a manager and forget about it. Inspect your property monthly and read your reports from the management company faithfully. You may decide, when you acquire many properties, to hire your own management team. This way you can maintain a firmer control over expenses and income.

For the first several months it's a good idea to manage your own property so that you can see the problems of managing an apartment building. Among the best books on the market about property management are Leigh Robinson's *Landlording,* published by Leigh Robinson, Express, Box 1639, El Cerrito, CA 94530 and *Landlording,* c/o Nick Koon Realty, 460 S. State Street, Westerville, OH 43081. If you plan on managing your own properties, reading these books is a *must!* As you grow, you may decide to turn over all of the headaches (and believe me, there are headaches!) to a professional company. The professionals know their business and will perform well as long as you monitor them carefully. In our example, I have included professional management at 7 percent.

11, 12, 13. Payroll and Resident Management.

The larger the apartment building, the more people you will need on your staff. Up to about twenty-five apartment units, you can probably expect your resident manager to handle all minor repairs and problems. The resident manager should be trained to collect rents and handle minor problems without calling in outside help; it's important to find a handyman for this position. His salary should be enough to motivate him to do his job well. You may pay as little as $25 a month off the rent or as much as free rent plus a small salary. This will depend on your area. In our example, we have a resident manager who receives $125 off his rent for the services he provides. This amount is *not* paid by the management company—it is paid by you, although the management company handles the mechanical aspect of giving him the money and will train him.

14, 15. Taxes.

Depending on your county, you will have to pay both personal property taxes and real estate taxes. You can determine what your current tax bill will be by calling the county assessor and asking for the tax assessment for the current year. Don't rely on your seller's past year's taxes. In many cases the taxes and insurance payments are paid monthly as a part of the mortgage payment; know what your mortgage payment includes, or you will be deducting these expenses twice. Count on at least 1 percent of the sales price.

16. Repairs and Maintenance.

These expenses usually amount to between 5 and 10 percent of the gross operating income. On newer buildings the figure will be closer to 5 percent; it could be 10 percent or more on older buildings. Try to obtain the seller's receipts for repairs during the past several years so you can see the trend. For our example, repairs were calculated at 5 percent.

17–22. Services.

Each of these expenses should be verified as closely as possible. Calls to various experts can help immensely; check with the firms that are currently providing the service to the seller. In our example, the resident manager takes care of the lawn.

23. Supplies.

There is always a need for small items such as tools, faucet rings, fertilizer, and so on. You should budget about 1 percent of your gross operating income for such expenditures. After a year's operation you can make a more accurate projection. You may give your resident manager a small petty cash fund so he can take care of these small items without having to bother you; if your property is professionally managed, all of these items will be handled through the management firm.

24–28. Utilities.

The cost of each utility item should be verified by going to the local agency and asking for the past several years' utilities records for the building. In my area the gas company will give you (with the seller's permission) a computer printout of the past eighteen months' gas bills. This can reveal any trends and can help you make projections for the coming year. In our example, I have made an estimate for water and sewer expenses. The tenants pay for their own electricity, gas, and garbage collection.

29, 30. Miscellaneous.

This is just an estimate of expenses which have not been included in other categories. It will amount to at least 1 percent of gross scheduled income. We are going to be conservative and plan on 4 percent.

31. Total Operating Expenses.

A total of all expenses is made here. The ratio of expenses to total operating income is an important figure. Across the country this ratio varies from 30 to 50 percent. In other words, from 30 to 50 percent of your total collected income will eventually be paid out as operating expenses. If the seller gives you a projection for expenses that is lower than 30 percent, something is not right somewhere. It is possible to have expenses lower than 30 percent if the building is new, if the tenants pay all of their own utilities, and if you do your own management. If property taxes are high in your state, your expense ratio will be 40 percent or higher. I have used 40 percent expense ratio in our example. Check with your local management firm to determine what your local expense ratio will be.

32. Net Operating Income.

Subtract all your expenses (line 31) from your gross operating income. What's left is called net operating income. If you have been conservative in your projection and have verified as many figures as possible, this net operating income will be the amount of money you should collect for a year's operation of the building—before paying the mortgage payment. This figure is a critical one in judging the value of the investment, as you will see later.

33. Total Annual Debt Service or Mortgage Payments.

Monthly mortgage payments multiplied by 12 will total the debt service figure.

34. Cash Flow Before Taxes.

After all expenses and mortgage payments have been figured, you should have a small cash flow.

. . .

By filling out the Annual Property Operating Data form on our subject property, we have learned some of the valuable information needed to make a good investment. Your projection should be conservative, based on conservative information. First of all, we have collected *all* of the necessary information needed to enable us to make a wise decision based on costs. The figures have all been verified and are conservative. This one sheet is all that any investor needs to do a preliminary investment analysis. Blank copies of this form are available by writing my company, Challenge Systems, Inc., 5931 Priestly Drive, Suite A, Carlsbad, CA 92008. Ask for information about APOD forms.

Second, we have been able to determine if there is a positive or a negative cash flow on this property. Just as in a land investment, it is possible to have a negative cash flow—an alligator—in an income property. If the mortgage payments are too high because of small down payments or if the expenses are inordinately high because the building is an older one (or income is very low because of low rents), there could be a negative cash flow. The only ways to eliminate a negative cash flow are to restructure the mortgage payments, pay less for the property, increase the rents, or lower the expenses. More on this later.

If you determine after your analysis that the property has a heavy negative cash flow, and it will not be possible to raise rents in the immediate future, you will have to be prepared to subsidize your investment on a monthly basis until the cash flow can be improved. If you are not prepared to subsidize the investment, then don't buy the property. It is better not to buy something than to lose it to foreclosure for failure to make the payments.

The bottom line of the analysis form tells how much debt you can amortize without going in the hole.

In short, make sure you do your homework at this stage of your investment planning. You will avoid costly mistakes later.

CHAPTER 7

It's Fun Figuring Out How Much Money You're Going to Make

Now that you've determined what kind of a cash flow will exist, find out what return you'll receive on your investment (ROI). Let's use the same example: We have invested $20,000 as a down payment toward the purchase price of the five-unit building. If we had taken the same $20,000 and invested it in a savings account at a local bank, we would be lucky to earn 10 pecent for one year. How well does real estate compare to a savings account's guaranteed return of 10 percent?

There are four kinds of return from a normal income property investment:

1. Cash flow is money left over after all expenses and mortgage payments have been made.
2. Equity buildup results as mortgage payments gradually reduce the loan.
3. Tax savings come from the favorable tax advantages of owning real estate.
4. Appreciation develops as the property (if well selected) increases in value over time.

If we analyze the five-unit building with respect to these four kinds of investment return, we discover some interesting figures that will answer the question of an investment in real estate versus savings accounts.

1. Cash flow.

$$\frac{\text{Annual net cash flow}}{\text{Down Payment}} = \frac{\$503}{\$20{,}000} = 2.5 \text{ percent}$$

This kind of cash on cash return seems extremely low. After all, you can go to the bank and get 6 percent or more without any trouble at all. But let's keep going.

2. Equity buildup.

As the mortgage payments of $1,700 are made each month, a portion applies toward the reduction of the $180,000 loan. Using a calculator with special functions (Hewlett Packard and Texas Instruments both make excellent calculators for real estate math), it is possible to determine that at the end of the first year of ownership and after paying the interest, the loan balance will be $178,432. If you then sold the building, you would collect the $1,568 in principal reduction that took place during your ownership of the property.

$$\frac{\text{Loan principal reduction}}{\text{Down payment}} = \frac{\$1{,}568}{\$20{,}000} = 7.8 \text{ percent}$$

3. Tax savings.

$$\frac{\text{Tax savings}}{\text{Down payment}} = \frac{\$500}{\$20{,}000} = 2.5 \text{ percent}$$

If you earn more than $50,000 per year these tax advantages drop to zero. We will assume a $500 tax savings and let your accountant show you how to work out the specific details.

4. Appreciation.

Appreciation is the gravy in real estate investing. It is not possible to project the increase in property values accurately, since the increase depends on inflation, investor demand, and supply of available units. But property values should at least keep pace with inflation. If appreciation rates change, so will your rate of return. But let's conservatively figure an appreciation rate of 5 percent. Our investment return is almost 60 percent!

$$\frac{\text{rate of increase in value} \times \text{value}}{\text{down payment}} = \frac{5\% \times \$240{,}000 \text{ value}}{\$20{,}000} = 60 \text{ percent}$$

Remember, by carefully searching for the don't-wanter seller we were able to buy this property at $40,000 below the market price. We thus made an immediate profit. If we were to put the property back on the market, we could recoup this profit and gain a 200 percent return on our $20,000 investment before sales costs, without waiting for any appreciation. If, however, we decided not to sell but to hold on to the property, then our rate of return from appreciation would be calculated by multiplying the appreciation rate (5 percent) by the value ($240,000) and dividing this by our investment ($20,000).

When all of the above rates of return are combined, your total rate of return from this real estate investment after one full year is found below.

Cash flow	2.5 percent
Equity buildup	7.8 percent
Tax savings	2.5 percent
Discount bonus	200 percent
Appreciation	60 percent
TOTAL RETURN	272.8 percent

That's right! *Almost 300 percent!* Compared to your 10 percent return at the bank, 300 percent looks rather exciting. This is, of course, your return on investment in the first year of ownership. The ROI will decline each year thereafter.

If you had invested your dollars at the bank, you would have $22,000 at the end of the year. By investing the same amount of money in an apartment building, you have made your $20,000 grow into almost $75,000. Of course, the 10 percent in the bank is guaranteed and paid without management hassle. You know your money will be there at the end of the year, without fail. You won't have to lift a finger to earn it. But you can put up with an awful lot of hassle to get the returns that real estate can earn.

Now, before you go charging out into the world to buy your first property, let me prepare you for the shock you are going to get. You can't expect every property you analyze to give you a 300 percent return on your investment. You can't even expect to buy every property with small down payments. Do not misunderstand me. My system involves buying property from highly motivated sellers who, because of their flexible circumstances, are willing to sell their property with excellent terms or at excellent prices or both. You must be willing to get turned down dozens of times before you find the right seller with the right property. This is a numbers game. You will be rejected by most sellers, real estate agents will tell you that what you are looking for is almost impossible to find, and everyone will tell you that you are crazy for wasting your time. But I assure you, from my own experience and that of tens of thousands of graduates of my seminars, that the bargains are there, right now, and are found by those who are willing to persist until they find them. If you want to play safe, put your money in a bank.

But safe as it may seem, there is no profit in keeping your money in a savings account (unless you are waiting for the right real estate investment), because inflation and taxes render your investment useless. You must take the risk that real estate investment requires: You must cope with management problems (or give them to a management company for a fee); you must learn that your financial independence comes at a price, but the price is well worth it. Nothing worth anything is free.

Two final elements need to be considered in an analysis of a real estate investment: the power of leverage and the determination of value.

Leverage makes real estate advantageous. Think of using a small lever to move a large boulder. You could never move the boulder by yourself; use a lever, and the job's easy. Leverage in real estate is the ability to control a large number of investment dollars with a small amount of money. Without leverage the $240,000 investment in our example would not have been nearly as exciting. In the example, you could control $240,000 worth of real estate with only $20,000 (and for which you paid approximately 80 cents on the dollar). You borrowed the remaining $180,000 from other people or you used other people's money. If you had purchased the building with your own money—$200,000 cash—then the return on your investment would have been very different.

Cash flow without mortgage payments:

$$\frac{\$20{,}903}{\$200{,}000} = 10.5 \text{ percent}$$

Equity buildup: Since there is no mortgage, there is no equity buildup.

Tax savings:
$20,903 cash flow × 40 % tax rate =

$$\$8{,}361 \text{ in taxes or } \frac{(8{,}361)}{200{,}000} = -4.1\% \text{ R.O.I.}$$

Appreciation:

$$\frac{\$12{,}000}{\$240{,}000} = 5 \text{ percent}$$

Discount Bonus:

$$\frac{\$40{,}000}{\$200{,}000} = 20 \text{ percent}$$

TOTAL RETURN:
10.5 − 4.1% + 5 + 20 = 31.4 percent

With leverage your return is almost 300 percent; without leverage, about 31.4 percent. That is the power of leverage. The more you can buy with the least amount of money, the greater your rate of return. The more leverage, too, the greater the risk—an element that must be overcome. Real estate is one of the few areas in which an average investor with average knowledge can borrow other people's money to use leverage in investing and, by doing so, can increase his own return. That's what the nothing-down concept is all about.

The final area of analysis is determination of value. After all, who is to say the building you buy today for $100,000 on fairly good terms isn't really an $80,000 building? How do you make sure you're not being swindled out of $20,000? Real estate land schemes have been notorious for selling property on good terms at prices much higher than market value. One of my clients insisted on purchasing sixty acres of desert property for $20,000, a price that is still too high ten years later. How can you avoid making the same mistake?

Determination of value is accomplished through three processes known as appraisal of value. The easiest way to determine a building's accurate value is to hire a professional real estate appraiser; you will find them listed in the Yellow Pages, or you can write to the American Society of Appraisers, Dulles International Airport, P.O. Box 17265, Washington, DC 20041. Appraisal costs will vary from $50 to several thousand, depending on the size of the property. A less expensive—and probably free—way to determine value is to ask a local real estate agent to do a comparative market analysis. You can do your own estimate of value by employing the same process as a professional appraiser.

Cost approach. Determine what it would cost at present rates to replace the building by talking with local building contractors.

Income approach. Determine value by analyzing the income the building generates.

Market approach. Determine what other, similar properties have sold for recently, which will give an indication of what the investor in the marketplace will pay for a similar unit.

Of these three approaches, the market approach or determining the market value is the most effective method of determining value. The prize for investing in real estate goes to the investor who *knows*—not who guesses—the current market price of similar units. The more time you spend studying the market, the more you will know about market prices and the more prepared you will be to judge them. This must be a continual process; with real estate values fluctuating in some areas of the country, you need to analyze the market every month.

Until recently, sophisticated investors usually arrived at a determination of value through the process of capitalization of the future stream of cash flow from an investment. They used this formula:

$$\text{Value} = \frac{\text{Income (net operating income)}}{\text{Capitalization rate}} \text{ or } V = \frac{I}{CR}$$

Most investors wouldn't invest in a piece of real estate unless there was at least a 10 percent capitalization rate on the investment. If a property had a net operating income of $10,000, then its value would be calculated by multiplying the net income by 10 or $10,000 × 10 = $100,000. In our example, the price was $200,000 and the net operating income was $20,903. The formula reveals a capitalization rate of:

$$\$200{,}000 = \frac{\text{Rate}}{\$20{,}903} \text{ or Rate} = \frac{\$20{,}903}{\$200{,}000} = 10.45 \text{ percent}$$

Therefore, the formula for determining the capitalization rate of any property is:

$$\text{Capitalization (cap rate)} = \frac{\text{Net operating income (NOI)}}{\text{Price}}$$

In some areas of the country, the capitalization rates are as low as 5 percent.

So what's the trend now?

Investors are looking less to the income from a building and more toward its appreciation potential as they calculate what will provide the greatest return on their investment. In other words, many investors have begun to speculate on the increased appreciation of the properties they buy. Obviously, this trend has caused real estate prices to escalate in many areas. As people have expected prices automatically to increase, they have sacrificed cash-flow return in anticipation of high appreciation profits. Since rents haven't kept pace with property values, cash flows from real estate are low and can even be negative, depending on financing.

What you must remember is not to get caught up in the feverish purchase of highly overpriced properties just for the sake of investing. Each property must be carefully analyzed on its financial merits before an offer is presented or accepted. Follow the steps outlined below:

1. Determine the gross operating income of the property you are considering buying (gross yearly rents less vacancy estimate).
2. As a rough guess, estimate what percentage of your gross rents will be spent on expenses. As you learned earlier, this may be as low as 30 percent or as high as 50 percent. As you gain experience in your particular area, you will learn how to estimate accurately. For the time being, use 40 percent until you learn if your area has a higher or lower average expense ratio. Of course, as soon as possible your estimate of annual expenses (ratio used here of 40 percent) should be replaced with the actual expense projection obtained by going into a more detailed analysis of the property operating expenses.
3. Subtract the expenses (2) from the gross operating income (1) to come up with Net Operating Income. Once you have this all-important figure, you are ready to use the capitalization formula to determine the property value.
4. Using the formula, determine the property capitalization rate. This is done as follows:

$$\frac{\text{Net Operating Income}}{\text{Seller asking price}} = \text{Capitalization rate}$$

For example, if your property has a net operating income of $12,600 and the seller wants a price of $194,000 for his property, then the cap rate (shortened in real estate lingo) is:

$$\frac{\$12{,}600}{\$194{,}000} = .065 \text{ or } 6.5 \text{ percent}$$

As a general rule, in most areas of the country, the higher the cap rate the better the price of the property. If the property has a cap rate of 10 percent or higher, you had better act fast. That property can't last long at such a price. On the other end of the scale, if a property has a cap rate of 5 percent or less, you can be sure that one of three things is wrong:

—The rents are too low.
—The expenses are too high.
—The price of the property is out of line.

You may still be safe in buying the property with a low cap rate if you are certain that you can immediately raise rents or lower expenses significantly and therefore raise the cap rate.

Generally, however, a property with a low cap rate is being sold by an individual who is trying to make a killing in the real estate market. Make sure you don't become his victim.

The higher the cap rate, the greater the possibility of a positive cash flow even with small down payments. As the cap rate approaches 7 percent or less, the greater the possibility that you will have an alligator on your hands. Since the price of real estate is going up continually (and thereby causing lower cap rates), it is easy to see why it is more and more difficult these days to find a property with a positive cash flow. In some areas of California, some properties show a negative cash flow even after the buyer places a substantial down payment to buy the building. I am of the opinion that a once-in-a-lifetime buy comes on the market about every seven days. I would rather be investing my time finding the best buys than spending my money feeding an alligator property which is overpriced. As a general rule, then, buy if the cap rate is close to 10 percent. Be careful if it is below 7 percent.

One last word about using the cap-rate formula. It is generally very difficult to find a home, duplex, or four-unit apartment building which has an adequate capitalization rate. This is not because the smaller property is not a good buy—it is because the smaller property has an additional reason for being built. The rationale for the smaller unit is to provide the owner with a way to live in his property and have renters pay enough to make the owner's mortgage payment. As a rule, it is better to rely on the market sales approach when purchasing smaller units. What have similar properties sold for recently? On properties over four units, the capitalization-rate formula will begin to be more accurate.

This is a rather simplistic view of an extremely complicated subject. If you are a beginner and don't quite understand the valuation process, hire a professional appraiser, or use a real estate agent who knows his investment market well. The best real estate agent to deal with will have a CCIM designation (Certified Commercial Investment Member). This is a strenuous program of certification which is granted by the Realtors' National Marketing Institute. For a listing of all CCIM real estate agents in your area, write RNMI, 430 North Michigan Avenue, Suite 500, Chicago, IL

60611 or call (312) 670-3780. Through practice your confidence will grow, and you will be able to make accurate market-value estimates yourself.

Now a word about rules of thumb.

Each area of the country has its own special rule of thumb. For example, California uses the Gross Rent Multiplier rule of thumb quite extensively. In other words, properties are valued by multiplying the property's gross scheduled rent by a figure which is average for the area. This figure might be anywhere from 5 to 10 or more. The gross rent multiplier for our book example is found by dividing the sales price by the gross rents:

$$\frac{\$200,000}{\$36,000} = 5.6$$

(But remember we bought this property at 20 percent below the market.) The lower the multiplier, the better the price. If the multiplier is ten or above, the price is very high.

Now, let's summarize. It goes without saying that the location should be good, the price in line with the market, the seller anxious to sell and flexible, and the financial details favorable. However, if the property condition gives us a red light, then we should not buy. The condition of the property is extremely important. What you should be looking for as you inspect the property are areas of structural problems. Is the roof sound? Is the foundation solid? Are the plumbing and heating systems adequate and in good condition? Is the electrical system working? Does the property meet current building codes? (A call to the city might help here.) Are there adequate parking spaces? What about termites? In many major cities an inspection company will come in and check each of these areas for you and give you an estimate of cost to repair deficient areas. I highly recommend such an inspection. It's cheap insurance. You should not be too concerned with *cosmetic* problems. These things include landscaping, painting, draperies, small appliances, carpets, and minor repairs. The cost of these items is small in comparison to the increase in value resulting from a minor fix-up (or touch-up). William Nickerson's book *How I Turned $1,000 into Five Million in Real Estate in My Spare Time* is the best book ever written about this subject.

With this in mind, how do you proceed? How do you gain confidence? Look at several properties each month and take note of their net operating incomes, their prices, and their other amenities. I use a comparative market analysis form whenever I do market research (see page 64). Whenever I hear of a new building that has sold, I try to find out what the sale price was and what the special terms of sale were. This gives me ammunition against sellers whose prices may be out of line with the current market value. There is another benefit: If I know that two-bedroom four-unit buildings are selling for $200,000 (or $50,000 per unit) in a certain area of town, I can be on the lookout for anything priced lower. If I happen to find a seller who hasn't kept abreast of the market and has priced his building at $175,000 for a quick sale, I know I am looking at an immediate profit of $25,000—and that I had better act quickly before someone else comes along with the same intent.

I can't stress enough the importance of learning the market. Go out and compare prices. This one simple exercise will prepare you for wise investments better than any other thing you can do.

Choose several pieces of property from the classified ads. Call the owners; visit the properties. Stop whenever you see a "For Sale" sign posted on a lawn. Ask the owner questions; record the answers on your comparative analysis form. Get a feeling for which areas of town have the best and the worst properties. Always be on the lookout for a don't wanter.

In the process, you'll get the best education in the nation.

Remember: You don't need to have a lot of cash in the bank before you start your search for the right investment. Practice first: Practice makes perfect.

CHAPTER 8

Help! It's Too Complicated for Me (Putting the Professionals on Your Side)

You're concerned. Income-producing property is the wisest way to invest your money. So you venture into the marketplace and make a few feeble attempts at investment. But you encounter a problem you hadn't anticipated: You can't understand what they're all talking about.

What's a trust deed? A warrantee deed? A title policy? A legal description? A contract of sale? A land contract? A wraparound mortgage?

Your head is swimming. A seemingly sane thought crosses your mind: Maybe you'd better put your money in a mutual fund or the stock market, where at least you understand the jargon.

Stop! Don't do anything foolish. There is a simple solution.

There are hundreds of experts in your area who spend their entire lives answering the kinds of questions that you need answered. And in many cases, these services are—or with ingenuity can be obtained—free of charge. You are literally surrounded by your own private team of consultants. Let's see how they can help you.

Real Estate Agents and Buyer's Brokers

A good real estate agent is one of the most important consultants on your team. This man (or woman) is a wealth of information because he understands something about every phase of the real estate business. He has walked through the entire purchasing (or selling) process dozens of times. He understands the vocabulary thoroughly. He can answer any questions you have, or he can tell you where to get help.

The best service a real estate agent provides is market analysis. His job is to take the pulse rate of the market. He knows what properties are selling for, how fast they sell, and for what terms, and where the hottest areas are. He has access to the local Board of Realtors file, where he can check information on any sales made during the last two or three months.

Many real estate offices provide free appraisal services for sellers. Your real estate agent, then, could help you appraise properties you want to buy and could give you an estimate of market value.

A real estate agent is a watchdog on the lookout for bargain properties that come on the market.

In addition to market knowledge, the real estate agent has information from contacts about the financial details of the purchase.

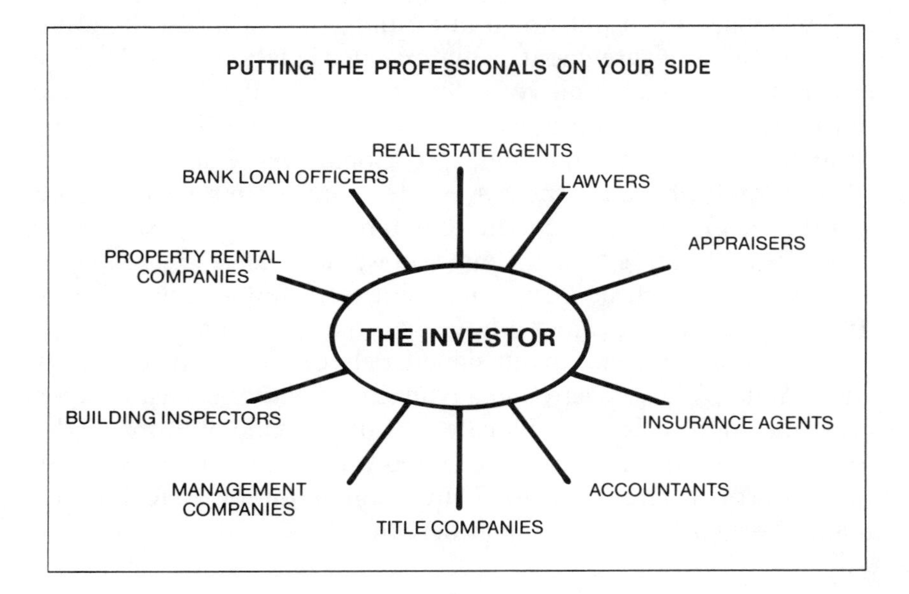

He knows which banks are easiest to deal with and which loan officers most readily lend money for real estate mortgages. This information could save you hours of research and legwork.

As a source of help, a real estate agent is a great benefit. But don't let that blind you to some of the disadvantages of working with real estate agents. A real estate agent's services are not free. He charges a commission, so you need to be prepared to pay him if you intend to use his services. Generally, the seller pays the real estate commission, but the cash to pay the fee comes out of the buyer's down payment.

There are other drawbacks to using a real estate agent: According to the law of agency, the real estate agent is legally and morally obligated to act for and in behalf of the person with whom he has signed a contractual agreement. This person is usually the seller, who has signed a binding listing agreement usually lasting from three to six months. In exchange for his services, the real estate agent is paid a commission in cash ranging from 3 to 10 percent of the sales value. He is paid by the seller. He is working for the seller. He is under signed agreement to represent *only* the seller.

This means that a real estate agent doesn't look out for your best interests first; he represents the seller, because the seller pays him. Generally it is illegal for him even to tell you if a seller is considering lowering the price or changing the terms. He must relate to you only what has been put down in writing, only what is already in the signed listing agreement. Anything else is taboo. (Just because he is not supposed to tell you a lot of these details does not mean that he will not. Each real estate agent is individually responsible for upholding professional standards. Some simply do not.)

Worst of all, because the real estate agent is supposed to represent the seller, he is going to be reluctant to present the seller with the kinds of creative transactions you want to offer.

So what can you do? Try something very few people think of: offering a real estate agent a buyer's-broker agreement. In simple terms, this is an agreement signed between the *buyer* and the agent. You, as buyer, agree in advance to pay the real estate agent a specific fee if he is able to locate for you the kind of property that you are looking for. I have included an example of a complete buyer's-broker agreement for your examination on page 106; it is much like an attorney's retainer agreement.

Questions and Answers on Employing a Buyer's Broker

Q. Who really pays the brokerage fee in a real estate transaction?

A. While the fee or commission may be deducted from the seller's proceeds, it is really "built into" the price and therefore is paid by the buyer. Most sellers think in terms of "net" to themselves and add on commission to their listing price or sales price.

Q. Who really receives the representation?

A. The seller, provided, of course, that the broker is living up to his employment agreement (listing) as the seller's agent.

Q. Can't I (as a buyer) get representation by dealing with a broker other than the listing broker?

A. If the co-broker will receive compensation from the seller, then he is legally a subagent of the seller and owes his allegiance to that seller. Suggesting prices below the asking price would be a violation of the agency relationship for either broker.

Q. For which client is a broker going to devote his time, effort, ability, and overhead?

A. In representing sellers, the broker spends most of his time on exclusively listed properties and little or no time on open listings or uncontrolled situations. The broker who has been employed by (is under contract to) a buyer to locate a specific or nonspecific property will concentrate his time to fulfill this obligation. A good broker will spend little time and effort with uncontrolled buyers who are shopping with every other broker and "for sale by owner" in town. In this latter case he will only try to sell his own exclusive listings.

Q. Under a buyer's-broker contract, can my agent collect two fees?

A. No! The contract precludes the broker from accepting a fee from anyone other than his client. The transaction is on a "net" basis to the seller with the buyer's broker negotiating the best possible price. The buyer then evaluates the benefits to be obtained in view of the combined "net" price and his broker's fee. If the seller pays a fee to another broker, he does so out of the "net" price.

Q. What if the broker I employ as buyer's broker turns out to be unproductive?
A. The contract can provide for cancellation on reasonable notice with protection for the buyer on any properties previously submitted to the buyer.

Q. Will the buyer's-broker arrangement save me any time?
A. Yes. Since the buyer's objectives and capabilities need only be explained to one broker, this saves time. It also keeps the buyer's affairs more confidential. Because of the closer broker/client relationship, the broker can eliminate many weak possibilities and wasted hours, and the buyer need inspect only properties with the "right benefits."

Q. What can I (as a buyer) expect from my buyer's broker?
A.
1. More conscientious representation.
2. A more thorough job:
   a. A seller's broker is interested in a ready, willing, and able buyer—no questions asked.
   b. A buyer's broker has a greater responsibility. Since his fee is protected he seeks the best property in the best location, with minimum problems and maximum benefits to accomplish his buyer's objective.
3. A better-negotiated transaction. Dealing direct with the owner or listing broker may put you at a competitive disadvantage. A buyer's broker becomes *your* negotiator. He can often negotiate a price down to the "real world" and save you more than his fee!
4. Preliminary negotiations. If you wish, the buyer's broker may submit preliminary offers on your behalf subject to your inspection and final written approval.
5. Anonymity! Selling prices tend to become very firm when the buyer is a well-known real estate investor, wealthy individual, or large corporation. The buyer's broker can now act as agent for an undisclosed principal.
6. After a successful transaction the buyer's broker becomes an important contributor to the buyer's continuing program.

Q. Can compensation to the buyer's broker be based on something other than a percentage of the purchase price?
A. Yes. Frequently buyer's brokers work for a flat fee! In some

cases they can be employed on an hourly basis but in these cases their fee is usually not contingent on the outcome of the transaction.

Q. Will I get maximum exposure to suitable properties using this buyer's-broker approach?

A. *Absolutely,* and this is the biggest benefit of all. Normally a good broker will show a buyer only listed properties in order to protect his commission and avoid having "customers" go around him. Since the buyer's broker is contractually protected on his fee, he can contact owners of any and all properties that will benefit his client, even those "not on the market." A buying broker who doesn't have to cloud up his approach to an owner by asking for a commission usually has a better psychological relationship with the owner. It is amazing how some owners who have not publicly expressed any interest in selling suddenly come to life if they think they can "save a commission." Some brokers who have exclusive listings of excellent, desirable properties frequently try to avoid dealing with other brokers because they want to keep the entire commission for themselves. The buyer knows what he is willing to pay for the property, including his broker's fee, and the benefits to be derived from the acquisition. If the benefits are there, why should the buyer concern himself with what the seller does with his money?

Q. How do I select the right broker to represent me in the capacity of a buyer's broker?

A. Ask people in related fields—attorneys, CPAs, bankers, title-insurance people—who are the most knowledgeable and experienced investment real estate brokers in the community. After a few inquiries, you will hear several names repeated over and over. Concentrate further inquiries on these individuals and learn of their specialties, methods of operation, and expertise. Select the one who seems to be the best qualified for your purposes, and make an appointment to discuss your situation. If the two of you decide not to work together, make an appointment with the remaining one and counsel with him or her. Usually, one or the other will be just the person you need to help you. When you feel you have found the right broker to represent you, then stop searching, place your trust and confidence in that person just as you do with your doctor, attorney, and CPA, and work with him to accomplish your objective.*

By using the agreement on page 106 you accomplish two very important things. First, you put the real estate agent on your side legally and morally. Now the real estate agent can be aggressive with any seller he meets, even if the seller has already signed a listing agreement with another broker! If that is the case, your broker will receive his buying commission directly from you, and the seller's listing broker will receive his normal percentage of listing commission from the seller.

Second, a buyer's-broker agreement gives you and your real estate agent greater flexibility and enables him to help find you good properties. Since you're not obligated to buy anything, you only have to sit back and wait until the real estate agent brings you a piece of property you think is valuable enough to invest in. This puts you in the driver's seat all the way. It also puts him in a stronger negotiating position with sellers who have not listed their property. He doesn't have to beg for a listing but can negotiate on your behalf, knowing that if you buy the property he will get paid.

One weakness with most real estate agent/buyer relationships is the real estate agent's lack of understanding of the many kinds of creative transactions you will need to make. Since the real estate agent has worked so much with sellers, he is accustomed only to the normal transactions: Seller has property. Buyer has lots of cash. Buyer gives seller lots of cash in exchange for the property. Real estate agent gets cash commission from seller. All live happily ever after.

Most inexperienced buyers become discouraged when they first approach a real estate agent about finding property for them with no down payment; the real estate agent usually listens to their story and then tells them that it can't be done.

I'm telling you that it *can* be done.

Picture how difficult it must be to have an unbelieving real estate agent present a creative offer to purchase to a seller who is not

* Questions and Answers material on pages 101–104 are

desperate. The real estate agent is flustered—perhaps even embarrassed—to have to present such an unconventional offer to the seller. The seller is equally upset, because the real estate agent virtually promised a cash customer. The seller counters with an angry full-cash, full-price deal. The real estate agent just looks at you hopelessly and says, "See, I told you so!"

There *are* ways to work with a real estate agent creatively, ways to overcome any lack of understanding. Use these guidelines:

1. Give the real estate agent specifics.

For example, whenever I work with a real estate agent, I give him the following restrictions: I tell him I am very interested in any property he brings me when the seller will

—Sell for 10 percent down payment or less
—Carry back at least a 25 percent second mortgage subordinated to new financing
—Sell his property for 15 to 20 percent below the market value for a quick cash-out.

Now my real estate agent has something concrete to use. Whenever he finds a suitable property he calls me up, and I inspect the property exterior within twenty-four hours. I reject most because of location or physical appearance. But if I'm interested I have him arrange for an interior inspection of the building. The real estate agents I work closely with will usually give me a list of properties to inspect at one time. I drive by and do the exterior inspection by myself without the real estate agent present. He doesn't have to give me a tour of the town or spend his valuable time giving me a sales pitch. I let my real estate agents know that when I find a property that interests me, I will act immediately to prepare a written offer through the real estate agent. I let them know I appreciate their efforts and that I will be fair with them.

2. If you have the time, always do your own negotiating.

If the real estate agent is not familiar with your *modus operandi,* he will try to convince you that he must act as a go-between, and he will try to present your earnest-money agreement to the seller

NCR (No Carbon Required)

BUYER'S BROKER EMPLOYMENT AGREEMENT *

The undersigned ______________________________, hereinafter designated as CLIENT, hereby employs ______________________________, hereinafter designated as BROKER, for the purpose of exclusively assisting Client to locate property of a nature outlined below or other property acceptable to Client, and to negotiate terms and conditions acceptable to Client for purchase, exchange, lease, or option of or on such property. This agreement shall commence this date and terminate at midnight of ______________________________, 19___.

GENERAL NATURE, LOCATION, AND REQUIREMENTS OF PROPERTY.
Apartment units and commercial building located in California preferably San Diego but not excluding Orange County or other areas depending upon the particular investment.

Size: Up to 36 units.

PRICE RANGE, AND OTHER TERMS AND CONDITIONS.
Price range/rental: Anything up to $75,000 down payment with maximum leverage for tax purposes.
If client or agent of client locates a piece of real estate in California without aid of Broker the 3% fee will be waived.
It is Broker's responsibility to analyze and do research and act as an investment counselor with the objective of determining the long-term value of the property as compared to other valuable properties. A $500.00 retainer will be paid by client as credit for a $50.00 per hour fee that Broker will charge for all time spent locating, organizing and closing the purchase of property.
The rider attached hereto is an integral part of this agreement.

RETAINER FEE. Client agrees to pay, and Broker acknowledges receipt of a retainer fee of $ N/A , as compensation for initial professional counseling, consultations and research. Said fee is non-refundable, but shall be credited against the Brokerage Fee.
In the event state law so requires, Broker shall deposit and account for said Retainer Fee in Broker's Trust Account.

COMPENSATION TO BROKER. Client agrees to pay Broker, as compensation:

a) For locating property acceptable to Client and for negotiating the purchase or exchange, a fee of $ N/A , or 3 % of the acquisition price, or $ N/A per hour.
b) For obtaining an option on a property acceptable to Client, a fee of $ N/A , and to pay Broker the balance of a fee equal to N/A % of the purchase price in the event the option is exercised or assigned prior to expiration of the option.
c) For locating a property acceptable to Client and negotiating a lease thereon, a fee of not applicable.

IF:

1. Client or any other person acting for Client or in Client's behalf, purchases, exchanges, obtains an option for, or leases any real property of the nature described herein, during the term hereof, through the services of Broker or otherwise.
2. Client or any other person acting for Client or in Client's behalf, purchases, exchanges, obtains an option for, or leases any real property of the nature described herein, within one year after termination of this agreement, which property Broker, Broker's agent, or cooperating brokers presented or submitted to Client during the term hereof and the description of which Broker shall have submitted in writing to Client, either in person or by mail, **within ten (10) days after termination of this agreement.**

NOTICE: The amount or rate of real estate commissions is not fixed by law. They are set by each broker individually and may be negotiable between the buyer and the broker.

AGENCY RELATIONSHIP. Broker agrees to act as agent for Client only in any resulting transaction, provided that Broker may cooperate with other brokers and their agents in an effort to locate property or properties in accordance with this agreement, and may divide fees in any manner acceptable to them. If Broker receives compensation from anyone other than Client, Broker shall make full disclosure, and such compensation shall be credited against Client's obligation hereunder.
In addition, Broker will provide appropriate Agency Disclosure as required by law.

BROKER'S OBLIGATIONS. In consideration of Client's agreement set forth above, Broker agrees to use diligence to achieve the purpose of this agreement.

CLIENT'S OBLIGATIONS. Client agrees to provide Broker, upon request, relevant personal and financial information to assure Client's ability to acquire property outlined above. Client further agrees to view or consider property of the general nature set forth in this Agreement, and to negotiate in good faith to acquire such property if acceptable to Client. In the event completion of any resulting transaction is prevented by Client's default, Client shall pay Broker the compensation provided for herein upon such default.

ATTORNEY FEE. If any action is brought to enforce the terms of this agreement, or arising out of the execution of this agreement, or to collect fees, the prevailing party shall be entitled to receive from the other party a reasonable attorney fee to be determined by the court in which such action is brought.

ENTIRE AGREEMENT. Time is of the essence. The terms hereof constitute the entire agreement and supersede all prior agreements, negotiations and discussions between the parties. This Agreement may be modified only by a writing signed by each of the parties.

Receipt of a copy of this agreement is hereby acknowledged. DATED: __________ TIME: __________

Buyer's Broker: ______________________ ______________________ Client
By: Robert Allen ______________________ Client
Address: 5931 Priestly Dr. Carlsbad CA 92008 Address: ______________________
Phone: 1-800-345-3648 Phone: ______________________

FORM 100 (2-89)

PROFESSIONAL PUBLISHING

* For a free Buyer's Broker Employment Agreement form call 1-800-345-3648.

himself. This is *not* always the best approach. When you talk to the seller face to face you can determine for yourself what kinds of things the seller wants and needs without trying to interpret these wants and needs through the eyes of a third party.

3. Work with several good real estate agents simultaneously.

To give yourself the maximum exposure to the marketplace, you should have good relationships with several real estate agents, and the only way to establish this is to talk to several every week. Explain your guidelines and let them know you will not give them a runaround. If you talk to twenty-five or thirty real estate agents, you will probably only have two or three who will eventually begin bringing you properties, because of your strict guidelines and because many real estate agents are looking for the same kinds of properties to buy themselves.

Don't get discouraged.

The last major problem in dealing with a real estate agent is the fact that he makes his living from selling properties. Since your criteria for buying property are rather unusual and strict, he will cut down his chances of making a sale by working with you. What's more, he needs to be paid in cash for his services. Therefore, if you want to get into a property with little or nothing down, you are obviously not thinking in terms of his best interests.

I find that the only kinds of properties I can work with a real estate agent on are those that require some kind of cash down payment and those that are too good to pass up. Since I am always buying properties with the same real estate agents, they know they can make money serving my account. Once I have established that, I can ask my real estate agent to let me give him a short-term note for his commission, which I can pay off as soon as I can find the partners.

And now a few words to those real estate agents who may find themselves reading this chapter: You are in the best position of all to find the kind of properties I have been discussing. You have first access to the multiple-listing books, to the new listings in your office, to well-known investors who may want to become partners with you, and so on. To top it off, you can use your commissions as part of the down payment on any property listed. This puts you a jump ahead of the rest of the world.

But having a license has its drawbacks. When I had my license I found that my liability was greater. Whenever I bought a property from a client and thereby received a commission, the seller had more grounds to sue me by maintaining that I acted with superior knowledge, took advantage of the seller, and was even paid for it. I also found that fellow real estate agents would not deal with me as eagerly because I wanted a piece of the action for myself. And finally, I found that sellers who had not listed their properties would always want to know if I was a real estate agent; when they found out that I was, they were always more reluctant to deal with me.

Because of all these disadvantages, I decided I would be better off surrendering my license and working as an investor on a full-time basis. You might consider doing the same, especially if your current broker frowns on your investment practices. If you are a full-time Realtor and you love what you do, I see no reason to stop selling. Keep your license and use it in your investment activities.

Other Professionals

The real estate agent is only one member of your private team of consultants. Let's look at what the rest of them can do to help you:

1. Accountants.

Don't undertake any major real estate venture without establishing a relationship with a good real estate–oriented tax accountant; he will keep you from paying all of your income to the government as taxes. It doesn't *cost* to have help from an accountant—it *pays!*

If you run into a property owner who doesn't want to sell his property because of the tax ramifications, you should find out as much as you can about the details and discuss them with your accountant. He may give you a new idea that might not have crossed your mind about how the seller could sell his property without major tax consequences.

I consult with my accountant constantly, and I have never regretted it. Don't be shy.

2. *Attorneys.*

Attorneys are oriented to finding out what could possibly go wrong with any given real estate transaction or agreement and to preparing ways to avoid adverse consequences. Because of their cautious stance, they are known among real estate investors as "deal killers." But you *need* to know what could go wrong and how to avoid it. You need to know how the deal should be written up to offer you the greatest possible protection.

Not all real estate transactions require the help of an attorney, but it is worth the extra money in most cases. It may cost you up to $200 for an hour's worth of specialized help, but that amount is minuscule compared to a default costing thousands of dollars because of a faulty closing document.

If you have any doubt about what is taking place, get an attorney to review your problem with you. Young attorneys just establishing themselves might offer you a free hour of counseling in the hope that you will become a permanent client. If you have never visited an attorney because of the cost involved, you should seek out one who has reasonable rates and who offers a free first visit so that you can get acquainted and comfortable. If you can trust him, then stick with that attorney throughout the rest of your real estate lifetime.

3. *Title Companies.*

Title companies provide you with insurance that the person who is selling you his property has been proved to own the property legally and has the right to transfer title of his property to you. The title company prepares a title policy that indicates all of the liens, mortgages, and encumbrances on the legal record against the property.

Can you imagine the catastrophe that would result without title companies? You would never know if a person was the legal owner of a piece of real estate. I heard of one instance where a con artist sold one piece of property several times to different individuals—each time collecting a down payment. Then the thief left town, leaving no forwarding address. There were several angry investors when they found out that they had been swindled—and that none of them owned the property, because the seller didn't either!

Even though title insurance is expensive, it is obviously critical. You *must* get title insurance for every property you buy. In most states the responsibility for paying the costs of title insurance is borne by the seller. If this is true in your state, you shouldn't hesitate to require that the seller purchase title insurance.

Title companies offer many services besides title insurance. In many states title insurance companies offer what they call a "listing package." If you promise to purchase title insurance through a company, it will research the title to any property you are considering and will provide you with information such as current taxes, legal descriptions, a photocopy of the property and its boundary lines as they appear on the county records, and the names and addresses of current owners. Some even find out what the property originally sold for and on what terms. Such information is helpful to you in preparing an analysis of a potential investment.

The competition among title companies can be very fierce. A progressive company will put you on its mailing list, and you will receive from local lending institutions monthly quotes on their interest rates and loan fees. These fees are called "points" and can be from 1 percent to 10 percent of the face value of the loan—e.g., 3 points is equal to 3 percent of the amount borrowed. I have had title officers accompany me to the courthouse and teach me how to locate divorce files, files on properties that are going into foreclosure, and other important information. Ask and ye shall receive.

Title companies also usually act as escrow agents and closing officers. In other words, if you have a complicated transaction, a title officer will give you information you need to complete the transaction. If you have questions about trust deeds or warrantee deeds, your first source of free information is a title company officer. He will be glad to help you with any real estate problem.

4. Appraisers.

Simply put, a professional appraiser can give you an accurate (and legally recognized) figure detailing a property's value. The appraiser can let you know whether the property is overpriced or underpriced, and you can use the appraiser's estimate as the basis to obtain funding.

5. Management Companies.

No one enjoys being awakened in the middle of the night by a frantic renter with a backed-up toilet. Management companies handle *all* these maintenance details. They're professional. They have staff members (or contacts) who can do repair work at the lowest possible prices. They have connections, too, so that they can often purchase supplies at wholesale prices—all of which means lower cost for you.

In addition to handling maintenance, management companies also collect rents, pay all utility bills (with collected rent money), and pay mortgage payments (with collected rent money). In short, they will handle all aspects of the operation of your building. They'll even provide you with a monthly financial statement including bills and a cash-flow check. In theory all you have to do is wash your hands of the whole matter, and concentrate your energy and creativity on your next investment. But you would be unwise to choose a management company without shopping. And by all means, watch over their shoulder. Don't delegate complete control and responsibility for your money to anyone!

If you do decide to use a management company, it will cost you about 5 to 10 percent of the property's gross income. The more units you have, the lower the fee; fees can go as low as 3 percent. The cost for the services is well worth it. You probably won't be able to afford one right away, so make sure your cash flow is adequate before you take the step.

Managing your own properties for a while can be a very good experience, though—you can get a feel for the problems that can arise and can understand better the process of property management. If you choose to keep at it, fine. Some properties involve very little hassle and would be a good management experience.

6. Property Rental Firms.

Every town has small companies that charge potential renters a fee for the privilege of examining their listings of vacant rental properties. If you are trying to rent some of your properties, contact one of these rental agencies. They are listed in the phone directory, their services are often free to property owners, and they usually refer good tenants (those who are willing to pay money to find a good place to live).

*7. **Bankers.***

The role of bankers is so important and so involved that several chapters are dedicated to a discussion of their services and methods of working with them.

If you feel overwhelmed with the details of the real estate business, you are only normal. Go to the professionals in the business and ask their advice. They are ready with answers. A confused mind always says "No"; don't let your confused mind tell you "No" simply because of a lack of confidence on your part. There are people who are ready to help. Use them.

CHAPTER 9

Negotiations: The First Person to Mention a Number Loses

All right. You've found a property with promise. Now what do you do?

Hang on. Here comes the fun—and critical—part of investing in real estate: negotiating with the seller.

Negotiating is an art that becomes easier the more highly motivated the seller becomes to sell his property. In other words, it's necessary to find a don't wanter if you want to have a successful negotiating experience.

1. If a seller is firm on his price, you must be able to negotiate flexible terms! If a seller is firm on his terms (usually meaning all cash), then you must be able to choose the price (usually lower). Whenever possible, try to choose both the price and terms.

If you can't obtain either your price or your terms, move on. The only time you should deal with an inflexible seller is when his original price and terms are already good enough to get excited about. You can't afford to waste precious time dealing with a seller who might not budge. Move on to the next deal.

2. Destroy all expectations of high profit in the seller's mind!

You must subtly and gently poke holes in the seller's expectations of high profit. Don't let the seller blind you with all of his fancy reasons why his property is worth a fortune. Go over the property with a fine-toothed comb and observe every single negative thing you can. You do this for two reasons. First, you may not really want the property after all. It may be just too much of a hassle; you may decide against it. Second, you want to show the seller that you are thorough enough to observe that his property has flaws and problems that need correcting. Later on, as a point for negotiation, you might require the seller to correct all of the faults you found in your examination before you buy his property if you decide to invest.

Almost every property owner (except the don't wanter) has learned to ignore the flaws in his property and to overemphasize the good aspects. Bring the seller gently back to reality. You might be able to bring his price back into the real world, too.

And if you sincerely follow my advice to notice all the flaws in the property, you may do yourself a big favor—you may destroy your *own* expectations of high profit. Don't buy a property if you can see all your profit going into deferred maintenance.

There are other ways of destroying the seller's expectations of high profit:

Act uninterested in the seller's property. Let the seller know directly or indirectly that his property is only one of several you will be visiting that day. Let him know, too, that there are competitive properties on the market every bit as attractive as his property. You might say to the real estate agent who is with you, "What time is our appointment to visit that ten-unit building on Charles Avenue?" Or "The bedrooms in this unit are not as big as the bedrooms in the Terrace Apartments." Or "This house is priced $4,000 more than the identical one on Seventh Street." Do your homework and let the seller know in no uncertain terms that the marketplace does not command a price as high as he is asking. Show him comparable figures on comparable units. If your figures are accurate and your analysis is convincing, you may cut thousands of dollars off the price the seller wants.

Teach the seller whose property has been on the market for some time a lesson that neither he nor you should ever forget: *The only reason a property doesn't sell is that the price is too high.* Any property in the world will sell immediately if it is put on the market at the right price. If a property has been on the market for more than three months, the property is not worth what the seller is asking, no matter what the terms are. Before I negotiate any transaction I always ask:

"How long has this property been listed or been offered for sale?"

"Before you listed this property, did you try to sell it by yourself? At what price?"

"How many offers have you had for your property? Why didn't you accept them?"

Don't be shy about asking questions like these. It's your right to have them answered before you buy the property. Don't stay silent out of a fear of offending the seller—as long as the questions are questions you wouldn't hesitate to ask in any normal, casual conversation. These are bold questions and should be asked carefully and with great sensitivity to the feelings of the seller. Don't push. Just ask in a straightforward manner. Notice the seller's reaction. Your objective here is not to offend but to obtain sensitive information. It may require time for the seller to "soften up" before he will respond to such questions. Give him space. Make a joke. Try again later. Remember, *your money* is at stake here. You need answers.

Other questions might affect your purchase decision; make a list of the questions before you meet with the seller. Some that might help are:

"When did you buy the property and from whom?"

"What did you pay for the property?" Even though this is a very personal question, more often than not the seller will answer you without hesitation.

"How much did you spend on repairs and capital improvements during your ownership? What structural changes did you make?"

"Why did you list your property for sale with XYZ Realty?"

"What is the worst thing you can think of about your ownership of these apartments?"

"Are there any major improvements that will have to be made shortly?"

The seller will more than likely answer these questions without hesitation because you asked in a straightforward manner. If he balks at any of these questions, ask him, "Is there any reason why I shouldn't know that information? Would the answer to that question keep me from buying your property?" Be sure to smile while you are asking this, to break the ice. If he says no, repeat the question and wait for his answer.

Success during this questioning phase requires that you visit the seller personally. A real estate agent—or any other third party—will reduce the effectiveness of the technique and will probably affect the honesty of the seller's answers. The more flexible the seller, the more effective the face-to-face negotiation becomes. If the property is listed for sale by a real estate company, you may have difficulty getting the real estate agent to arrange a face-to-face meeting with the seller. The agent feels an obligation to act as go-between in the negotiations and generally does not want the two parties to meet. This sets up an adversarial frame of mind—with the buyer as the enemy. And if this frame of mind prevails it is difficult to create a problem-solving spirit which makes the buyer an ally or friend. If the real estate agent refuses to let you visit his client, you can do one of three things. (1) You can try to get as much information about the seller's flexibility from the real estate agent and make your best offer. (2) You can sleuth out the whereabouts of the seller and arrange your own meeting (realizing, of course, that the real estate agent may not appreciate this and that there is no legal or ethical way to cut the agent out of the commission which the seller has agreed to pay). (3) You can decide to look for don't wanters who are selling their properties without the aid of a real estate company.

3. Interpret and relieve the seller's fears.

In essence, try to understand why the seller is selling his property. The answers you get will probably surprise both you and the seller. The seller probably hasn't really been asked these kinds of questions before. As you probe deeper into the seller's motivations and show an interest in his needs, he will become more confident in your ability to solve his problems.

You need to ask and understand the answers to questions like these:

"What would happen if you didn't sell for six months?"

The answer will help you determine just how much the seller

wants to sell. If he says he can wait as long as necessary, he's probably just speculating and hoping someone will come along and pay his price. If he says he must sell before the first of the month, your seller might consider creative terms. The closer you are to the deadline the seller sets, the more anxious the seller will become.

"Do you have other property for sale?" This might lead you to a property that isn't listed that might better suit your needs.

"What are you going to do with the cash proceeds of this sale?" The seller may say that he intends to pay off some nagging debts. Offer to pay the debts for him; you might be able to prolong the payment of these debts, permitting you to come up with less cash at the closing. If the seller says that he plans to buy a plane ticket to Rome, offer to buy it for him as part of the down payment. Then buy the ticket with your MasterCard—another way to defer the payment of cash at the closing. Do you get the point? Try to find ways of solving the seller's dilemma without investing any of your precious cash. Probe deeply. It can probably be done.

"What is the lowest cash price that you will accept if I give you all of your equity within forty-eight hours?" This is a critical question; it reveals the rock-bottom price. Sometimes you should look for a way to raise the cash quickly instead of pressing for terms. Your profit potential may be much greater this way. Don't avoid the question. You might make a lot of money as a result.

"What is the real reason that you want to sell?" Now you'll really find out if you have a don't wanter. He'll tell you he has management headaches, financial headaches, physical-plant problems, personal problems, or partnership problems. You solve his problem. But don't oversolve! Remember the last time you had an itch? You could scratch all around the itch, but until you scratched the itch itself you still had that nagging itch. The don't wanter has the same problem: an itch of sorts. And all you have to do is listen, determine where the itch is, and scratch *only* the itch—no more. Whatever he says, solve his exact problem. If the management is too much for him, stress your management skills. If he has a deadline to meet, stress your ability to close now, today. If he is afraid to sell with a low down payment, offer him security on other property you own. If he is concerned about closing costs, you sell him on the fact that he will pay no closing costs whatsoever (of course, you lower the price to compensate you for having to pay the seller's closing costs). If he is afraid of tax consequences, take him to your accountant; let your accountant show the seller the many avenues open for him to reduce his tax liability. Whatever his problem or fear, come up with a solution. This technique will be your strongest selling point.

Once you understand the seller's position, you will be in a better position yourself to proceed with negotiation. Remember these rules for the buyer:

1. Decide beforehand the benefits you want for yourself. Pick a price and terms beyond which you will not bend. Get up and walk out graciously when you can see that you are not getting what you had hoped to gain.

The seller may realize that you are not bluffing and back down on his terms so he won't lose a good prospect.

2. The first person to mention a number loses.

If you wait long enough, the seller will tell you exactly where he will go. You don't need to mention any numbers; if you do you may weaken your position. An anxious seller becomes even more anxious in the presence of a silent negotiator. Your conversation might go something like this: "I've got to have $100,000 or I won't sell." Silence. "Because that's the figure that I said I needed." Silence. "Well, I guess I could settle for $90,000 if you pay all the closing costs." Silence. "I won't go a penny below $85,000." Let the seller do the talking. Silence is devastating if used in the right places.

3. Keep it simple.

Don't say, "We'll have to draw up a wraparound mortgage with a substitution of collateral agreement and we'll place them in escrow." Using the vernacular of real estate with a novice seller will just confuse him; remember that a confused mind always says "No." Keep it simple. Say, "We'll have everything done legally so that you won't have anything to worry about."

4. Make sure the seller is well aware of the problems you will be saving him from.

5. Try the would-you-take technique.

Once you have listened to the seller's reasons, test your own ability to listen by using the would-you-take technique (pronounced "woodjatake"—a term used frequently by real estate exchangers). Would-you-take questions expose the flexibility of a don't wanter. For example:

"Would-you-take a duplex equity for your fourplex equity?"

"Would-you-take some raw ground instead of cash?"

"Would-you-take a new car in exchange for your equity in your home?"

"Would-you-take a note due in a year for part of your equity?"

Try to give the seller dozens of alternatives to choose from. This will prepare him for your final offer, which will probably incorporate some of the successful would-you-takes. The seller needs to be reminded that cash is only one form of payment for equity. Point out that there may be other more suitable solutions short of a large cash down payment. Use the would-you-take technique to give you a little advantage in the final round of negotiations.

6. As soon as you have as much information as you need, leave the seller, go somewhere where you can analyze all of the data that you have collected, and prepare a formal offer to purchase.

CHAPTER 10

The Final Round of Negotiations: The Effective Nonuse of Cash

You've had some time alone to consider your investment, and you've decided to go ahead. Even though you've negotiated verbally, nothing's legal yet. You still need to make final negotiations.

In most states of the union, negotiations become legally binding when both the seller and the buyer have affixed their signatures to a written agreement called an Earnest Money Receipt (also referred to as an Offer to Purchase, a Purchase Money Receipt, or a Deposit Receipt). Any real estate agent in your city can show you one of the state-approved forms, or you can obtain one at any stationery or office-supply store.

Even if a particular form is not legally required in your state, the law still requires that you show your earnestness to buy the property by giving the seller a cash deposit; the seller or the seller's agent will hold the deposit, and the seller will keep this deposit as liquidated damages if the buyer defaults.

Three rules will serve as guidelines as you fill out an Offer to Purchase. First, try to negotiate price. Get it as low as you can before you do anything else. Second, start to think of your cash as a precious commodity—a disappearing species, so to speak. One millionaire referred to his tight-fisted policy as the Effective Nonuse of Cash. Many of us, on the other hand, spend our cash as if our policy were the Noneffective Use of Cash. Guard your investment capital with your life. Negotiate for low-down or nothing-down deals. Set this goal now. You'll be more successful. Third, you need to be aware of a hierarchy of negotiation. What does it mean? Examine the chart below:

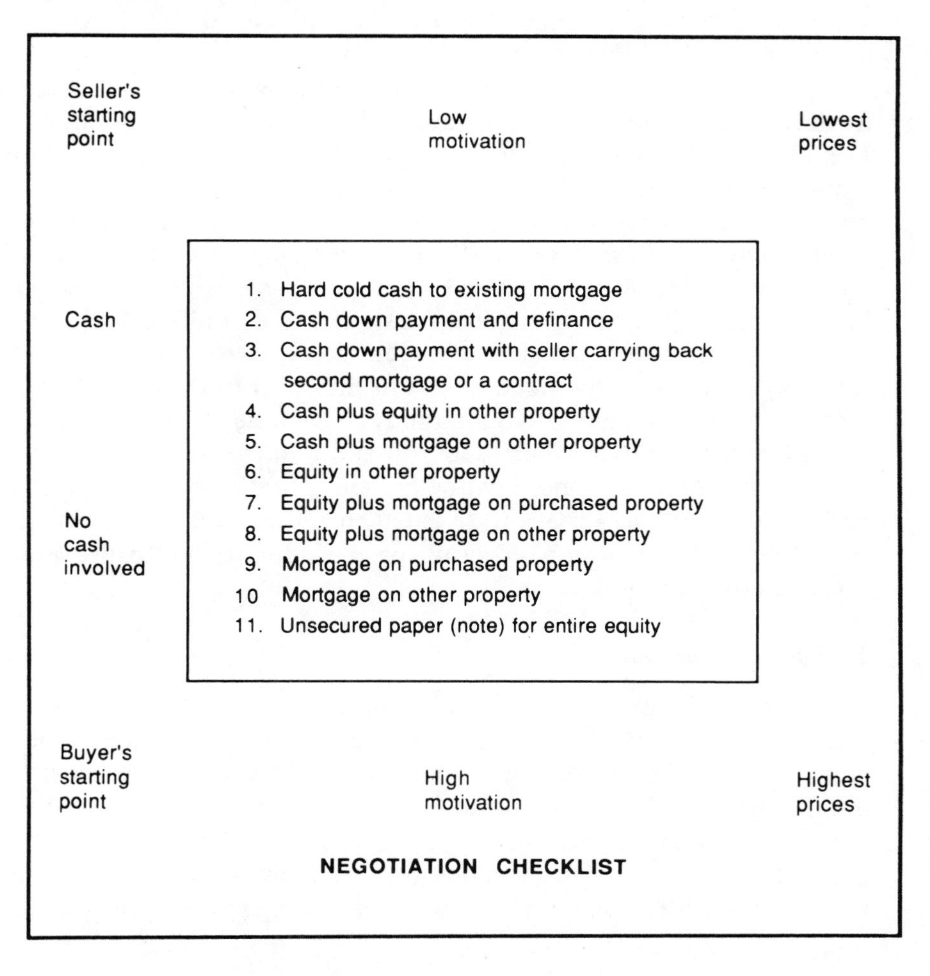

NEGOTIATION CHECKLIST

You can see this checklist has eleven basic alternatives for you and the seller to choose from as you arrive at a price and terms for the final purchase.

At the top of the list is the seller's first choice: The buyer pays all cash. The buyer, of course, wants to start at the bottom of the list at number eleven: The seller accepts an unsecured note for his equity with no cash changing hands. You will learn soon enough that neither the buyer nor the seller ever gets exactly what he wants.

In between the top and the bottom are nine other choices. As you conduct your negotiation, always begin at the bottom, and don't get too close to the top! Stick to your guns. If your seller is a don't wanter, he'll come down to meet you closer to the bottom of the chart.

You will see why the chart is organized the way it is as you read further in this book. Items 6 through 11 do not involve cash at all. For example, if you were to make an offer using number 7, you would offer equity you have in another property (perhaps a motorcycle or another piece of real estate) plus a note for the rest of the seller's equity. With number 10, the seller may agree to accept a second mortgage on another piece of property you own as full equity in his property. The point is, avoid using cash if at all possible.

Once your negotiations have been completed and price and terms agreed upon, you need to fill out the Offer to Purchase form. At this stage in the game, you may involve the real estate agent as a third-party negotiator between yourself and the seller. I always recommend that you speak with the seller first, to determine his flexibility, then use a real estate agent, if there is one involved, to complete the negotiation. Follow these guidelines to ensure that you are covered in all cases:

1. Name of Purchaser.

This should always read "John Doe [your name] or his assigns." This phrasing should appear anywhere on the form where your name needs to be listed. Where the name to be used on the closing document is to be listed, write "To Be Designated at Closing." Why? You might decide before closing that you want to sell the property and make a profit. You don't want the Offer to Purchase to limit your flexibility. Your new buyer can legally qualify as your "assigns."

2. Amount of Earnest Money or Deposit.

Start low ($1,000 or less). The law says that $1 is legal and binding, so offer as little over that as possible. This limits your liability; if for some reason you are forced to default, you want to suffer as small a loss as possible. Early in my career I put up $1,000 with a partner as earnest money and committed to coming up with financing for a duplex in one week. It was sheer stupidity on my part. I ended up paying back the $500 I borrowed from the bank to make up for not coming through with the money. That taught me to be stingy with my earnest money. If a seller asks why you offer so little in earnest money, you might reply, "I often make several offers on different properties at the same time, and I don't want to tie up my capital needlessly."

If the seller demands more earnest money, tell the real estate agent that the seller can request this in a written counteroffer. Stress that you have good reasons for the small amount. Let the seller give you a good reason that justifies coming up with more money. If you do come up with more, designate it as "additional deposit, not to be called earnest money." Then if you default you'll forfeit only your original earnest money depending on the laws in your state, of course.

If you are working through a real estate agency, it will collect the earnest money from you and will hold it in a trust account until fulfillment of the terms and conditions of the Offer to Purchase is completed. If you are dealing directly with a seller, you can either give the funds to the seller or to a third party. I feel more comfortable giving the money to my title company, which acts as an escrow agent between me and the seller; I know that my money is safe with an independent third party. I have been known to give a $500 check to a seller with instructions not to cash the check until the closing. This way I could use the funds until closing, but I also had to trust that the seller wouldn't cash my check and disappear. It's a risky proposition at best.

3. Closing Date.

Sometimes it is best to prolong the closing as long as possible; this gives you the flexibility to raise the needed capital for the down payment, to search for a partner, or to sell the property to another individual for a higher price. If, however, you can sense that the seller will not last long in an extended closing situation, negotiate a short closing. Use your judgment. I generally allow myself at least four weeks to close, and longer if I have to get conventional financing.

Engineer the closing to fall on the day the rents are due if you are buying a rental property. You are normally not required to make your first mortgage payment for thirty days after closing, but you are allowed to collect all of the rents on the first day of ownership. In some cases you will have thousands of dollars' worth of rents and tenant deposits, and no obligation to make a first mortgage payment for thirty days. Depending on the laws in your state you could even use the money as part of your down payment!

4. "Subject-to" Clauses.

These are better known as "weasel clauses." They are clauses that you insert into the Offer to Purchase (wherever indicated on your form) that limit your liability even further. Here you state that the offer is *subject to* certain limitations and conditions that must be fulfilled before the offer is valid, such as:

—Subject to the inspection of my partner, whoever he may be, within three days of the seller's acceptance of this offer. (If you decide within three days that you don't want the property after all, just have your partner write a letter saying that he does not give approval to the purchase. Your partner can be anyone—your wife, your doctor, your next-door neighbor, a friend.)

—Subject to all appliances, heaters, refrigerators, stoves, air conditioners, and all other equipment pertaining to the operation of the property being in good working order as of the day of the closing. (Then, if anything goes wrong before the closing day, the seller has to pay for repairs or replacement—not you!)

—Subject to the seller's obtaining a termite inspection of the property. (This applies equally to a building-code inspection, a roofing inspection, or any other kind of inspection you want conducted.)

—Subject to having all the things done to the property that need to be done to bring it up to standard. Be specific—list repair to cracked foundation, grounds cleanup, and so on. Make the seller bring the property up to your standard.

—Subject to obtaining suitable and adequate financing (specify the amount and interest rate) on or before the day of closing. (If you can't obtain financing, you can get your earnest money back.)
—Subject to the seller's providing clear and marketable title to his property. (You might request a survey to verify the title search.)

Your possibilities are limitless.

Of course, the real estate agent, acting as the seller's agent, will try to get you to eliminate most of these "subject tos" because they stand in the way of an easy closing. But be sure that you include enough of the clauses to limit your liability. Make sure that if anything goes wrong, you've got something to fall back on.

One last "subject-to" negotiation technique: the front porch offer. Among many creative investors a "front porch" inserted in an Offer to Purchase refers to a final concession you want the seller to make (such as painting the front porch). While the main points of your offer require you to obtain an excellent price and/or excellent terms, the front porch is not critical to the negotiation.

Some common front porch clauses are:

—Seller must pay all closing costs.
—Seller must relinquish all of his tax and insurance impounds.
—Seller must paint the property inside and out.
—Seller must pay any FHA or VA points.

If the seller accepts your front porch offer without any changes, then you just got a free paint job for the front porch. If he refuses your offer, it's no skin off your teeth.

Visit your local office-supply store and ask to see its supply of legal forms. Buy a large supply of Offers to Purchase real estate forms and put them in your car, and in your briefcase or purse; in short, have one with you at all times. You never can tell when you'll need one. Look at as many properties that are for sale as time permits.

Make offers on everything. Even if you don't have the time to go through the long process of formal negotiation, at least get in the habit of making acceptable offers. Set a goal to write a certain number of offers each week. Be specific. This is a numbers game: The more offers you write, the greater your chances of buying property will be. Make as many offers as you can, and don't be afraid to offer low. You might find a taker. One real estate agent I know wrote offers to over 1,700 properties in a California listing book, offering all cash down to the existing mortgage with a price 20 percent below the listed price. Forty of his offers were ultimately accepted!

What about a counteroffer? Suppose the seller doesn't like your offer—which is not uncommon. What do you do next? The seller will inform you, usually in writing, that your offer is unacceptable, and he will usually propose a counteroffer. This process of offer/counteroffer is a critical one, as both you and the seller are jockeying for position, seeing just how far the other party will bend. If you have had previous discussions with the seller personally, you will have a fairly good idea of how flexible he will be. Just remember not to bend yourself beyond your limits to pay. If you can't see the light at the end of the tunnel, you may decide to back out of the negotiations quickly and move on to your next project. You can't afford to waste time and mental energy with an inflexible seller. If the property is an excellent buy, then I would suggest moving rapidly. I have known properties to be sold out from underneath a negotiating buyer because he persisted in demanding minor concessions. Remember, you snooze, you lose. If you find a seller who completely refuses to negotiate because he is offended by your first "creative" offer, you should respond in this manner:

"I have taken considerable time and spent precious money analyzing your property. I have even been courteous enough to put my offer in writing. Please be courteous enough to give me a written counteroffer if my original offer is not acceptable to you. Don't tell me what you won't do; tell me what you will do."

Practice making your offers. Your chances of being able to negotiate and close properly when you do find a good buy will be greatly increased.

Now get ready to buy your property!

CHAPTER 11

Paper: The Difference Between Success and Failure

Before you proceed with your investment plans, you need to familiarize yourself with a term commonly used in the real estate business: *paper*. Paper refers to mortgages or notes either secured or unsecured by real estate or other collateral. *Hard paper* comes from a bank or lending institution. *Soft paper* is a note with lenient, flexible terms.

A typical first mortgage held by the bank that financed your house is called *paper*.

When you buy your first investment property with nothing down, the seller will take back 100 percent *paper*. (Maybe it is a $100,000 first mortgage on the property, with monthly payments of $500 over the next thirty years.)

When you borrowed $2,000 on your signature from your bank, you filled out a personal note that said you owed the bank $2,000; that note is *paper*. (The note would still be *paper* even if it was secured against other property.)

Whenever you buy real estate with little down payment, there will be paper involved. The creative use of paper makes the difference between success and failure in those investments.

How can you make the best use of paper? Let's start with notes.

The obligation to pay a note (1) should be unsecured by collateral if possible, (2) should be negotiated at the lowest possible interest rate, (3) should be negotiated with the longest term acceptable to the seller, and (4) should not require monthly payments or should require only low monthly payments. These conditions are critical to success.

The key to borrowing money and making good use of paper is to incur debt by deferring the obligation to repay as far into the future as possible. This concept is against the seller's goals, which more often than not include the repayment of loans as soon as possible. The more the seller is a don't wanter—and the more serious a don't wanter he becomes as the negotiations proceed—the better your chances of working paper to your advantage.

The hierarchy of paper is clearly illustrated below:

High interest rate	Short-term payoff	High monthly payments
•	•	•
•	•	•
•	•	•
•	•	•
•	•	•
Low interest rate	Long-term payoff	Low monthly payments or no monthly payments

Always start at the bottom of each column in your negotiating. Avoid the top like the plague. High monthly payments can kill you.

Using paper to your benefit is *critical* to the success of any investment you make. Let's look at an investor who ignored the conditions that would have ensured his success:

John is just beginning to invest in real estate and wants to build up a portfolio for future retirement. He has little money saved, and has about $250 extra cash flow a month to invest.

John locates a fairly sound three-unit apartment building selling for $150,000. The seller is a don't wanter, but he needs $10,000 in cash. The seller's existing first mortgage of $125,000 is payable at $1,000 a month; the seller wants to receive the balance of his $15,000 equity over a seven-year period at 10 percent interest (a very good interest rate), secured by a second trust deed (mortgage) on the property. Monthly payments would be approximately $250.

John is so excited about what seems to be a great deal that he ceases to negotiate and hurriedly signs the Earnest Money Receipt. He arranges for a personal loan of $10,000 from his credit union, due and payable in six months with an interest rate of 18 percent.

The closing date arrives and John becomes the proud owner of an "alligator." John hasn't done his homework. The seller had told him rents were $500 per unit and that monthly expenses were about $300. But the first few months are a real revelation. Two of the units are rented out for $400; the other one is rented for $350. Expenses during the summer do run about $300 a month, but during the winter, when gas bills are higher, monthly expenses go as high as $600.

John took possession in September. Financial details were:

Monthly gross rents	$1,150
September expenses	($300)
First mortgage payment	($1,000)
Second mortgage payment to seller	($250)
Monthly negative cash flow	($400)

Even though John really only has $250 to spare each month for negative cash flows, he manages to come up with the extra $150

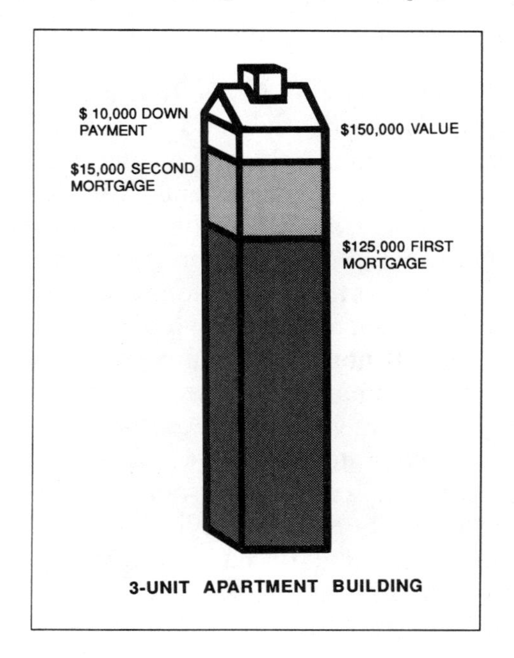

3-UNIT APARTMENT BUILDING

needed to feed his alligator. (And John is lucky; if a major repair had been needed or a unit went vacant, he really would have been in trouble.)

Then suddenly winter is upon him and monthly costs go up dramatically. John is starting to feel the pinch. What's worse, his six-month note is coming due soon.

John has learned the hard way what happens with a "short-fuse" note: It explodes. He doesn't want to sell the building, so what are his alternatives? Can he convert the credit union loan to a monthly payment? That monthly payment will be about $250 over a five-year period with 18 percent interest.

John obviously can't handle an additional $250 each month. His alternatives, then, are rather limited.

John becomes a serious don't wanter. John has learned that when you don't feed your alligator, it eats you. And a person who is being eaten alive by an alligator is the most desperate don't wanter of all.

Today's real estate investor must be on the lookout for alligators every time he negotiates to buy a piece of real estate. The lower the down payment, the more probable the creation of an alligator. You must learn how to cage the alligator from the very start. See the illustration on page 131 prepared by my brother Richard J. Allen.

There are five surefire ways to avoid negative-cash-flow properties. The first and most effective is to cut the seller's price. If this is not possible, then you should analyze the rents and expenses to see if there is room for improvement. How long will it take to increase rents to a level at which there will be no negative cash flow? Can you afford to feed this property until the rents break even? If the answers to these questions are not satisfactory, then you may consider giving a larger down payment, thus lowering the mortgage payment. If none of the above solutions seems to solve the problem, then you have only one avenue left to you: structuring the mortgage payments to meet your cash-flow needs. This must be done in your negotiating with the seller from the very beginning. That's why it is so important to know as much as you can about the property you are trying to buy before you enter formal negotiations. Once you have bought the property it is impossible to go back and ask the seller to accept a different payout schedule.

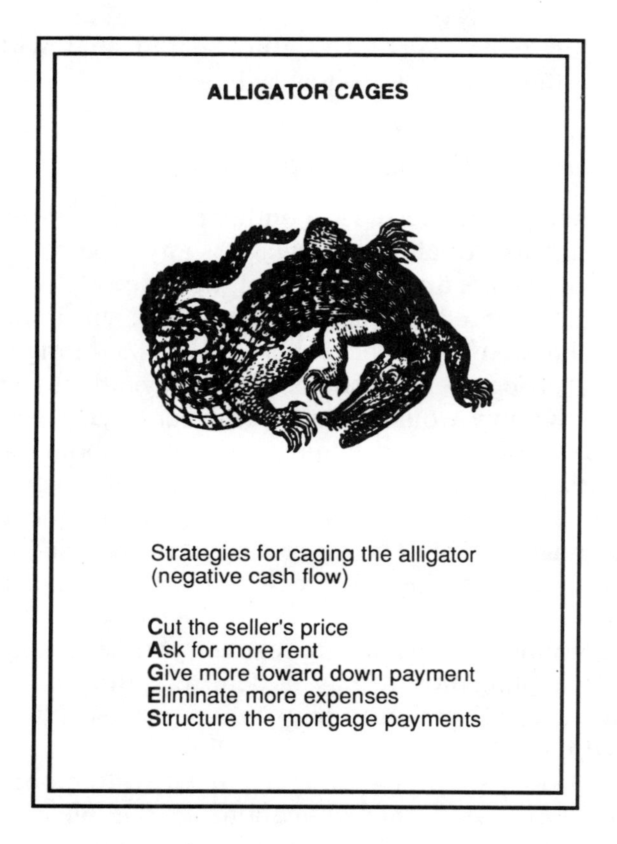

Let's rework John's situation so there is some comfortable leeway. Consider these solutions:

Paper Formula #1. Structure the seller's note to seasonal demands.

In John's situation, summer monthly expenses were $300 for six months; winter monthly expenses were $600 for six months. Yearly total was $5,400. If the seller is really anxious to sell, he should agree to receive payments on his note that coincide with your payment schedule. Suggest that during the summer months he will receive $350 ($100 a month more than originally negotiated) and during the six lean months of winter his monthly payment will be only $150 ($100 less than normal). Such a payment plan will give you extra money when you need it and structure extra payments when you have extra money to spend.

Remember: Note payments are not sacred. Play with the numbers so that they come out to your advantage.

Paper Formula #2. Structure a balloon mortgage.

Rather than giving the seller monthly payments, throw a balloon mortgage at him. A balloon mortgage is any type of note that has lump-sum payments during the life of the note.

If John had wanted to apply a balloon payment in his situation, he would have offered the seller a $15,000 mortgage secured against his property with no monthly or yearly payments. The interest on the note would accrue from year to year, and the entire balance would be due in one lump sum or "balloon" at the end of seven years. (If a seller balks at this situation, calculate for him what his balloon payment will be in seven years: the $15,000 will have grown to $29,231. The figure may have some influence on the seller who is considering retirement and who will need something to live on.)

Having no monthly payments relieves you of an additional burden, and the obligation to pay is deferred. But don't forget that you *do* have an obligation to pay. Your extra cash flow should be reinvested into something else that will be used to help defray the large future obligation. The property itself will be one of the best sources for repaying this obligation. If the building is worth $150,000 when you buy it, it could be worth more than $200,000 at the end of seven years if it appreciates at an average rate of 5 percent per year. You could then refinance the building and come up with the necessary money.

This method sounds easy. But there are cautions. It is always a good idea to protect yourself against the future possibility that it will be impossible to refinance the property. What if mortgage money is tight and you can't find a lender who will make you a loan? Ask the holder of the note for a grace period if mortgage money is impossible to find. Perhaps you could make a token payment of $5,000 every six months until you find a willing bank, or you could negotiate to pay a nonrefundable fee of $500 for the right to extend the balloon payment date for one full year if necessary. And let the holder of the note do his own checking; he might be able to find a source of financing *for* you.

Paper Formula #3. Try reverse paper.

This is sometimes called walking the paper backward. Rather than agreeing to such a high monthly figure to the seller ($250), John could have agreed to make only a $100 monthly payment. Although this amount is not enough to cover the interest charges (thus the name "reverse"), it will at least help the seller in his cash-flow situation and will reduce the final amount owing. Of course, the note will still continue to grow, but not at as great a rate.

Paper Formula #4. Increase the length of the amortization with a lump-sum payment (or balloon payment).

This formula is successful because sellers usually like to receive a monthly payment on their notes but would like to receive their cash as soon as possible. Have the seller accept the monthly payment of his note *as if* the note were going to be paid over a period of twenty-five or thirty years. At the end of seven years, balloon the remaining balance to the seller. For example, if you owed $15,000 and it was set up on a thirty-year amortization, the monthly payments would be only about $132. That's less than $250 and might give you some breathing room. In seven years the remaining balance on the note will be $14,197, and you will have to pay it in one lump sum. Again, consider cashing in on the increased property value.

The chart on page 134 shows some different amortization schedules.

The longer the amortization without a balloon payment, the better. Balloon payments are *not* good except when the property they are used on has such an excellent price it is hard to pass up—then use a balloon *only* if you feel confident that you will be able to obtain the money at the end of the period.

Paper Formula #5. Increase the interest rate.

Depending on his motivation, you might be able to convince the seller that you will have a rough time making payments under the stringent terms he demands. You may ask that the interest on

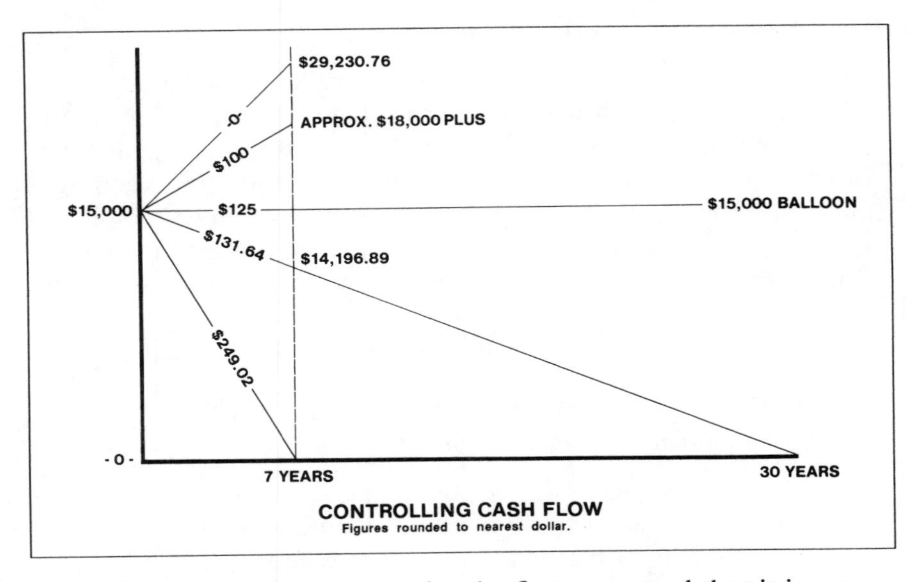

CONTROLLING CASH FLOW
Figures rounded to nearest dollar.

the $15,000 note be 6 percent for the first year, and that it increase a percentage point each year until you are paying 12 percent on the remaining balance. With this formula your payments at first would be lower, escalating in line with your increasing ability to pay.

Paper Formula #6. Pay interest only.

Rather than amortizing the loan, negotiate a semiannual or annual interest-only payment. In John's situation he would make a $750 payment twice a year or a $1,500 payment once a year. This situation relieves the constant monthly burden of a fully amortized loan over a short period of time and allows John a full year (or half a year) to obtain the needed money.

Again, there are some cautions. Many a poor soul has hung himself out to dry with such short-term payments. This formula breeds potential don't wanters—those who are unprepared on the due date. You must have the discipline to save for the payment date or to be ready for it when it comes.

Paper Formula #7. Moratorium on interest payments until cash flow increases.

If John had done his homework, he would have realized that he would be experiencing a substantial negative cash flow during part of the year. Until he had a chance to raise the rents to a level that would cover all of his expenses, he should have negotiated a note with the seller that did not have any payments for the first twenty-four months but that converted to an amortizing loan at that time with monthly payments of $250 or higher.

Paper Formula #8. Convert any balloon notes to amortizing notes when they are due.

Whenever possible, defer payments until you have a chance to become comfortable with your situation. John should have negotiated with the credit union on his due date to have the $10,000 balloon note converted into a monthly amortizing loan; in fact, he should have written that into the note at the beginning of the arrangement. If the loan officer balked, John could have offered him a higher interest rate on the unpaid balance of the loan; a loan of $10,000 fully amortized monthly payments of just over $250. John could have raised rents enough in a six-month period (an increase of $50 an apartment) to cover most of the added cash flow needed to amortize the new monthly payment.

These first eight formulas work well to increase your flexibility when you've written a note.

But what about mortgages?

Most people mistakenly believe that once a mortgage is placed on a property it cannot be removed unless it is paid off in cash. While banks and lending institutions are rather rigid about creative maneuvers with mortgages, you *can* be creative with mortgages assumed from private persons.

Mortgages are not riveted to a property once a property is mortgaged. A mortgage is nothing more or less than a note for the repayment of a debt and a collateral agreement in case the note is not repaid. If you understand that, you can work all kinds of creative twists in your purchases.

Paper Formula #9. Move the mortgage.

If you are buying a piece of property from a seller who is going to carry back a second mortgage (or trust deed) for part of his equity, tell the seller you want to move the mortgage to your home (or some other piece of property you own). He might question you. Explain that his mortgage will be just as secure against your own home as against the purchased property—in fact, it will be more secure because you don't intend to lose your own home to foreclosure. Since a mortgage is simply a security arrangement anyway, he may feel secure enough with what you are offering.

Moving a mortgage has several advantages. If you don't want to sell your home, another mortgage on it shouldn't bother you. Chances are, there's not enough equity in your home to profitably borrow against for a bank loan. Transferring the loan to your own home frees you to sell (or trade) the newly purchased property at any time and to collect all of the equity instead of paying part of it to the previous owner. It leaves you with greater flexibility.

Several years ago I counseled with a client who had a four-unit apartment building; he wanted to trade up to a twelve-unit building I had found for him. He began to arrange for a sale of his four-unit building that would give him $25,000 in cash for his equity, but he still lacked enough for the necessary down payment of $50,000. He approached the holder of a $25,000 note against his four-unit building and asked if the note could be secured instead against a twelve-unit building. The note holder gave the go-ahead. When the sale of the fourplex was finally completed, my client collected the $50,000 in cash for the fourplex and used it as a down payment on the twelve-unit building. The holder of the note transferred his note to the new property. Everyone was satisfied. Without this technique my client would have had to seek a $25,000 loan from a conventional source, and he might have been denied. The transaction may not have taken place. The diagram on page 137 tells how it worked.

How can you convince a holder of a second mortgage to move it to another piece of collateral? Following a few guidelines will help you convince him that he will be protected.

Give him the right to refuse the move if he feels his security is inadequate. Let him inspect the new building and feel comfortable about the move.

As an inducement to move, offer the seller one of the following alternatives: (1) an increase in position from a third to a second mortgage or from a second to a first (use only as a last resort); (2) an increase in interest rate after the move (a good way to give him

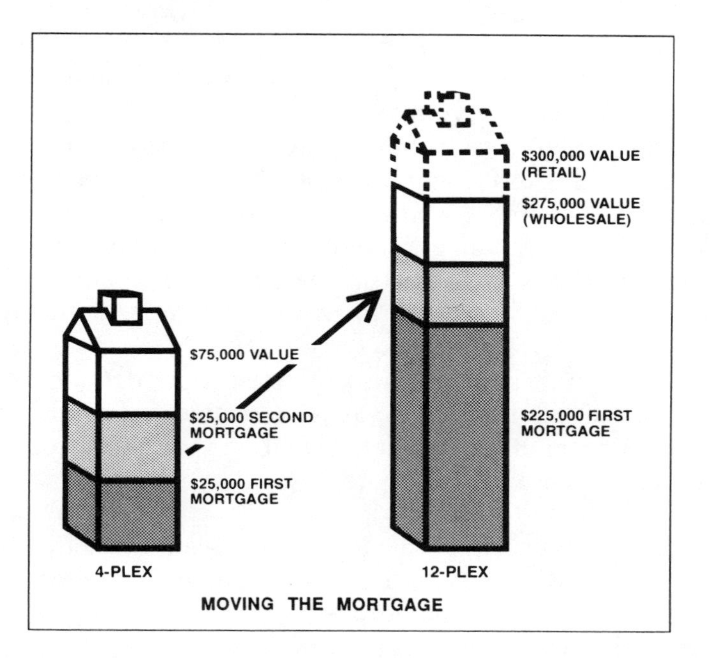

MOVING THE MORTGAGE

something without giving up much yourself); (3) an improvement of the value of the collateral with more equity or a larger building; (4) payment of a portion of the note in the move, a technique that will give him some cash and shorten the length of your obligation to him; or (5) agreement to increase the monthly payment without paying any immediate cash (with this offer he will have more cash to spend monthly).

Try to include the "move of mortgage" concept in all notes secured by your property, because you will need greater flexibility as you progress into your investment program.

The legal terminology of moving the mortgage is called "the substitution of collateral." In other words, the seller agrees to accept a different form of collateral for security on the note you owe him. In the note, you will want your title company to include a clause such as:

"The seller agrees to accept a substitution of collateral for this note at any time in the future as long as the seller has the opportunity to inspect the new property and can feel comfortable that his note is adequately secured. Of course, this approval will not be unreasonably withheld by the seller."

As another example, I had title to a sixty-acre piece of property in a sparsely inhabited Utah region. There was a $12,000 note against the property. There was virtually no way I could have sold or exchanged the property unless I had the right to move the mortgage off the property and offer it free and clear as an exchange equity. The holder of the note was flexible and willing to remove the mortgage any time I wanted to sell the land. So whenever I made an offer on a building I always included a sixty-acre tract of *free and clear* property as part of the equity. If a seller accepted my offer, all I had to do was to transfer the note onto my new property.

This kind of transaction is also referred to as *definancing:* the process of either paying off an existing indebtedness or moving the indebtedness to another collateral location. With this technique, your possibilities are endless!

—It allows you to borrow against unborrowable assets.
—It gives you flexibility to fix up new property and sell for cash to raise cash for buying property.
—It provides a pyramiding potential.
—It allows you to borrow cash without having to sell your property.

Paper Formula #10. Use the security blanket.

The security blanket is used very successfully when a seller balks at one of your creative financing formulas. Consider, for example, 100 percent financing. The seller's first concern is: "Where is my security for the note you owe me? How do I know that you won't trick me out of my money?" The seller is obviously insecure. Play on that insecurity—give him more security than he bargained for. For example, if the seller of a three-unit building was concerned about a $15,000 note against the property (since you will be highly leveraged and might not be able to make your payments), offer him a "blanket mortgage" that not only gives him a mortgage of $15,000 on his own property, but also gives him additional collateral in the form of other equities in other properties you own and don't intend to sell in the near future. You can also use the blanket-mortgage technique simultaneously with the moving-the-mortgage technique to placate a dubious note holder. Don't make the blanket mortgage permanent—you don't want to tie yourself up for the length of the note—but make it long enough to satisfy the seller that you will make your payments and that they'll be made on time. Then renegotiate the mortgage and free up your properties. Use a blanket mortgage as a last resort. But remember that it is extremely effective. Many of the sellers who are initially reluctant to accept your original offer will be agreeable to a blanket mortgage.

If the seller is still concerned about his security, buy a life insurance policy (term, of course) with a face value equivalent to the mortgage, in this case $15,000. If you die, the policy will be paid to the holder of the note (since he is the beneficiary of the life insurance policy), and the mortgages will be removed. A term life insurance policy for $15,000 could cost as little as $100 a year—a small price to pay for something that might ensure your long-range success. (There's an additional benefit in this technique: If you do die, your family will be better off financially because they will be clear of the mortgage in question.)

Paper Formula #11. Create paper.

As long as you own the property, you can create paper against it to use as down payments on other property. Consider this example:

Suppose you find a don't wanter who is extremely flexible. Offer to buy his $100,000 apartment building; give him a $15,000 note for his equity and assume his $85,000 loan. You'll need to offer him collateral for his note, so suggest he take a $15,000 mortgage on your home. The monthly payments would be $150 until the mortgage is paid in full.

You just created a note out of thin air and attached it to a property you already owned. You could do it forever! Now you can create a note against the equity in the $100,000 building and use it to buy another building. Whenever a bank turns you down, use this technique to finance your down payments.

In essence, the power of the creation-of-paper technique lies in allowing an investor to borrow out 100 percent of his equity in the real estate holdings. He can structure the repayment schedule on the "created" note to fit his personal situation. All it takes is to find a don't wanter who would rather have a note than his property. For the nothing-down investor, the benefits are multiplied:

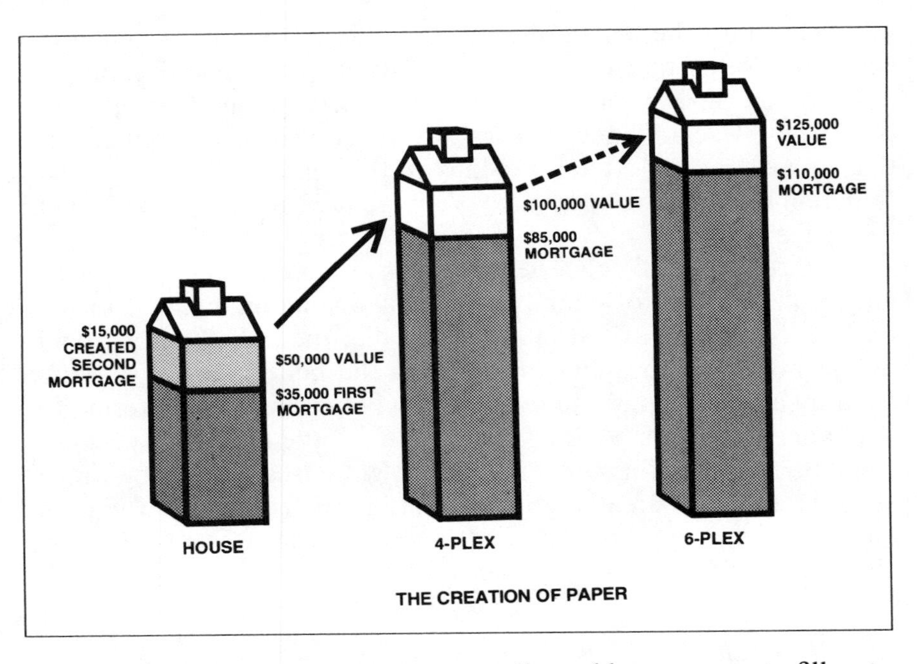

THE CREATION OF PAPER

no qualifying for bank loans, no complicated loan papers to fill out, no high interest charges, no high monthly payments, no credit checks.

Take this technique a step further: "Create" an unsecured note against your future earnings. Write out a note on a standard promissory note form attainable at any stationery store. A highly motivated don't wanter would be happier with a note secured against your future earnings than he would be with his property. Very few buyers will accept a proposal like this, but you'll never know unless you ask. I've found several. Remember that it's worth a try.

Paper Formula #12. Trade discounted paper for the down payment.

Try buying an existing second mortgage at a substantial discount from someone who wants cash now. Then trade off the note at full face value and pick up your profit going in. In our three-unit building example, the seller was expecting a $15,000 note secured by his own building. If he is a real don't wanter he won't care if the note is secured by another piece of property. Your seller doesn't have to know that you paid $8,000 cash for the $15,000 note only two weeks earlier. Just sit back and enjoy your $7,000 profit!

not fixed? You probably can't make a smaller-than-normal payment, but you *can* make a larger one. A small increase in your monthly mortgage payment can have a drastic effect on your mortgage balance.

Let me illustrate. Suppose you just received a mortgage of $60,000 with monthly payments (for principal and interest only) of $663.72, interest at 13 percent over a thirty-year period of time. By increasing your mortgage payment by only $50 a month, you will pay off your mortgage in eighteen years and nine months instead of thirty years. That meager $50 a month was an extra $11,250 outlay over the eighteen-year period, but you saved $89,602 that you would have had to make over the last eleven years and three months of the loan.

If you were to make an extra $100 payment on the same loan, your total loan payment would be cut to less than fifteen years. It's a fast way to build up equity.

Make sure you check with your mortgage company to verify that the extra payment is being applied to the principal each month. Each company has different rules about extra payments.

Study these paper formulas. Apply them when you invest in real estate. There are limitless combinations and variations; tailor them to meet your specific needs. You'll find they can bring success and enhance the final negotiation process.

CHAPTER 12

Running Out of Cash Before You Run Out of Good Buys: Creative Solutions to the Money Problem

Why would anyone want to buy real estate with little or no money down?

First, the smaller the investment in terms of down payment, the larger the rate of return, because of the power of leverage.

Second, most of us don't have much money, if any money at all, for investment purposes.

This second reason is the most compelling reason behind the nothing-down philosophy: We have no other choice.

So you're a cash-poor novice investor. The real estate investment world is still open to you if you understand money and if you know how to make money (or the lack of it) work for you.

Consider a building that is selling for $100,000. The seller wants $10,000 down.

The property is a great investment as it stands, but there is one glaring problem: Who has $10,000 sitting around in a bank account waiting for the right deal to come along? The majority of us barely have enough money in savings (if we have any savings at all) to buy a new lawnmower. Obviously, we'll have to come up with some rather creative solutions.

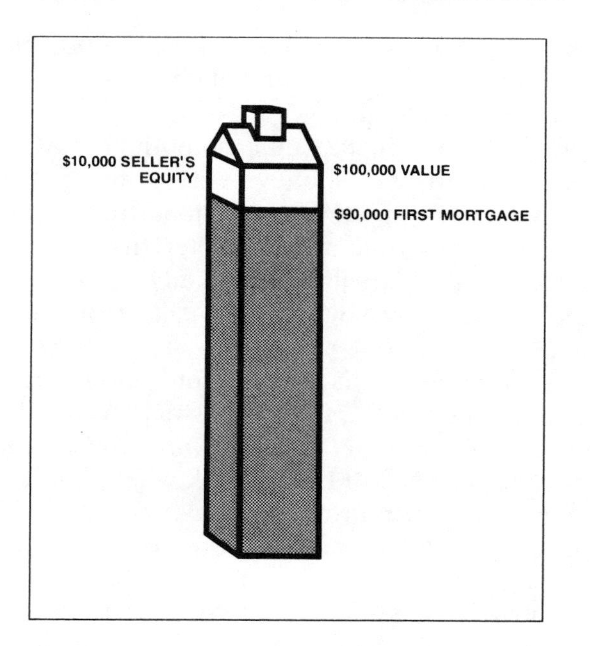

There are eight major sources of creative down payments:

1. Cash saved by living the guns-and-butter theory (the hard way)
2. Soft paper notes used with all parties involved—including the seller
3. The use of rent and deposits, or creative splits involving the subject property
4. Short-term borrowings from hard-money lenders
5. Long-term borrowings from hard-money lenders
6. Exchanging and the use of other equities
7. Partnerships
8. Options

The first source is up to you. You must begin to save money. Limit your current consumption of butter items in favor of future, long-term gun items. A savings account isn't the best solution. Even if you were able to put $200 a month into an account paying 10 percent interest, it would take you almost four years to raise the $10,000 needed for the down payment in our example. By that time the $100,000 building would have increased in value much beyond your reach with your $10,000. You will obviously have to turn to other sources to obtain that $10,000. We will now examine all of the areas open to you.

Meanwhile, you must realize that the nothing-down concept involves the use of borrowed money. This money may come from the seller himself, or from banks, or from partners—just as long as it does *not* come from your own pocket. This process requires a creative mind, one that is willing to try any solution. Basically, it is a process of borrowing yourself to wealth using other people's money.

The process of creativity is a mysterious and interesting one. It is brilliantly described in the following story, from Alexander Calandra's book *The Teaching of Elementary Science and Mathematics*. A student refused to parrot back what he had been taught in class. When the student protested, Calandra was asked to act as arbiter between the student and his professor.

"I went to my colleague's office and read the examination question: 'Show how it is possible to determine the height of a tall building with the aid of a barometer.'

"The student had answered: 'Take the barometer to the top of the building, attach a long rope to it, lower the barometer to the street, and then bring it up, measuring the length of the rope. The length of the rope is the height of the building.'

"A high grade is supposed to certify competence in physics, but the answer did not confirm this. I suggested that the student have another try at answering the question. I gave the student six minutes, with the warning that his answer should show some knowledge of physics. In the next minute he dashed off his answer, which read:

" 'Take the barometer to the top of the building and lean over the edge of the roof. Drop the barometer, timing its fall with a stopwatch. Then, using the formula $S = 1/2at^2$, calculate the height of the building.'

"At this point, I asked my colleague if he would give up. He conceded, and I gave the student almost full credit.

"In leaving my colleague's office, I recalled that the student had said he had other answers to the problem, so I asked him what they were.

" 'Oh, yes,' said the student. 'There are many ways of getting the height of a tall building with the aid of a barometer. For example, you could take the barometer out on a sunny day and measure the height of the barometer, the length of its shadow, and the length of the shadow of the building, and by the use of a simple proportion, determine the height of the building.'

" 'Fine,' I said. 'And the others?'

" 'Yes,' said the student. 'Take the barometer and begin to walk up the stairs. As you climb the stairs, you mark off the length of the barometer along the wall. You then count the number of marks, and this will give you the height of the building in barometer units. A very direct method.

" 'Finally,' he concluded, 'there are many other ways of solving the problem. Probably the best,' he said, 'is to take the barometer to the basement and knock on the superintendent's door. When the superintendent answers, you speak to him as follows: "Mr. Superintendent, here I have a fine barometer. If you will tell me the height of this building, I will give you this barometer." ' "

Creativity is born when you have a problem to solve. And as you can see from the above story, there are many ways of solving a problem. Creativity is the art of looking for solutions that are out of the ordinary, different, unorthodox.

Most of us spend countless hours trying to solve ordinary problems in the same old ways. We enter school at age six and exit some years later with hardly the bare essentials we need to solve problems. We have usually been drilled to see only the *obvious* solutions; we haven't learned to dig just a little bit deeper for fresh ideas. We haven't learned to devise creative solutions to both ordinary and complex problems.

Consider, for instance, the most common problem of every real estate investor: lack of investment capital. Some of us don't even have enough cash to make an initial investment. To make matters worse, most of us have been trained to believe that it is impossible to buy real estate unless we have cash down payments bursting our bank accounts wide open. So most of us—lacking that kind of bank account—never even *try* to invest.

There are other solutions to the cash problem. These solutions require creative thinking. Some of the solutions presented in this book will appear ridiculously contrived. That kind of thinking, though, is a trap. Don't let it muddle your creativity. Be concerned only with whether or not the solution will work.

Stretch your mind to new dimensions. Begin to be creative. To do these things, you will have to make a firm commitment to the following:

Positive thinking. Positive solutions require positive thoughts. If you continually tell yourself, "It can't be done," you will find exactly that. It can't be done. Creativity is born and nurtured in an environment of "can do" thoughts. It *is* possible for you to buy hundreds of thousands of dollars' worth of real estate in your own area. I have done it with little or none of my own money. Each year the graduates of my seminars buy tens of millions of dollars' worth of real estate. You can, too.*

Broadmindedness. Regard the obvious real estate solutions, such as large cash down payments, as only a small percentage of the solutions that will ultimately work. Look for these solutions as a prospector looks for gold. They are just as precious as gold to you, because they will enable you to buy real estate without having to invest the cash you either don't have or don't want to spend. Whenever someone says, "I must have cash," dig deeper for a better solution.

Disdain of the ordinary solution. Develop a healthy disdain for the ordinary solution. Try your hardest to practice creative solutions whenever possible. Deal with buyers and sellers who are creative. You can learn from them.

Brainstorming. Discuss your problem. The real estate agent, the seller, the seller's attorney, and anyone else who could have an impact on the decision to sell or buy should be involved. Search for solutions other than cash. Ask probing questions. Forget that cash is even a solution.

Deep thinking. Ponder. Don't give up. You'll learn the excitement of flashes of creative genius.

Cultivate a creative mind. Treasure it. Some will tell you that the only avenue that leads to successful real estate investment is paved with cash. Don't believe it. You will eventually run out of cash—probably very soon. You'll never run out of creativity. Plunderers can rob you of your cash. No one can steal your creativity. Cash loses value. Creativity never will.

It is your most vital asset.

Commit to it now.

* For a catalog of available seminars call toll free now: 1-800-345-3648.

CHAPTER 13

Nothing Down: Five Success Stratagems

Your goal is to buy real estate with nothing down. "Nothing down" does not mean that the seller receives no down payment. It means that the down payment comes from somewhere else. It means that *the down payment rarely comes out of your pocket.*

You've learned to incorporate creativity in your life. Now use it. Study the sample solutions I've listed in this chapter. Use one alone, or combine them to increase your effectiveness.

Let me involve you in an actual example of the nothing-down concept. The numbers may seem outdated, but the principles are timeless!

One evening I received a call from a man who had been attending my investment seminar. He described a fourteen-unit building located in a small town; it had been advertised for several months in our local newspaper, and I had checked it out with the real estate agent when it first appeared on the market. I had not been impressed. The seller required too much down payment. The units were too small. The rent was too low.

My student had gone a step further. After the unit had been on the market for several months, the seller had become a serious don't wanter. My student realized that the seller would be willing to be a little creative in the terms of the sale.

Here are the facts pertaining to the property. Let's see if you can be as creative as my student was:

Description of property: 14 one-bedroom units (a converted home and motel)

Listed price: $180,000

Mortgage information: $155,000 contract with payments of $1,250 @ 9 percent interest (Oh, for the good old days of 9 percent interest!)

Down payment: Seller would like $25,000

Average monthly rent collection: 13 units @ $150 + 1 unit @ $200 = $1, 875 (Rents were all too low.)

Tenants' deposits: $100 per unit = $1,400

Real estate agent's commission: 6 percent of sales price = $10,500 (based on final $175,000 price)

Reason seller needed to sell: a don't wanter

Seller's outstanding obligations: $7,000 small incidental debts at hardware stores, lumberyards, and so on

Make a guess! How much cash out of your own pocket will you need to buy this property? How will you come up with it?

The first thing my student (we'll call him Harold) did was to offer less—$175,000. Now he had to solve the problem of the $20,000 down payment. As it eventually turned out, Harold only had to come up with $2,000 in cash—for closing costs; to get the cash, he formed a partnership with his father, and his father funded the venture. In addition to forming a partnership, Harold used five fundamental creative ways to lower the amount of the down payment. Let's look at them one by one:

1. Use of Rents and Deposits.

Harold learned early in the negotiation process that rents were due on the first of each month. Because of this, he knew that barring any major vacancies before the closing, there would be

$1,875 in rents and $1,400 in total renter cleaning or security deposits that would become the property of the buyer on the closing day. He also knew that the first mortgage payment would not be due for thirty days following the closing date, so he negotiated the closing date to coincide with the day the rents were due. He also made sure that his first regular mortgage payment to the seller would fall due thirty days after the apartment building had been purchased. Harold ended up collecting over $1,800 in rent at the closing; after taking care of some minor operational expenses, Harold could apply what remained to the down payment. When the thirty days were up, Harold just collected the next month's rent and applied it to the mortgage payment.

Harold also used security deposits (amounting to $1,400) toward the down payment. But don't deposits belong to the tenants, and don't they have to be returned to the tenants when they move out? Yes. But when one tenant moves out, another moves in—and the deposit from the new tenant can be given as a refund to the old tenant. In some states deposits can be held (commingled) in the bank account of the building owner; in other states the law requires the funds to be held in a separate escrow account which cannot be touched. Make sure you know the law and obey it; if you are allowed to hold the money in your account, you can apply it to down payments instead of taking money out of your own pocket.

2. Time Payment of the Real Estate Agent's Commission.

One of the seller's first obligations at completion of the sale is to pay the real estate agent his commission. In our example, the real estate agent's fee was 6 percent ($175,000 × .06 = $10,500). That $10,500 amounts to a large share of the required down payment. Harold approached the real estate agent about lending him some of the commission; in return, Harold gave the real estate agent a personal note guaranteeing to pay the money in two payments: $2,000 in cash and the balance—$8,500—on a note due in three years. The seller wasn't involved in the transaction or the negotiation—he doesn't need to know what happens to the commission.

Not all real estate agents will agree to lend you part of the commission, but the ones who do will probably not charge you a high interest rate, will not require credit checks or extensive paperwork, and may not ask you to secure the note against any property. You should be able to negotiate some excellent terms. One way to convince the real estate agent to take a note is to tell him that if he doesn't help you out, you can't buy the property—then there will be no sale and no commission at all. If necessary and if you can handle it, give him a small monthly payment.

It will be much more difficult for you to arrange this kind of loan if the real estate agent is not his own broker. If the real estate agent works for another broker, he must share any commissions he earns—sometimes up to 50 percent of the commission will go to the broker. This leaves a real estate agent little to live on, let alone to lend out. Try to deal with the listing agents or brokers if you plan on borrowing commissions. The more people involved in the commission split, the less you will be able to borrow. Try always to deal with the listing agent on a large piece of property. If he can list and sell a property at the same time, he earns so much that he thinks he can afford to lend you some of it. In Harold's case, the lister, seller, and broker were the same person. The situation is ideal.

3. Assumption of the Seller's Obligations.

The seller's major reason for dumping his property was to relieve himself of some financial obligations. Harold sensed the seller's motivation and agreed to transfer part of the seller's obligations to his own name. This offer appealed to the seller, so Harold contacted all of the seller's creditors to explain that he, not the seller, was going to pay the notes off. Harold was able to extend the notes' due dates and in some cases he was able to get a discount by paying cash. Harold then subtracted the amount of the obligations he assumed from the down payment. Harold assumed obligations totaling $7,000, so he subtracted that amount from the down payment he owed the seller.

You could arrange something like this in several ways. One seller had not paid his bills for several months. An astute buyer entered the picture and visited each of the seller's creditors (who had understandably become quite anxious) and negotiated to pay them off in cash if they would accept 50 cents on the dollar for their outstanding notes. Many took him up on his offer, and he was able to lower both the price of the property and the amount of required down payment substantially.

4. Prepaid Rent as Part of the Down Payment.

Harold discovered early in the negotiation period that the seller and his family—who lived in the apartment building Harold was buying—would have to find somewhere to live while looking for a house to buy. Harold offered to let the seller and his family live in his apartment until he found a new home or for at least six months. The rent of $250 a month would be applied toward Harold's down payment. In this case, the six months' rent prepaid was $1,500, which reduced the amount of down payment Harold had to take out of his own pocket.

5. Satisfaction of Seller's Needs.

Harold learned from spending some time with the seller that the seller needed to buy some appliances and furniture for a home he was building. He bought $2,000 worth of needed items using credit cards and stores' credit. He then offered the package to the seller for $2,000 as part of the down payment, substantially reducing the amount of cash required for the down payment.

Look at Harold's final negotiation on the building:

He was able to receive credits totaling $22,000.

Real estate agent's fees borrowed	$ 8,500
Rents and deposits	3,000
Seller's obligations assumed	7,000
Seller's furniture bought on credit	2,000
Prepaid rents to seller	1,500
Total credits	$22,000

Of course, there were some cash items that had to be paid out at the closing:

Real estate agent's cash	$ 2,000
Closing costs	2,000
Seller's down payment	20,000
Total debits	$24,000

The total amount of extra cash needed to close this transaction was only $2,000 (the difference between the debits and the credits).

Harold borrowed that from his father. Harold took *nothing* out of his own pocket toward the down payment; he virtually purchased the building for *nothing down*.

Two things will make you successful in efforts to reduce a down payment. First, talk to the seller. Find out his needs, his obligations; try to determine why he is selling. Such information can give you clues to a workable approach. Second, use the techniques listed simultaneously in creative combinations. Look at what Harold did with all five.

And there are more. Keep reading!

CHAPTER 14

Seven More Nothing-Down Techniques

Before you learn other techniques to reduce down payment, understand that as far as a down payment is concerned, the seller is your best friend. Talk to him. Learn what you can about his situation. Let him tell you (without knowing it) which of these techniques will bring a favorable response:

1. The Ultimate Paper-Out.

I was once working with a very close friend (we'll call him Louis) as a partner on a subdivision. He wanted to invest in more real estate as a way of bettering his tax position, but he didn't have any cash to use for an investment.

I had recently been talking to another friend of mine who owned a four-unit apartment building; his time was spread so thin that he couldn't handle the management, and he desperately mentioned that he would gladly sell his building for nothing down. *He was a serious don't wanter.* He had all the symptoms: a rational decision to sell with totally irrational terms, the motivation to act immediately, and the willingness to be as flexible as necessary.

I considered buying the property myself, but my time was

spread too thin, and I soon would have been a don't wanter for the same reason my friend was. But the property was perfect for Louis. Within one week we had the property signed over into his name. Here are some of the financial details:

Sale price	$70,000
First mortgage	55,000
Second mortgage	12,000
Third mortgage	3,000
Seller's required down	– 0 –

The seller arranged for a second mortgage of $12,000 through a lending institution he worked for. He paid the loan fees and interest fees to set up the new loan. Louis assumed both the first and second mortgage loans. The remaining $3,000 of the seller's equity was put in the form of a note secured by a third trust deed against the property; 12 percent interest accrued on the note for the first three years, but there were *no monthly payments!* At the end of the first three years the note would begin a monthly schedule for a payout over a ten-year period.

A quick look at the cash-flow situation revealed that the income from the rents was not enough to cover expenses and mortgage payments on both the first and second mortgages. Louis would have to come up with an additional $80–100 a month!

Wasn't it a crazy move to make? Shouldn't income from rental properties cover mortgage payments? Isn't it wrong to invest in something like this?

In Louis's case, no. Remember—he wanted to improve his tax situation. Paying out the extra $100 a month did just that—and didn't alter his life-style because of an adequate cash flow from other sources.

About two months before he'd owned the property for a year, Louis placed the following ad in the local newspaper:

Fourplex for sale by owner
$78,000
Call Louis, 555–1234

Three days later he sold the property for $78,000 cash. The original owner received his $3,000 from the sale, and Louis received $8,000 in cash.

Louis's down payment was nothing at the time of the purchase, but he had to make a "deferred down payment" of $100 negative cash flow each month. His total down payment amounted to about $1,000 during the ten months he owned the building. His net profit for his ten months of ownership was $7,000 in cash.

Louis is not an isolated example. This kind of transaction happens every day in every major city of our country. It might as well start happening to you. The technique is called the paper-out formula because the seller actually takes his equity in the form of paper or mortgages. No cash is transferred. The buyer gives his promise to pay the seller's equity over a specified period of time. The buyer has 100 percent leverage. Total leverage almost always results in a negative cash flow.

What about negative cash flows? Don't be scared of a negative cash flow *if* you have the money to cover it, *if* you can eventually raise the rents to cover it, or *if* you plan on keeping the property only a short while and expect to sell it for a substantial profit.

One word of caution: Be deadly accurate in your projection of the expenses. Most owners with negative cash flow end up in trouble because they didn't project accurately enough what the expenses would be, and the negative cash flow gets greater and greater. Do your homework carefully before you buy something that appears to be a marginal property.

2. *The Balloon Down Payment.*

In this transaction the buyer gives the seller part of the down payment in cash and then negotiates to pay the rest in several "balloon payments"—for instance, on a down payment of $3,000 the buyer might pay $600 at the time of the sale, $1,200 six months later, and $1,200 a year after the sale.

This approach is really quite logical. The seller who must have a majority of his equity in cash—and who therefore requires a cash down payment—may be persuaded to sell his property if he receives a portion of the down payment immediately and the rest in a relatively short period of time. You can take possession of the property with a relatively small down payment and a promise to pay the rest.

This is a gutsy technique, but it allows you to have some breathing room, some time in which to search for the remaining down payment. You may just want to fix the property up and put it back on the market for a quick profit. Your new buyer would provide you with the money to cover the balloon payment. A word of caution: Have other sources to bail you out in case you can't sell quickly enough.

It is common practice for a seller to accept part of a down payment in cash and the rest in the form of a second or third mortgage.

"Taking out a second mortgage" does *not* mean that you go to the bank and borrow the money secured on a second mortgage. Banks are not involved in any way in the process; it's a transaction you work out with the seller.

Let's look at an example.

Upon graduating from college I began looking for properties to invest in. The first newspaper I picked up ran an ad in the income-property section of the classified ads that read something like this:

> Income property, duplex close to campus, reasonable down payment. Seller anxious. Call Terry at 555–4321.

I called immediately and got an appointment to visit the property that afternoon.

The property was rather run-down in appearance but was well built, and the location was excellent. The sellers, a mother-and-son partnership, had been trying to sell for some time. They were serious don't wanters. A real estate firm had tried for months with no success to sell the property at $26,500. In desperation the mother and son had canceled the listing and had begun to advertise the property themselves for $25,500. Their loan was $19,000 and they wanted to cash out.

After examining the property "thoroughly" (at the time I didn't really know what to look for), I called up the least expensive appraiser in the Yellow Pages and had him do a quick appraisal. He estimated that the duplex was worth $22,500 without the furniture, which was probably worth $1,000.

That wasn't much consolation. I went to visit the seller at his apartment so I could assess the situation. The son was attending school and was in the middle of a master's degree program. He didn't have time to manage the duplex, and he needed the money.

After several hours of talking, we reached a solution. He would accept a price of $25,000. I would assume his loan of $19,000 at the bank. The remaining $6,000 equity would be paid as follows: (1) $1,500 upon closing, (2) $1,000 in two months, (3) an additional $1,000 in another two months, and (4) the remaining $2,500 in equal monthly installments of $75 until paid in full (about four years). The $75-a-month payment was secured by a second mortgage on the duplex.

Four days after I bought this property for $25,000 with a $1,500 down payment, a neighbor approached me and offered me $28,000 for the property. He had been in Mexico and had not known the property was on the market. He agreed to continue to pay the balloon payments as I had negotiated with the seller. And he paid me back my original $1,500 down payment plus the $3,000 profit.

3. Using Talent, Not Cash.

Depending on who your seller is, you may be able to trade the seller some of your valuable services as part of the down payment. If you are an accountant or an attorney, you could give your seller credits toward the use of your services—for instance, offer to do his taxes for the next ten years. I once offered a building contractor a partial equity in a building lot I owned in exchange for the use of his labor on my own personal residence. He agreed to do all the carpentry work on my home for free in exchange for my equity in a $14,000 building lot upon which he could build himself a home. We both came out ahead—and happy.

Take advantage of any services you have that can be traded in part for real estate equities. One of my students was in the business of selling home food storage. He could buy the merchandise at dealer's cost and trade it for full retail value as equity in a piece of property. Let your imagination run wild.

4. High Monthly Down Payments.

If you are blessed with a high monthly surplus cash flow but don't want to wait to save for the down payment, consider offering the seller his equity in the form of a very high monthly payment. For example, suppose a seller wanted to sell, but he needed some cash for his $100,000 home with a $6,000 equity. Offer to buy his home with no down payment, assume his existing loan of $94,000, and make him a $500 monthly payment at 12 percent interest on his remaining equity. An anxious seller may bite because he knows that he can get his full price this way rather than a lesser price and an all-cash offer.

This technique offers you the flexibility of having at least thirty days to find another buyer if you are going to sell the property for quick profit. It also acts as a forced savings plan: At the end of twelve months you will have been forced to pay over $6,000 cash to buy the property, but the property will probably have appreciated during that period of time. Compare the return to that of a savings account: $500 a month into a bank account plus 8 percent interest (if you can get it) will grow to about $6,225 before taxes. The same $500 toward equity in a home nets you at least as much including loan equity build-up, if the property appreciates in value by only 5 percent ($100,000 x .05 = $5,000). You could more than double your money.

The obvious winner is the real estate purchase.

5. Raising the Price, Lowering the Terms.

If you determine that the seller is more concerned about his price than about what he receives in the form of cash, appeal to his sense of greed. Using the numbers from the previous example, offer him a price of $105,000 if he will sell the building to you with no-down or low-down terms. Tell him he can choose: $95,000 all cash or $105,000 with no cash down. The real estate industry operates on a universal rule: The more cash involved in the sale, the lower the price. The converse is also true: The lower the cash, the higher the price and profit to the seller. *It may be to your advantage to offer a higher price for a lower down payment.*

6. Splitting the Property.

I once bought a twelve-unit apartment building from an attorney who had purchased it less than eighteen months before. When he bought the building there was a small two-bedroom home on the same piece of property included in the deal. Since the property was commercially zoned and located near the city's downtown section, he simply split the home out of the legal description of the original property.

He paid $140,000 for the property. He sold me the twelve-unit building for $141,000, and he sold the small home to a title company for $19,500. His profit for an eighteen-month holding period was about $20,000.

One of my students came across the same sort of situation not long ago. He and his wife had been looking for property ever since they had mortgaged their home to buy a fifteen-unit building. The wife made an offer on three duplexes; they asked me if there was a way for them to buy all three units without using any of their own cash. We decided they should sell two of the units for a higher price; the profit they earned would give them some cash to pay the owner of three units. They had negotiated a three-month closing date. The properties were substantially underpriced, so they went looking for someone who would pay a higher price on two of the units before the closing date arrived. Then they would have sold the two units to the new buyer in a simultaneous closing that would have given them enough profit to be able to buy the third unit without investing any of their own cash. This technique is discussed in more detail in the chapter on options. As it turned out, my students located a man who was willing to lend them the money for the down payments on the three units, and they decided to buy the properties and keep them.

Another example clearly shows the splitting technique. A friend purchased an older thirty-unit apartment building which had a large amount of antique furniture in it. He removed the furniture and sold it to an antique dealer for $20,000. This helped him with the down payment he had negotiated, since he had given himself ample time to sell the furniture for cash.

Other splits? Several years back I bought a house that had a very deep, weed-covered back lot. The neighbor around the corner approached me before I closed on the sale and asked if I was interested in selling the back lot to him. I agreed to sell it for $2,900. Since my down payment to buy the home was only $2,000, I was able to apply $2,000 of the money from the sale of the back lot to the down payment on the house and put about $900 in my pocket. Of course, to accomplish the sale of the back lot I had to have it released from the mortgage with a lending institution. This required a new survey, a new appraisal, a new title policy, and some paperwork. But it was well worth it!

7. Deferring the Down Payment With No Mortgage Payments.

My students are always teaching me new techniques. At one of my seminars one of my repeat students related this story to me. I thought it was creative enough to include as one of the arsenal of nothing-down techniques.

After having taken the Nothing Down Seminar this student went out into the marketplace to find some property to buy. He located an older six-unit building which the seller owned free and clear of any mortgages. The property was in an excellent location and was priced right. There was only one problem. The seller wanted a $10,000 down payment, which my student did not have at the time. He began to use his head instead of his pocketbook and came up with the following solution. He reasoned that the seller had no mortgage payments to make each month and that he was wealthy enough so that the lack of monthly income for a few months would not be a burden to him. So my student proposed that the seller turn over the property to him with no down payment and *no mortgage payments* for six months. Interest would accrue on the mortgage for six months; at the end of this period, normal monthly payments would commence and continue for the next twenty-five years until paid in full. The seller reluctantly agreed, since he was able to obtain his full asking price and terms with the small exception of the six-month delay in the down payment. As soon as the buyer took over the property, he was able to collect the rents and the security deposits and put them in his bank account. And as each month rolled around he collected the rents and let them accrue in his bank account. He paid out only necessary expenses and did all of the maintenance work himself to save money. As you can guess by now, since he did not have a mortgage payment to make, the majority of the income he collected went right into savings, and during the next six months he was able to save enough money to come up with almost all the required $10,000 down payment. (E.g., six units renting at $275 per month gives a gross monthly income of $1,650. In six months' time, over $9,900 has been collected from rents, not counting the tenant security deposits. If he can be frugal with his expense money, the $10,000 down payment is generated from the property rents.) In effect, the buyer borrowed the down payment from the seller, who let him repay it over the next twenty-five years. Not bad.

So far we've discussed twelve creative ways to come up with part or all of a down payment. There are times, though, when you will be forced to come up with cash. To do that, you might have to turn to banks and other lending institutions. Let's examine the best ways to use those sources.

CHAPTER 15

Funds from the Philistines: Short-Term Loans from Hard-Money Lenders

So you've located the perfect deal, a real bargain! How are you going to get your name on the deed if you don't have something put aside for a rainy day?

You'll need to borrow the money, probably from someone I call a "hard-money lender." Hard-money lenders offer you hard terms: The loan has a high interest rate and a short-term payback period, and, as a consequence, high monthly payments. In addition, hard-money lenders always try to secure the loan by using another piece of property as collateral. There's another good reason for calling them "hard-money lenders"—the loans are hard to get! If your income is low, your monthly obligations are high, or you are self-employed, watch out. Hard-money lenders are wary of a borrower like you, especially if you are planning on investing the borrowed funds in real estate. For some reason most hard-money lenders haven't realized the potential such investments have. There is a saying in the banking business: "We don't give unsecured lines of credit to bullfighters, parachutists, and real estate investors."

Of course, you should turn to hard-money lenders only after you have exhausted all other sources of income and only if you are sure you can make a good profit. Under those circumstances and equipped with a little know-how, you can make banks and other lending institutions work for you.

There are five kinds of hard-money lenders: commercial banks, thrift institutions and finance companies, credit unions, money brokers, and cash-by-mail companies. Each has its particular lending guidelines, and each has different goals and objectives.

As you gain experience you will find out which lender to contact first for the best terms; I've found that my own banker has given me the best service at the lowest interest rates. When I began investing in real estate, my strategy was to establish a strong credit rating so I could borrow large amounts of money quickly on an unsecured basis. I approached the banker who handled my checking account and explained my objective. I then began to borrow small amounts of money so I could establish a history of prompt repayment. My first loan was for $500; I worked my way up to a credit limit of $5,000 unsecured.

That's when I ran into trouble. As soon as I reached $5,000, the loan committee was reluctant to lend me any more money on an unsecured basis. As a result, I promptly moved all of my accounts to another more flexible bank that was confident of my ability to repay large amounts of money.

Since then I have deposited my money in several banks in order to achieve the capacity to borrow thousands of dollars from each of four or five banks. Even though this relationship was a long and tedious one to establish, it has proved worthwhile and necessary.

If you don't already have a good credit rating, open checking accounts at several banks. Find those whose loan officers are friendly and interested in helping you establish a credit rating through borrowing small amounts of money. There will be plenty of banks in your area to deal with, and banks are in a keenly competitive business, so don't be afraid to get up and walk out of a bank that is not responsive to your needs and wishes. Write letters to the officers of banks where you are treated poorly; let them know how you feel.

Constantly cultivate your sources for short-term funds by visiting with lenders weekly. Learn how their business operates and get to know the managers in each office. You will soon realize that bank officers and lending institution personnel are ordinary human beings, not fiery dragons. The more you know about borrowing, the more confident you will become about your ability to borrow money.

It is simultaneously amusing and exasperating to realize that the person most concerned about security usually finds himself employed at a bank, where there is a lot of money in the vault. The banker's salary is notoriously low, but he has all the security in the world. And he holds the pursestrings to your financial future. It's ironic that a man so security-conscious stands in the way of the enterprising investor who dares risk everything to make his dream come true. An odd couple, indeed.

So before you begin to borrow money, try to understand your banker's goals and objectives. They're probably in conflict with your investment goals and objectives: He is concerned about high security, while you are trying to negotiate the highest possible leverage. He wants collateral; you would rather have an unsecured loan. He needs appraisals, credit checks, approval from loan committees, title policies, and a pile of other paperwork; you want to borrow money in the most simple and straightforward manner. Whenever possible, try to supply what your banker wants, but explain that once you have proved your prompt repayment ability you would like to start doing business your way.

If you recognize that your personalities clash, go to another bank. Life is too short to waste your time dealing with someone who questions your integrity, points out all of the weak spots in your financial situation, reduces you to begging in order to get the loan, and then makes you pay for the "privilege" of doing business with him. There are plenty of good bankers in your area. Go to them.

There's a good analogy that describes the banker-borrower relationship. When you go to the doctor for a checkup, he asks you to strip to your shorts, stick your tongue out, and cough at the appropriate time. A banker interviewing you for a loan asks you to strip to the shorts financially. That's where the similarity ends, though. The banker is concerned with *his* security, not yours. Don't be fooled by all the advertising that portrays the friendly banker who is anxious to lend you money. Just remember: The people who are writing the ads aren't making the loans!

Try to locate a young, nonconservative, aggressive banker who has enough experience to understand your request but who has not been around long enough to be influenced by the "lifers" on his loan committee. Ask your loan officer if he owns any real estate besides his own home. If he does, your chances of getting a loan for real estate ventures will be increased, because the loan officer will understand your goals.

Let a banker know that he is competing for your dollars. There are plenty of banks, and he should be trying to attract you to his bank. Remember—*your* business is important to the bank, not the other way around. Adopt that attitude, and you will begin to win.

Try to help your banker—and yourself. Be prepared with typed financial statements, income tax statements for the last two years, pictures of some of your properties, and other supporting documents. Try to present as stable a picture to your banker as you possibly can. You might consider putting all of your highly leveraged properties in your spouse's name to reduce the loan-to-debt ratio.

Be as realistic with your financial statement as possible. If you want your banker to believe your statement, be sure that you enter the value of your car below the car's current market value; your banker can check values very easily with his used-car books. If he can see that you are realistic on the things he does understand, he will trust your values on the things (such as real estate holdings) he may not understand.

Critical questions that a banker will want answered are: How much money do you want or need? Why do you need to borrow it from me? Where is your bank account now? Why don't you borrow the money from your own bank? What are you going to use the money for? How will you pay the loan back? If you can't pay the loan back within the specified time limit, how can I be sure that I will be able to collect the money from you? Be prepared with answers to all of these questions. Keep your requests simple, and don't go into full detail about your creative transactions. *A confused mind always says "No."* Don't confuse your banker with complicated real estate deals. Simply tell him how much money you need and how you intend to pay it back.

A banker's chance for promotion comes with his capacity to make good loans. That's why he's concerned about your highly leveraged position. Convince him that you are not a threat to his security and his chance to get ahead. From time to time drop in to discuss your progress with him. Let him know that you are successful and that you are a person of integrity.

When you find a good banker, let everyone know about him. When your banker finds out that you have been favorably advertising him and his bank, he will appreciate it.

Once you've begun to establish good relationships with bankers, jump at the chance to borrow money. By borrowing money and repaying it on schedule, you can establish a credit history that could be worth hundreds of thousands of dollars later. Do what you can now. You might borrow $500 from one bank and deposit it in a savings account at another bank. When the note comes due, you can pay it off by withdrawing the money from the savings account. The interest charges on the loan will be largely offset by the amount of interest accrued from the savings account.

Or you could deposit $500 in your savings account and then ask the same bank for a $500 loan secured by your savings account deposit. You could then deposit the $500 loan in a savings account at another bank, where you would request another $500 loan. You could do this in four or five different banks simultaneously, proving to several bankers that you are able both to borrow money and to have a savings account. This method requires $500 initial capital plus accrued interest for the term of the loan, but even if interest is $100 during a six-month period, the stronger financial position you will gain will be well worth the price.

Why use so many banks? First, when you can borrow funds from any of several sources, you have increased your flexibility and your capacity to buy larger properties. Second, if you have a short-term loan of $5,000 due at one bank, you can always go to another bank in your system and borrow the $5,000 to repay the first bank. This way you could keep a $5,000 note floating forever, and the only cost would be the interest. All the time you would be improving your credit rating through prompt loan payment.

Let's take a closer look at the five major kinds of hard-money lenders:

1. Commercial Banks.

It is feasible for a person with good credit history to be able to borrow up to $50,000 on an unsecured basis from one bank. If you were able to borrow this amount from five banks, you could secure up to $250,000 in cash in less than a week. Of course, it would take you many years to attain this level of borrowing, but you will make the most money when you are able to use other people's money to buy properties at good prices.

In the initial stages of your borrowing program, the banks may wish to secure your small loan on a piece of property you own. This is a normal procedure. But you should request that your loans be moved to an unsecured basis as soon as possible so that you do not encumber properties you might want to keep free for trading purposes.

2. *Thrift Institutions and Finance Companies.*

In addition to commercial banks, there are a host of financial institutions that specialize in making loans for buying cars, boats, trailers, and other "butter" items. These thrift institutions borrow funds from customers and loan it out at higher rates—up to 18 percent in many cases, and sometimes as high as 36 percent. Thrift institutions usually require a monthly repayment plan, while banks are equipped to lend money on a balloon basis for three to six months or up to a year. These thrift institutions charge higher interest rates and are not prone to lend money on an unsecured basis. They should be avoided; if you *do* use this kind of financial institution, settle only for the best terms you can find. Several loan companies allow you to miss up to two payments per year on your loan without penalty; search for the terms that will give you the most flexibility.

3. *Credit Unions.*

If you belong to a credit union, your chance of obtaining a loan at reasonable rates is good. One of my former seminar graduates who did not have a high-salaried job applied for a $20,000 loan from his credit union to use as a down payment on a fifteen-unit apartment building. His loan was approved, and he was able to arrange for repayment terms that did not strap him with negative monthly payments. It's a good idea to join a credit union and to establish a good business relationship with one of the loan officers.

4. *Money Brokers.*

These people make their living by introducing those who have money to those who need to borrow money. The brokers charge a fee ranging from 1 to 10 percent of the loans they arrange. You can locate a money broker by checking the classified section of your local newspaper under "Loans" (or some similar heading). You may also find brokers listed in the Yellow Pages along with other financial institutions under "Loans."

Money brokers primarily locate long-term loans for real estate, but some money brokers also find short-term second mortgage money. Their rates will be comparable to those of loan companies, but brokerage fees may be higher, so use these kinds of short-term monies only if you are certain you can make a healthy profit on your real estate investment after all interest charges are paid and only after you have exhausted all other sources.

5. Cash-by-Mail Companies.

Some loan companies offer a *loan-by-mail service,* often advertised in airline and executive magazines. These loans are unsecured, but the rates and monthly payments are high. To qualify you must have a substantial income and you must not be self-employed.

Whichever type of institution you decide to borrow from, search for the lowest rates available and, if possible, do not get locked into inflexible monthly payments. If such payments are required, always negotiate for the longest possible payback period, since this will lower your monthly payments. Commercial banks may have three-, six-, or nine-month commercial notes that do not carry monthly payment obligations, but you should *always* be prepared to come up with the lump sum when the loan comes due either by taking out another loan or by converting the balloon payment to a monthly payment until you are able to pay the loan in full.

There *are* some borrowing options open if you are unable to obtain an unsecured or a conventional loan. First, consider a second mortgage on your home. If you own your own home, you've probably built up a rather large equity because of the increase in the value of real estate over the years, and you might be able to borrow the down payment for your investment program by taking out a second mortgage on your house. Your spouse may disapprove of a second mortgage because it exposes the family's financial situation to risk. But if the real estate purchased with the borrowed funds is well selected and underpriced in relation to the market value, the risk is minimal, and at best, it increases the family's long-range financial situation. Sometimes you need to take a risk to improve your position.

As an example, consider a family that owns a home valued at $80,000; they have a loan of $30,000. After checking with several financial institutions to find one with low interest and a long repayment period, the husband locates a company that will loan funds for a second mortgage with a ten-year term and 16 percent interest with no closing costs. The monthly payments on the $10,000 loan will be only $167.51.

The family has decided to invest in a duplex. The duplex is selling for $80,000 with a down payment of $10,000 cash; the seller agrees to carry the balance of the $70,000 with monthly payments of $686 for the next twenty-five years. This payment will be covered by rent paid by tenants of the duplex, and will have a break-even cash flow after the payment of all expenses (since the husband will make all minor repairs himself). The second mortgage payment, of $167.50, is not too burdensome a commitment, and will be largely offset by the tax advantages of the investment property.

What will the long-run picture look like? Suppose both the house and the duplex appreciate at the rate of only 5 percent annually for the next ten years. At the end of ten years, the home will have appreciated to about $120,000 and the duplex will have appreciated to the same value. Taking into consideration the loan the family had to obtain on the home to buy the duplex (and at the end of ten years the loan has been paid off completely), the family's risk of using a second mortgage has paid off to the tune of about $40,000.

Using a second mortgage is an excellent technique to raise capital for an investment program. Yes, it takes some fortitude to overcome the security complex, but the results only add to your family's security if the funds are well spent. Under *no* circumstances should any of the funds from a second mortgage be spent on butter items. Leave your house equity alone unless you plan to use it on a solid investment.

If your banker doesn't like the idea of lending you money on a second mortgage for investment purposes, apply for a home improvement loan (which can be easily arranged). Many banks have home improvement loan programs which are very lenient about where the funds are used. Maybe you could use the money to improve another home you buy.

If you can't use the second-mortgage technique because you lack equity, try refinancing your car, boat, or trailer or trying using your furniture, stereo, or some other valuable item as collateral for a loan. The monthly payments may be higher using this approach, but it provides a ready source of cash if the need arises.

While you are establishing a credit history, don't overlook the use of credit cards. Apply for as many credit cards as you can, especially those without a monthly surcharge. Use one of the cards for yourself, but reserve the others for investment purposes. How? Use your imagination. For example, one young investor found a homesick European couple who desperately wanted to return to Germany. The home they owned here had an equity of about $8,000. The investor recognized the situation and immediately bought two one-way tickets to Germany with his MasterCard. He offered the couple the two tickets in exchange for the equity in their home. They gladly accepted it: It solved their problem quickly. I'm sure the sellers would like to have received more for their equity. But when they thought about it they decided they would rather be back in Germany than wait around for another offer. The investor paid for the tickets at $100 a month over the next year, and the home was his. Some sellers might accept a number of brand-new items you could buy with a credit card.

Don't get caught thinking that you can only possess one MasterCard and one Visa card at one time. Each bank has the ability to qualify you for a separate credit card, regardless of how many cards you might have acquired through other banks. For example, in my area at least five different banks offer the MasterCard to their customers. In fact, I could easily apply for a separate MasterCard from each of the banks and not be stepping out of the bounds of the law. If each bank allowed me a credit limit of $1,000 on each of the cards, I could borrow $5,000 quickly and easily just on my signature alone. If the opportunity arose to put $5,000 to use quickly, I would have the money ready and available. For this reason, I suggest that you have several cards in your possession for use in an emergency.

As a summary to this chapter, look at the following program of building your credit. Begin now to establish your credit and borrowing ability in as many places as possible. I offer you a challenge that you build up your borrowing ability so that you will be able to borrow $10,000 on your signature from at least three separate banks in your area. Armed with short-term money in the amount of at least $30,000 you are much better prepared.

Remember that whatever route you take to finance your real estate investments, you need to be flexible. Settle only for terms you are comfortable with, and don't get trapped into a bad situation. The money is there for the borrowing; take what steps you can to get established so that the money will be there for you.

Short-Term Funds from Hard-Money Lenders

How to build your credit:

1. Choose three banks in your area immediately.
2. Pick a loan officer you can relate to.
3. Go to another bank if you feel you are not welcome.
4. Ask your loan officer if he owns real estate.
5. Determine what the loan officer's credit limit is.
6. Ask him if it is possible to establish an unsecured line of credit. If so, how long does it take?
7. Borrow as much as you can, either secured or unsecured, as soon as possible.
8. Repay your loans early, but not too early.
9. Repeat the borrowing process with a larger amount.
10. GOAL: TO BE ABLE TO BORROW $10,000 SIMULTANEOUSLY FROM AT LEAST THREE SEPARATE BANKS WITHIN THREE YEARS.

CHAPTER 16

From Bankers to Crankers: Working for Long-Term Loans

Mastering techniques for borrowing short-term funds will help you establish a credit rating and a good working relationship with several cooperative bankers. Sometimes long-term loans are more difficult to obtain; bankers may want you to have a good credit rating that has built up over several years. So if you establish the groundwork through short-term loan processes, your credit will help you get started.

Long-term loans (fifteen to thirty years) secured against real property are called mortgages. You can find lenders who like to loan money for mortgages by looking in the Yellow Pages. Many lenders like to deal in government-sponsored loans such as GI veteran loans and FHA loans. These loans usually call for lower down payments (GI loans require nothing down to qualified veterans) and lower interest over the life of the loan, and they are always available. But they are also more difficult to get because of endless government paperwork involved. In addition, appraisals are generally below the market. If you are buying a home to live in and you have a good credit rating, the FHA offers the lowest down payments and interest rates available.

If you're borrowing money to buy property you won't be living in, watch out. It's a whole different story. Interest rates on loans for purchase of buildings that are not owner-occupied are much higher, and the down payments required are sometimes higher than 25 percent.

Be prepared to answer these questions when you apply for such a loan:

—What is your total monthly income?
—Do you have copies of your last three years' income tax returns?
—Can you verify your down payment requirement?
—Have you borrowed any portion of your down payment?

The last question is especially critical; lending institutions want to keep their risk at a minimum. They realize that if an investor has saved at least 25 percent of the purchase price of a property he is buying, he will be less likely to lose the property to foreclosure. If they know that any portion of your down payment has been borrowed, they'll probably try to deny your loan.

Don't be dismayed. There are specific ways of dealing with lending institutions, even if you have little or no down payment. Let's examine those techniques:

The Second Mortgage Crank

I call this the second mortgage crank because it involves the use of second mortgages and is done in such a way as to allow me to "crank" the required down payment out of the property I want to buy through a refinance. This technique can also be called subordination. When mortgage money is loose, this can be the most powerful technique in your arsenal. The first time I ever tried to use it, I held my breath during the whole transaction. I just couldn't believe it was going to work. But it did!

I called the owner of a twelve-unit apartment building located near a large local university to see if he wanted to sell his property. It was the spring of 1976. I had a real estate license and was farming the area for listings. He wasn't interested.

Several months later he decided that since he lived so far away from his property, he wanted to sell it and invest his money closer to his home. He called an old friend who was in the appraisal business and asked him to do an appraisal on the property. His appraisal came in at $225,000—an extremely low estimate and a surprise to both me and the seller. He told me that he had to net at least $300,000 or he would not sell. With that in mind, we listed the property for $315,000 with a 5 percent commission to be paid to me if I sold the property.

I did a thorough analysis of the property and determined that the net operating income was about $28,000 per year—quite high because each unit was rented out to six girls, each paying $65 a month. The capitalization rate, then, was almost 9 percent, not bad for a unit located in such a good area. I listed the property, turned the listing over to a colleague, and went to Europe for two months.

When I returned, the unit had not been sold, and no buyers were in sight. Suddenly I realized that I was a better buyer than a seller. I knew that the property was a great buy. I knew that I wanted it badly. But I also knew that I had no money to buy it with.

When the listing expired I began to get imaginative. I attended some creative real estate courses in California to expand my thinking. In the middle of October, while I was in Los Angeles attending one of the seminars, I received a telephone call from the seller. He told me that he had an offer of $295,000 from a neighbor, but he felt an obligation to let me have the first crack. I told him that I would pay $300,000 and that I would fly there and meet with him that weekend.

When I hung up the phone I knew that I had committed myself. Until that telephone call, my ownership of the building was just wishful thinking. Now I had to produce. I had no idea how I'd do it.

When I returned to the seminar room I began to concentrate more on what the instructor had to say than I had ever done in any other classroom situation. I began to play with the numbers as I knew them.

Since the seller's equity was a whopping $220,000, I felt that he would be a little more flexible if I could give him most of his equity in cash.

I finally reached a solution. I would go to a local savings and loan association and borrow 75 percent of the purchase price; in addition, I'd ask the seller to accept a second mortgage that would

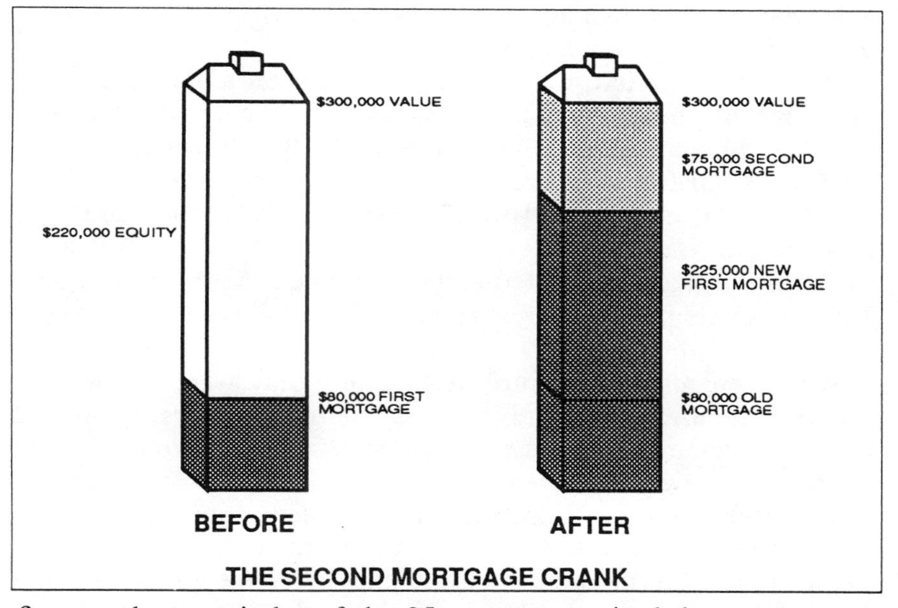

THE SECOND MORTGAGE CRANK

finance the remainder of the 25 percent required down payment. My proposal looked like the "After" drawing in the illustration above.

When I arrived in San Jose, the seller and I sat in his living room to discuss my proposal. He went along with most of it, but insisted that he would accept only a $60,000 second mortgage instead of a larger one, and he would have to have 12 percent interest. The most important motivating factor for the seller was the fact that he would be receiving $160,000 in cash, so he could afford to give me a break by lending me most of the necessary down payment.

There was a problem: I had wanted to close six months from the date of our conversation, and he wanted to have all of his money by the first of the year. He feared that I would tie up his property for six months and then not be able to put the deal together. His worries were probably well founded: I was a young, single, basically inexperienced real estate agent. He wanted $5,000 earnest money.

I didn't have it. I finally persuaded him to let me have six months to try to put the deal together by offering him my duplex—and its $8,000 equity—with no strings attached if I defaulted at the end of six months.

I told him that if I *could* raise the money, he would receive

$160,000 in cash plus a note for $60,000 earning 12 percent interest, and I would get my duplex back.

He accepted. We drew up our agreement on a napkin and we both signed. The financial picture is shown in the diagram below.

I still had some monumental financial hurdles: I needed to come up with $15,000 in cash for the additional down payment. And I needed to be able to borrow $225,000 from a savings and loan association.

The first problem wasn't as bad as it seemed. As the new owner, I'd immediately receive approximately $15,000 in rents and deposits.

When tenants moved into the building, they were required to pay one month's rent in advance. As the new owners, we would also receive the rent and security deposits. This would be the source of our down payment.

To solve the second problem, I persuaded a good friend who had a strong financial statement to become my partner. He had the ability to get the money; I had the expertise. We applied for the loan together. He was the borrower, I was the co-borrower.

We were extremely lucky. Things fell into place. The money market was loose, the loan officer ignored any extraneous financing we were planning on making, and the building was appraised

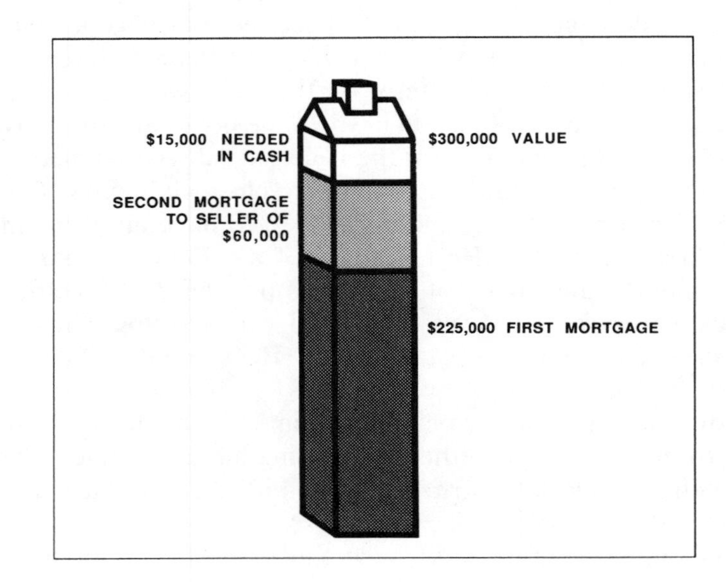

high enough to qualify us for the loan because I convinced the appraiser with some of my own homework. There was only one remaining obstacle: the approximately $5,000 in closing costs.

Our luck held out. My partner and I were able to obtain a six-month loan for the $5,000 on our signatures.

Let's examine the financing:

Borrowed from savings and loan:	$225,000
First month's rent, deposits:	10,000
Borrowed on signatures:	5,000
Seller's agreed second mortgage:	60,000
AMOUNT OUT OF OWN POCKET:	- 0 -
Total	$300,000

Incidentally, three months later my partner offered to let me buy him out for $5,000 in cash. Instead, I persuaded him to take a recreational acre in a beautiful mountain location that I had $5,000 equity in.

So the property became all mine—with nothing down.

I call this technique the second mortgage crank, because I am able to *crank* out my down payment by borrowing it from the seller. Essential ingredients for a successful cranker are:

—A seller who has a very low mortgage balance and lots of equity
—A property in a good location
—A bank willing to loan up to 75 percent of the appraisal price (and, of course, an ample money market), and
—A buyer who has a strong financial position or who can find a partner to provide the financial strength.

The illustration below shows what a potential "cranker" property might look like. The property has a low loan and lots of equity. If you could persuade the seller to accept only a part of his equity in cash and carry a second mortgage for the balance of his equity, then you have the makings of a nothing-down transaction. The first step is to determine how much a local bank or savings and loan association will lend on a potential new mortgage. Generally, on a property that is not owner-occupied, most banks lend up to 75 percent of the value of the property. The difference between the potential new loan and the existing loans will be paid to the seller at the time of closing. This is, in essence, a cash down payment. You now only need to persuade the seller to accept for the balance of his equity (25 percent in our example) a second mortgage on the property he is selling, with monthly payments or terms agreeable between you. He receives a great deal of cash at closing. The real estate agent involved also receives cash. And you are able to buy a property with absolutely no down payment—although closing costs for your end of the purchase price may be as high as 3 percent of the purchase price.

Since most banks will refuse to lend you the money if they think you've borrowed part or all of the down payment, you need to find a way to convince the banker that the down payment has been taken care of. Try one of these ways:

Moving the mortgage. Ask the seller to place the second mortgage on another piece of property you already own. Use your other property as collateral to the seller until the refinancing is completed. If the bank officer requires proof that the down payment has been made, have the seller draft a letter stating that he has received the amount in the form of an *exchange* for other property or that he has already received "consideration" for his equity.

Uniform Real Estate Contract. Ask the seller to sell you the

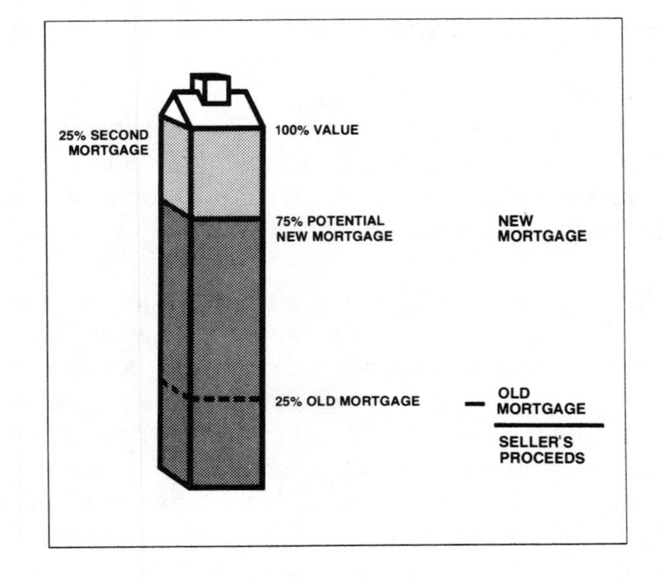

property on a Uniform Real Estate Contract with a $100 down payment. When you go to the bank, you will then be listed as the legal owner of the property, and the loan officer won't question you about a down payment. When the refinancing is complete, pay the seller the remainder of his equity and negotiate the terms for the second mortgage. In some instances the banker will require that you be the owner of record for at least six months before you can refinance. This limits your flexibility, but if the seller agrees to wait, it is an option that may work.

Seller refinance. If the seller refinances his own property first, before selling to you, the question of down payment is not raised by the banker. When the refinance takes place, the seller deeds the property to you and you take over his payments on the new loan. He gets the cash from the refinance plus a second mortgage from you for the rest of his equity. You get in for nothing down.

While using the second mortgage crank can at times be extremely complicated, the paperwork is worth it if you are able to invest in an excellent piece of property. And sometimes the returns are good: I could have sold my $300,000 building one year later for $350,000. After discounting my closing costs and partnership costs, I could have pocketed over $38,000—enough to get me started on my next deal!

If you really want to get fancy, consider doing something like what Gary and I did. Gary and I used to have our offices in the same building. He indicated an interest in buying some real estate for his own investment. I told him that I had a full-time "finder," Rex, searching for properties, and if I found something I couldn't handle myself I would let him know.

A few weeks later Rex located a four-unit apartment building in a nearby town that was advertised in the newspaper:

> Older fourplex.
> $55,000; appraised at $58,000.*
> Seller anxious.

* Isn't it amazing what has happened to real estate prices in the past ten years! You couldn't touch this property today for less than $100,000. And the same goes for rents. Real estate really is the best way for the average American to reach financial security.

Rex visited the seller. He turned out to be a serious don't wanter for the property. His family had just moved to Oregon, and he had stayed to clean up his last-minute red-tape messes. He wanted to sell—now!

Rex drove me past the property, and I didn't like what I saw. It was a frame structure—I am very partial to brick—and it was in terrible shape. It needed new paint, yard work, and extensive general repair. The stench was incredible. I told Rex I wasn't interested at any price.

But Rex was paid only for finding properties that I bought, so he persisted: "Come on, Bob, surely you would buy the property at the right price. Make him an outrageous offer. You never know—he just might accept it."

So we offered him $45,000 with a $3,000 down payment, and we sent the offer in the mail, never expecting to hear back from him.

To our surprise, he replied immediately. "I will accept $48,000 with $3,000 down," he said over the phone.

I gave Gary a call and told him about the property we had found. I told Gary that the property had real potential but that I didn't have the time or inclination to clean and repair the building. He drove out to the property with me a few days later and said that he wasn't afraid of the cleanup problems involved if he could purchase the building for an extremely low down payment. We put our heads together and analyzed the details:

Selling price:	$48,000
Seller's loans:	13,000 to a loan company @ 18 percent
	10,000 first mortgage to a bank
Seller's equity:	$25,000

We offered to give the seller $10,000 in cash if he would subordinate $15,000 of his remaining equity on a new first mortgage loan of $33,000. The $15,000 note would be secured against Gary's home until the refinance took place and thereafter would be transferred to the fourplex. The note would bear 8 percent interest with no monthly payments and would come due in five years.

Gary applied for a $33,000 first mortgage loan, but since money was scarce, the mortgage loan was approved for only $28,000.

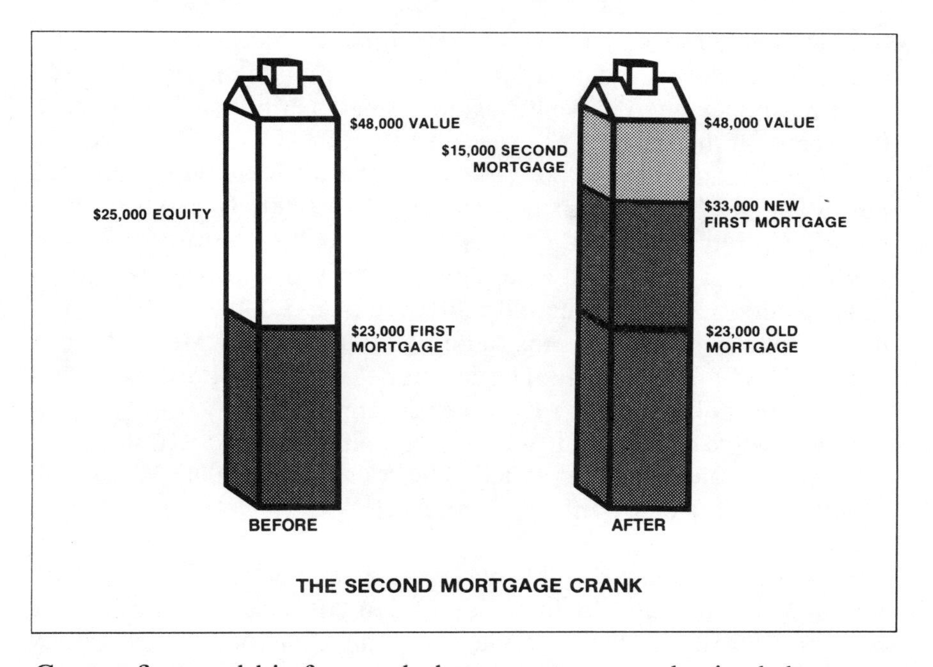

THE SECOND MORTGAGE CRANK

Gary refinanced his free and clear sports car and raised the extra $5,000.

Everyone was happy.

I received a $1,500 finder's fee. I gave Rex $300.

The seller got rid of his property, and he received $10,000 in cash.

But happiest of all was Gary. He bought a property with little down payment. But there's more: Gary's property was appraised at $58,000, so he made a paper profit of $10,000 the day he bought the property. Within three months of his purchase, after some minor cosmetic improvements, he had the property reappraised. It came in at $70,000.

Gary's off and running. You can be, too.

The Overfinance

This is just an extension of the second mortgage crank. It is possible to buy a property and in the process put cash in your pocket using the second mortgage crank technique with a little twist. Suppose we locate a $100,000 building which has a $25,000 existing mortgage. The seller wants some cash but is willing to be flexible with the balance of his equity. We know that we can obtain a new mortgage of $75,000. Obviously the difference between the new loan of $75,000 and the old loan of $25,000 is $50,000. This money should come to the seller, since it is his equity. However, we agree to give him only $40,000 cash from the proceeds and he must agree to accept a second mortgage of $35,000 for the remainder of his equity. This seems to be fine to the seller. After all, he is receiving $40,000 in cash. The figure below shows how the transaction will look once the refinance is complete.

If you look closely you will notice that there was $50,000 cash which came out of the refinance. The seller got $40,000. Where did the other $10,000 go? Into your pocket!

Great?

No—not so great. While there is a place for this kind of deal, you need to consider the financial burden you assume by promising to repay all of the loans. Unless you have negotiated extremely good terms, the property will probably generate a negative cash

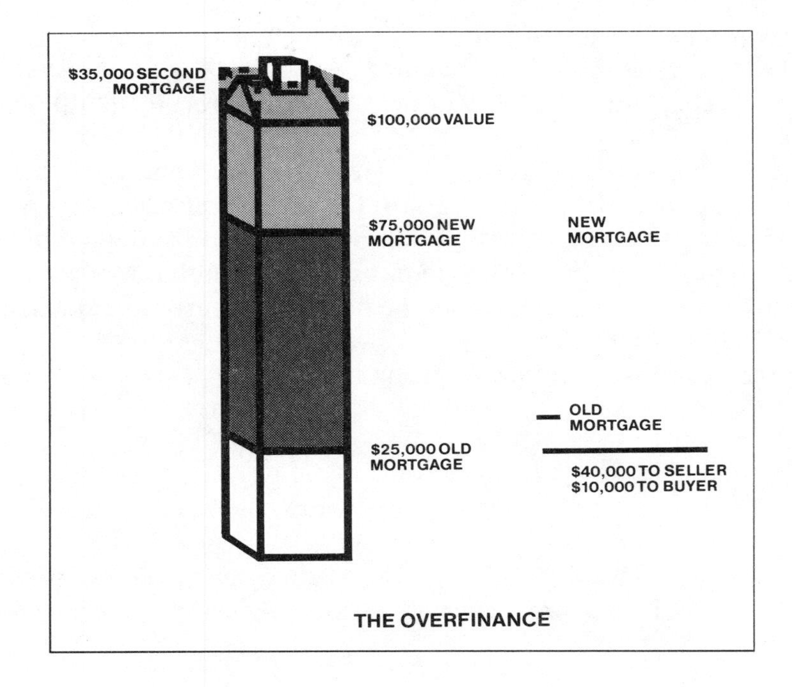

THE OVERFINANCE

flow. You'll need to dig into your own pocket every month until the rents can be raised. The higher the overfinance, the more acute the problem becomes. You should only overfinance a property if you have an absolute profit-maker in which to invest the leftover funds. *Never* spend them on butter.

There is another more serious problem. A seller who finds out that his mortgage may not be completely secured could sue you for fraud. If you do decide to overfinance, *always* explain the benefits to the seller, make sure that he understands the implications, and ask him to sign an affidavit agreeing to the overfinance. (One way to persuade him to agree to the overfinance is to offer him security on both his property and on another piece of property you own. You can remove the mortgage from your second piece of property once the seller is satisfied that you'll make payments promptly. This should take no longer than a year.)

There is an alternative to borrowing from the seller: *Borrow the down payment from holders of existing first, second, or third mortgages, or people who sold on a real estate contract or wraparound mortgage.*

How does this technique work?

Suppose you found a home selling for $80,000. The seller had an existing loan of $60,000 and wanted his $20,000 equity in cash if possible. If you don't have the $20,000, how can you come up with it?

First, find out about the existing $60,000 mortgage. To whom is it payable? Will the holder be flexible? Is a bank involved?

In our case, the $60,000 mortgage is really a Uniform Real Estate Contract payable to Mr. Harrison at $600 a month including 11.25 percent interest. Harrison bought the property from Mr. and Mrs. Peterson, and he owes them $30,000 at $300 a month at 9 percent interest. Mr. and Mrs. Peterson, who owned the property free and clear, owe no money on the property. The picture looks something like the figure on page 186.

Further investigation reveals that the Petersons are an older couple who are extremely nervous about the fact that the property they loved so much is not being cared for properly. They are unsure about the security of their $30,000 investment. They complain regularly to the owner, and even tried to repossess the property once due to breach of contract. Every time the property changes

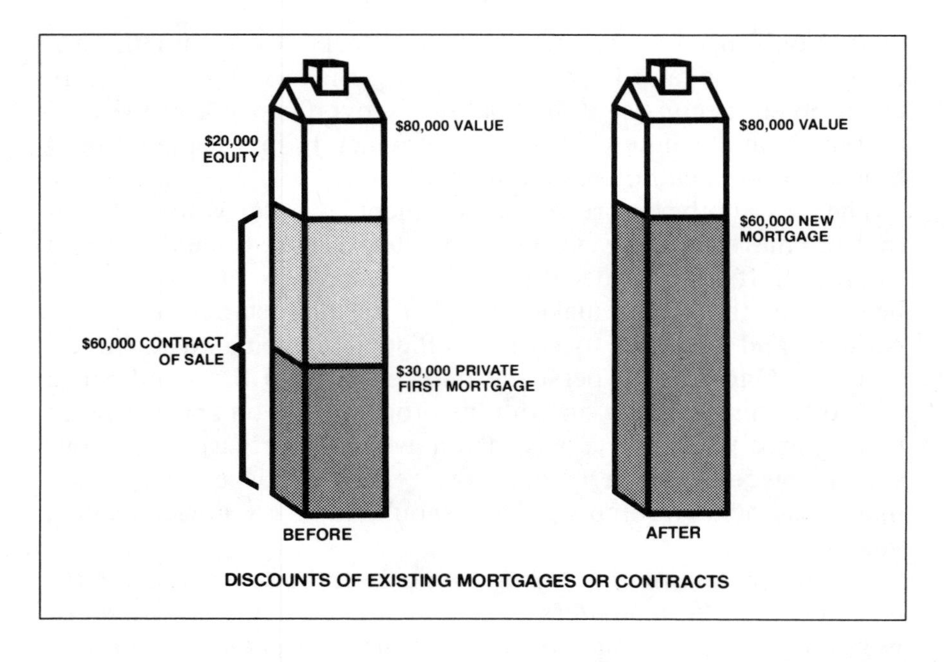

DISCOUNTS OF EXISTING MORTGAGES OR CONTRACTS

hands they become increasingly nervous. It's obvious they might be interested in a payout of their equity.

Harrison purchased the property and sold it to create for himself a monthly cash flow; for the last four years he has enjoyed $300 a month net cash flow. But his business has recently declined, and his wife has asked for a divorce. He hasn't been able to raise enough money to settle with his wife, and he desperately needs extra cash. He doesn't think his mortgage in the building is salable, and he considers himself stuck.

Armed with this information, do you think it is possible to bargain with the holders of the underlying mortgage, pay the present seller his $20,000 equity in cash, and still purchase the building with no cash investment?

Yes.

There are two possible alternatives available to you. First, you can approach each of the mortgage holders and offer to pay them $20,000 *cash* for their $30,000 mortgages.

Prepare for some moans and groans, but once the dust settles, remind the Petersons that they'd be much better off with $20,000 in cash than with their worries about future security and with the hassle of collecting $300 a month for the next fifteen years. Remind

Harrison that the $20,000 in immediate cash will remedy both his business losses and his divorce obligations to his wife.

Then draft a simple document that reads something like this:

> I, [seller's name], agree to sell my interest in a home located at 22556 Peacock Lane, Centerville, Va., for $20,000 cash. The funds should be delivered to Greenacre Title and Escrow Company, where this note and instructions will be held in escrow pending delivery of the required cash by [your name] (or his/her assigns) on or before the 3rd day of September, 1990.
>
> Signed this 1st day
> of July, 1990.
>
> ____________________
>
> Notary signature
>
> ____________________

Get Harrison and the Petersons to sign. You just made $20,000.

"How?" you ask.

Approach your bank or mortgage lender about getting a new loan on the property. Since you paid $80,000 for it according to your agreement with the seller, apply for a 75 percent loan of $60,000. The banker will want to know where your down payment is coming from; just tell him that it is being held in escrow at Greenacre Title and Escrow Company and that the $60,000 mortgage money should be delivered to the title company for final dispersal.

Upon approval, your money will be delivered to the title company. The following events occur:

—The title company will pay $20,000 to Harrison for his $30,000 interest in the property.
—The title company will pay $20,000 to the Petersons for their $30,000 interest in the property.
—The $20,000 that remains will be paid to the seller as a $20,000 cash down payment on his $80,000 building.

You just purchased an $80,000 building for a total price of $60,000, and the $20,000 equity you earned is clear profit.

The only loan you have to pay off is the $60,000 first mortgage. Of course, you will have to pay closing costs on the new loan plus title charges and other miscellaneous expenses, but most of these outlays can be covered by the rents and deposits that you will receive as the new owner. One more thing: There should be a steady, monthly cash flow from the rental units which you can put into your pocket.

The holders of the underlying mortgages might not be as generous as you would like them to be. What happens if both the Petersons and Harrison decide to discount their mortgages by only $5,000 instead of $10,000? You'll be $10,000 short. But your only limits are the limits of your imagination and creativity. Try one of the following alternate plans.

Plan #1. Persuade the seller to receive only $10,000 in cash instead of $20,000, and have him take back a second mortgage of $10,000 as soon as the refinance is complete. The result will look like this:

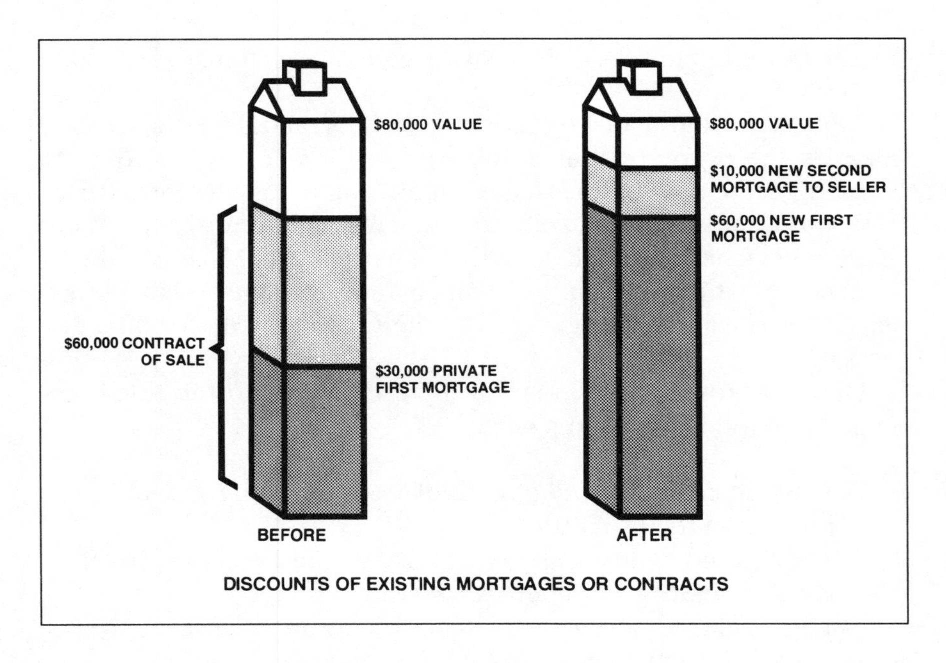

DISCOUNTS OF EXISTING MORTGAGES OR CONTRACTS

Plan #2. Persuade the Petersons or Harrison (or both) to receive $20,000 in cash and a $5,000 personal note for the rest of their equity. The results are as shown opposite:

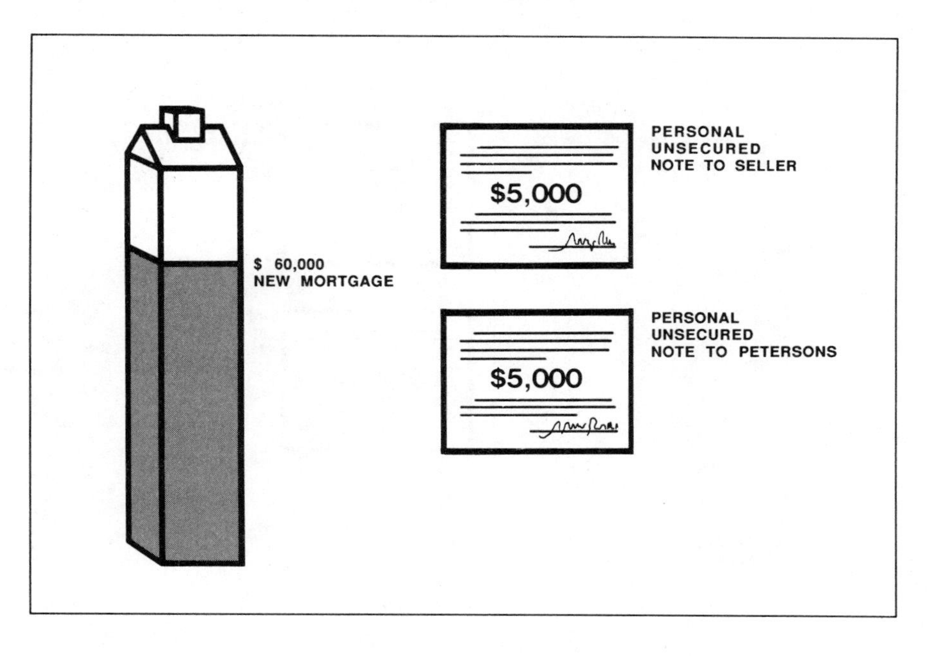

Plan #3. Persuade the seller to receive $15,000 in cash and a $5,000 note. Then negotiate with Harrison and the Petersons concerning who takes the discounts and the notes. Perhaps Harrison will take a $10,000 discount, but the Petersons will discount their note by only $5,000. You will still be able to accomplish your nothing-down transaction. (See illustration on page 190.)

You might even be able to crank some cash out of the transaction to put in your own pocket. Suppose that the seller would take a personal note (not secured against the real estate) for $5,000 and that Harrison will discount his note from $30,000 to $20,000 cash. The Petersons will discount their note by $5,000, and they want $20,000 in cash with a $5,000 personal note for the rest.

The results would look like this:

First mortgage proceeds	$60,000
Cash to seller	15,000
Cash to Harrison	20,000
Cash to Petersons	20,000
Total cash paid out	55,000
Your net proceeds	5,000

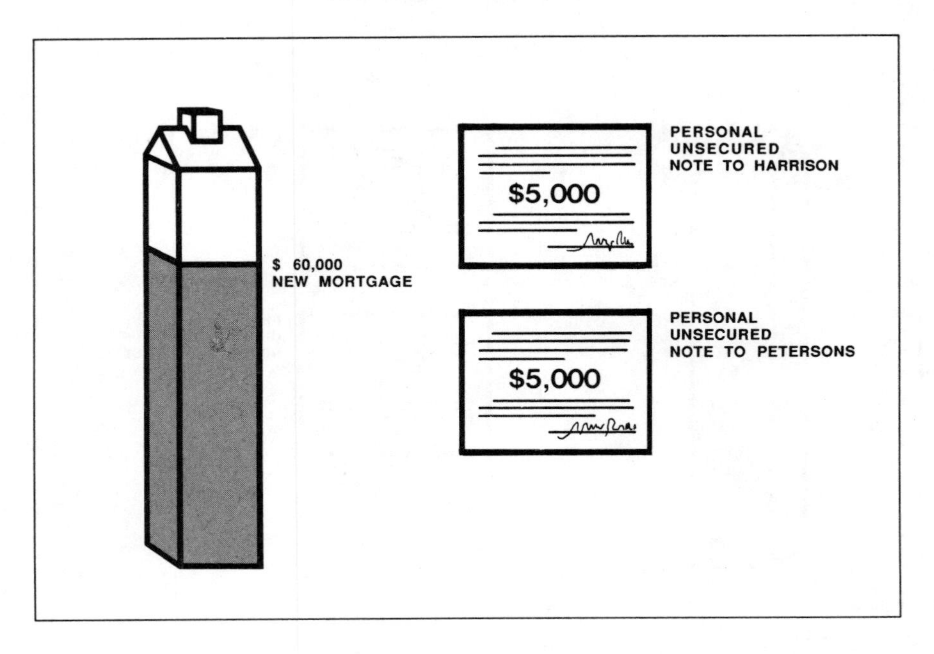

Situations like this never just happen. They are *created*. Spend some time and use some imagination, and you'll be able to pocket some cash on most of your real estate transactions.

Buy Low, Refinance High

Of all the techniques we've discussed, this one is easiest to use and simplest to understand for both buyer and seller. In essence it consists of finding sellers who are willing to sell their properties immediately for a substantial discount and all cash.

Here's an example. One afternoon as I was talking with a broker friend, I asked if he had any properties for sale involving a seller who was willing to accept a lower price for his property in exchange for a quick cash-out of his equity. He mentioned that he had recently taken in a house on a guaranteed-sale program, and he was ready to sell it for a great price.

A couple of weeks later his wife showed me through the house, and I was flabbergasted. The house had been newly painted and carpeted, and new drapes had been installed. The grounds were beautiful and well cared for. The place was immaculate. It took me about three seconds to make my mind up; a few minutes later I was in his office with an offer.

The property had a new loan on it for $36,000; the seller wanted a $45,000 price and $9,000 cash for his equity. I knew that the market price was at least $55,000 because I was in the process of building some new houses that didn't look as nice and that cost more. Within a few days the seller had his $9,000, and I owned the property with a partner who put up the cash.

How? Our strategy was to get a new first mortgage on the property as soon as possible to refinance our initial down payment. In a situation like this, if you can obtain an 80 percent loan you can obtain a $44,000 loan on a $55,000 appraisal. Most of your down payment will be returned; you can use it on other deals. In addition, rents will cover mortgage payments and other expenses, resulting in a break-even cash flow.

The basic ingredients of this technique are (1) a seller who wants cash now and is willing to discount his equity for the privilege; (2) a property that can be purchased for 75 percent of what a bank will appraise it for in order to obtain a new first mortgage; and (3) your ability to use your own cash or that of a partner.

There are some twists to this technique. First of all, you don't have to give the seller any cash on the front end if you can convince him that you can raise the cash within thirty days. Every time you talk to a seller, ask him, "What is your lowest cash price if I give you all of your equity in cash within thirty days?" For example, suppose you found a small $100,000 condominium for $80,000 cash. Negotiate with the seller to pay him $80,000 cash in thirty days; then apply for an $80,000 loan from a local lending institution based upon its $100,000 appraisal. Your only investment is to cover closing costs—about $2,000 in this case. This sounds easier to do than it is. The better your relationship with your banker the more easily these kinds of situations can be structured to your advantage.

Another twist is to find a property which, in its present condition, is only worth what the seller is asking but which, with some minor cosmetic repairs, would appraise for a lot higher. Buy the property from the seller at a low price, make some minor improve-

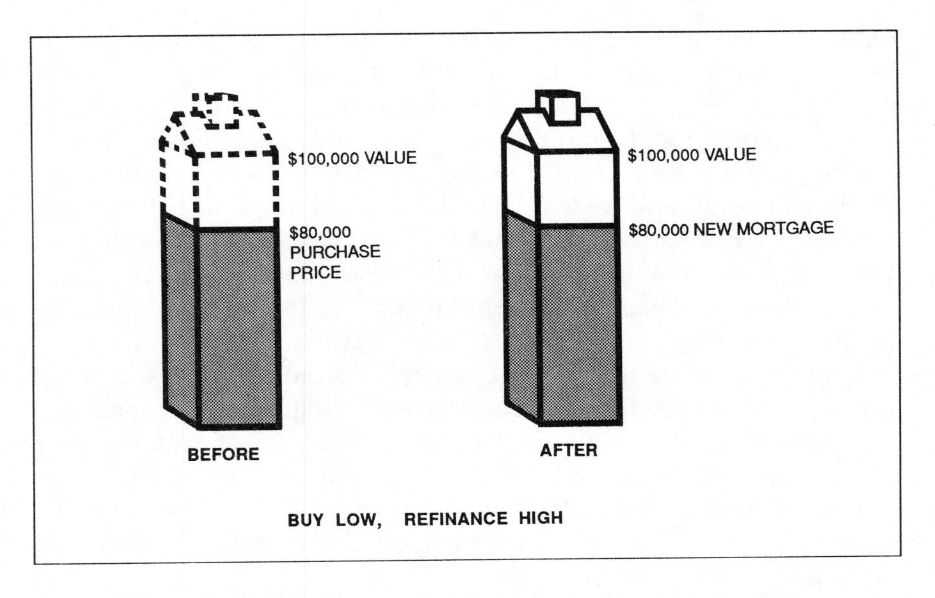

ments, and refinance the higher-valued property for enough money to pay the seller and to cover the expenses you incurred in fixing up the property.

Sometimes the sellers can't wait for thirty days for you to refinance the property. They need their money now. How can you take advantage of a low price? You have to cultivate your cash sources well so that when a "steal" comes along, you will be able to come up with immediate cash. This is one of the main reasons I always keep my bank lines of communication open. If I need a quick $20,000 for six months, I can get it. It also doesn't hurt to have a few partners who can come up with cash within forty-eight hours' notice.

Using the "buy low, refinance high" technique you could take a $25,000 investment and use it over and over again—buying first one property and then refinancing your cash out again and repeating the process several times a year. You would not need extra capital, and each time you would end up owning a piece of property which had been purchased substantially under the market price. There is no question about the fact that cash is more effective in this circumstance. It is like buying real estate at wholesale prices. When you buy real estate with small down payments and high leverage, you generally have to pay top dollar—retail prices. When a lot of cash is involved, the prices come down in a hurry.

You can continue to spread your money into as many properties as possible, but if you have the resources, the "buy low, refinance high" technique can make you more "real" dollars in less time than any other method.

How do you raise cash to take advantage of the wholesale opportunities which exist all around you?

—Establish yourself with short-term lenders.
—Explain the program to a partner.
—Sell another piece of property to raise cash.

As you can see, there are all kinds of possibilities. I have the most confidence in the "buy low, refinance high" technique.

CHAPTER 17

Greed and Need: Using Partners

Fred Astaire and Ginger Rogers, Batman and Robin, Laurel and Hardy. The Lone Ranger and Tonto. Mutt and Jeff.

They're all famous partners. One wouldn't be the same—or as effective—without the other.

The same thing can happen for you in real estate investment. If you need more money than you can get alone in order to purchase that perfect property, consider letting a partner come up with the cash. You'll have to give your partner half the profits, but remember: Half a pie is better than no pie at all!

My first experience with partners took place several years ago when I purchased an option on a very valuable piece of apartment ground. At the time I didn't have much experience and was naive enough to think that I could do anything. I found a three-and-a-half-acre piece of ground in an excellent location that was ripe for development. It belonged to a major church organization in the area whose agent was in the process of trying to sell it.

I contacted the agent and established a friendly relationship with him. He had offers on the property for $150,000, but he thought it was worth more. I offered to buy the property from him in a year for $200,000; I agreed to give him $2,500 as option money. He accepted. I was bound to keep my part of the bargain.

The deal was a good one. There was only one problem: I didn't have $2,500. At the time, I hadn't established sufficient credit to borrow even as little as $500 from my bank. I approached a good friend who had a growing dental practice and drove him over to the property. I convinced him that it was worth the gamble. My friend's banker thought the investment was a stupid one, but my partner persisted and, with some difficulty, was able to borrow the money.

I went ahead with the option and began trying to find a buyer for the property. I had one year. To make a profit I needed to find someone who would buy the property for more than $200,000.

About eight months later we were approached by a builder who was looking for ground; we negotiated a purchase price of $275,000. When the sale was completed I took a check for $10,800 to my dentist partner—his share of the profits. The rest of the money was split with my real estate broker.

The ingredients for success in this story are simple. I found a piece of property that had potential, and I persuaded a partner to finance the property. Without the partner I would never have seen any of the $30,000 I eventually put in my pocket.

Start now to cultivate partner relationships. Try to have at least three or four partners in the wings to use when you need them. If you are careful you will *never* have to use your own capital for any real estate venture again. You will always be able to rely on other people to provide all of the investment capital you will ever need.

There are two main motivations that bring people together to form a partnership. It's usually your need for money and his greed and desire to earn more than 10 percent on his invested dollars. If you treat your partners fairly, you will never lack for people who will be willing to lend you money for your investing. The word spreads fast. If you burn anyone, word will get around. But it will also get around if you return good profits.

There are numbers of people who have sizable amounts of money sitting in savings accounts earning less than 10 percent interest. Your job is to convince them that the returns are higher if they will join with you and invest in real estate. Let's look at the ways to influence partners and to form partnerships, and how to treat partners as far as profit is concerned and how to dissolve partnerships when the time comes.

There are some good basic rules concerning partnerships:

1. Don't ever form a partnership unless you absolutely need to.

It's too expensive. If you have adequate funds, adequate experience, adequate time, and adequate fortitude to do it yourself, do so. If you're weak in any of those areas, the partnership is probably a good idea.

2. At the beginning of the relationship, define exactly what each person will contribute to the partnership.

For example, your partner's responsibility might be to provide the money; your responsibility would be to negotiate, deliver the Earnest Money Receipt, and complete closing procedures. Obvious contributions that a partner would make include cash, equity in other property, the ability to borrow money readily, strong credit history, and good connections in the right places. Obvious contributions you could make include your time, your knowledge, and your fortitude. Whatever you decide on, get it down in writing and make it specific so that there will be no misunderstandings.

One interesting way you can use a partner is to buy his financial statement—in other words, if he's got a good financial statement and a strong relationship with a progressive banker, have him refinance a piece of property. As soon as the refinance is completed, have him give you a quit-claim deed transferring all rights, title, and interest to you, even though his name is on the mortgage and stays there until you are able to assume it. You might pay him $2,000 for the service. It's well worth it.

By the same token, you could make it worthwhile for a seller to take out a loan against his own property and in turn lend you the proceeds. Secure the loan on another piece of property you own, and pay a good rate of interest. The possibilities are limitless.

3. Maintain maximum control of the relationship.

If you feel in any way that a partner is limiting your freedom, end the partnership as soon as possible. Don't waste valuable time with a partner who does not trust you or who does not understand a good deal when he sees one. A good relationship sometimes takes time to establish, and the best thing you can have on your side is a good track record of making profit for both yourself and your partners. When you have established a good track record, you will be able to call one of your former partners and say, "I've found a great buy on a ten-unit building. The required down payment is $30,000. Do you want in or don't you?" It will be that simple. If partners have made money with you before, they will find a way to say yes.

4. Keep each partnership on a property-by-property basis.

Each project should be evaluated on its own merits, the profits should be split when the property is sold, and the partnership should then be dissolved. This practice allows you to be more flexible when other opportunities arise. For instance, if you have an agreement to buy properties with a partner and he runs out of money, you should be free to look elsewhere for another partner if you run across a good deal. It should be clear from the very beginning that your partnership is temporary.

5. Decide from the outset what procedure you will follow if one of the partners decides to sell out to the other.

Establishing this early will prevent misunderstandings if one partner does decide to sell out.

6. Decide early how you'll divide profits.

Try to negotiate the best arrangement you can for yourself while still making it attractive enough for the partner who is putting up the money. Here are some ideas to incorporate:

If you're sure that your project is going to be a winner, don't give large percentages of the profit to your partner. Offer instead to pay your partner 25 percent return on his money or 25 percent of the profits, whichever is less. That's still several times what he'd earn in a bank. Most people are very satisfied with 12–18 percent yields on their investment. Be careful of your state's usury laws.

If your partner is financially established, he will probably wish to forgo your offer of a guaranteed percentage return and will opt instead for your less guaranteed program of a percentage of the *profit*. The harder the bargain you drive with your partner, the better off you will be when it comes time to divvy up the profits. I never give away more than 50 percent of the profit to anyone in a partnership, and I try to retain as much as I can for myself. You may say that your partner's dollars are the first to be returned upon the sale of the property, after which all remaining profits are to be split 60 percent to you and 40 percent to your partner. Or you may decide that a 50/50 relationship is best for both parties involved. Whatever you decide, get it in writing! And whatever happens, guarantee that the partner will *at least* get his original investment back. And then stand behind your guarantee. A partner should understand (and should be guaranteed) that he will not lose one penny of his original investment, regardless of whether or not he makes a profit.

If you plan on being a nothing-down investor, you've got to begin living a borrower's life. The key to maximum leverage is OPM—other people's money! You have to learn how to overcome your reluctance to ask people for money. From now on, every person you meet is a potential partner. You are looking for people who will trust you with their money—it's as simple as that.

Let's look at the various sources of investor capital. We'll save the most conventional ones for last.

1. Relatives.

Most people find it very difficult to borrow from a relative. Granted, it has its drawbacks and could cause serious problems if anything negative happened. But there are also obvious benefits. Relatives are more likely to lend you money because they know you.

2. Friends and Business Associates.

Word travels fast when you know what you are doing and you prove it by making money for yourself and others. Talk up your latest adventures with every crowd you have a chance to talk to;

someone there will want to spend a little money for a profitable cause. Just make sure you are selective and careful.

3. The Seller Himself.

The seller ends up lending money to the buyer in over half of the real estate transactions that I am familiar with by agreeing to let the buyer pay him a portion of the remaining equity over a period of time. The borrowed equity is secured by a mortgage on the property purchased, a mortgage on other property, or a personal note. Whenever a seller takes back a second or third mortgage he is, in essence, lending his money to the buyer.

Some methods of dealing with partners will help ensure a successful experience:

1. Choose your partners carefully, make sure all of the terms of partnership are in writing, and stand behind your investments. You'll find that teaming up can provide a good solution to an otherwise troublesome money crunch.
2. If necessary, reduce the fears of the partner who needs some added security by placing the property in the name of the money partner. Retain a written agreement with him that whenever the property is sold—and since the property is in his name, he alone can make the decision on when to sell—the profits will be split according to your written agreement. It can be a simple agreement drafted in mutually satisfactory language and signed by both of you, or you can ask your attorney to formulate an agreement. The simple, do-it-yourself method can work just as well and be legally binding, but using a competent attorney is the best route.
3. Agree to pay the partner his profit and invested capital first after the sale of the property. He will thus know that your profit is subordinated to his and that you will probably work harder to see that things happen as you say they will.
4. Do not get mixed up in limited partnerships. These are not for the investor who likes to have any control over the situation. The fewer the partners, the better. If you don't have the time to do your own looking for properties, visit a real estate agent with a CCIM (Certified Commercial Investment Member) designation in your area. (See page 95 for more infor-

mation on CCIM.) These real estate agents will give you professional counsel and help you determine the best route for you to take in real estate.

5. Avoid if at all possible investing your own dollars into a partnership. In lieu of cash, give your partner confidence in your ability to raise cash from other sources. Remember, your contribution to any partnership is the talent, the intangible experience that makes the whole partnership have life and meaning.
6. Don't be discouraged by those who aren't interested in being your partner. You may have to talk to twenty people before you form your first partnership. Once you prove yourself, however, you will find people beating a path to your door to lend you money.
7. Partnerships were made for man, not man for partnerships. When you find yourself in a bad partnership, get out as soon as possible. Learn your lesson and don't make the same mistake again.

Let me challenge you to find in the next two years five people, each of whom will be willing to lend you $5,000. You would have a tremendous financial resource at your disposal using the $25,000 you borrowed from your partners. And your partners would love you for it because you would be doing something for them that they could not do for themselves.

How do you overcome your fear of asking other people (perhaps even total strangers) for money? Easy! Go out into the real estate market and locate a fabulous property which could be bought for below market value, if you could only raise the cash. Then we'll see how shy you are. At that point you have a very important decision to make. Either you get up the courage to ask a partner to join you in making a tidy profit or you let your fear cost you thousands of dollars. It's up to you. Whenever I talk to a group of people about real estate investing, I ask for a show of hands of those who either have $5,000 in the bank or who could get $5,000 in thirty days if I would double it for them. Generally, over three-quarters of the people raise their hands. It's amazing how fast people can come up with money when they smell a profit. This same principle can work for you. If you don't have the money, somebody in your city does—and he's just waiting for you to ask him for it. Show him how he can make a profit and you'll both laugh all the way to the bank. And you'll have a friend for life.

Of course, as soon as you can afford to, get out on your own. Partnerships are great, but if you can afford a whole pie, why should you give half of it away? Until the day that you can go it alone, I challenge you to find five partners who would lend you $5,000 each for real estate investing. I think you could find five partners easily within a two-year period of time if you use the techniques outlined in this chapter. Just think of what you could buy if you had $25,000 cash to play with!

CHAPTER 18

Bundles of Benefits: Everyone Wins on Exchanges

Exchange.

Back in the days when an Indian brought his beaver pelts to the trading post and swapped them for a blanket, we called it barter. Today, when we swap services or property—when we get what we want without using money—we call it *exchange*.

For example, if you are a painter, you might offer to paint a dentist's house *in exchange for* having some bridgework done or *in exchange for* outfitting your daughter with braces. There is no reason for you to use cash as long as you can find someone who wants your services more than he wants cash for his own.

You can utilize this philosophy to its fullest in real estate investment. Let me illustrate:

Suppose you own an acre of ground in the country that you bought many years ago. The property has increased substantially in value; since you don't want to build on it, you have decided to sell it and reinvest the money in a new home in the city. You place an ad in the newspaper to sell the property, and you receive a telephone call from Mr. Bellamy Brown, a local contractor. He owns a new home that he just finished building, and he wants to know if you will exchange your land for equity in the new home.

Let's look at how the exchange would benefit you:

—There's no need for you to search for a cash buyer for your ground.
—Since the cash buyer usually wants to dicker for lower prices, you probably would lose part of your equity.
—You won't have to look for a new property.
—There are tremendous tax advantages.

There are benefits to the builder, too. He doesn't have to search for a buyer for his home. He doesn't have to look for more land to build on. And he saves time so that he can be about his business—which is building, not buying or selling.

Basically, you'd both come out ahead.

Exchange isn't a magic cure-all for every transaction you get involved in, but it can be a valuable tool to use when you need it. Let's examine the basics behind the technique of exchange.

Every piece of property is a "bundle of benefits" that can be sold or traded for other bundles of benefits. In our example, you received a property that had the following benefits:

—It was located in the city.
—It had a house built on it.
—It had equity that approximated the equity of your land.
—It was readily usable.

The builder also received a "bundle of benefits":

—Vacant land that could be built on.
—No need to waste time searching for a building site.
—Disposal of his property.
—Relief from the financial burden of paying a mortgage on the home.
—No transfer of cash.

Both parties are happy. You both received what you wanted—and completely without the use or transfer of any cash.

Since benefits are of such great importance, a successful creative buyer must understand the benefits he is seeking and the benefits he has to offer. It is critical that you understand the seller's situation: Learn what benefits he is seeking. If the seller is seeking relief from the burden of management, step onto the scene as a benefit. Offer to take the property off the seller's hands and thereby relieve the seller of his problem *in exchange for* certain terms.

There is an important point to remember here: *There are no problem properties, just problem ownerships.* In our example, there was nothing wrong with your property out in the country; you just didn't want it anymore because you had decided not to build a house on it, and you didn't see what else you'd need it for. And there was nothing wrong with Brown's house. It's just that he had finished building the house, and he wanted to build another one. To do that, he needed vacant land. There was nothing wrong with the properties; the problems were strictly ownership. Remember—one man's poison can be another man's feast.

1. Two-Way Exchange.

My first experience with exchanging came early in my career when I began calling property owners in a specific area of town to find sellers who wanted to list their property with my real estate company. I found a large company that owned two big apartment complexes in town. They had been managing the properties from out of town and, because of an incompetent resident manager, had found that the management was more than they could handle. In a board of directors meeting they had decided to liquidate the properties and invest instead in other units closer to their base of operations.

I sold one of the units to a group of doctors for cash.

The other apartment complex, a student rental apartment consisting of sixty-five units with space for about 330 students, was a little more difficult to move. It was situated in a marginal location and was an older property that needed a major face lift to make it competitive with newer properties. In analyzing the needs of the sellers, I determined that the major motivations for selling were: (1) the distance factor, (2) the seller's lack of knowledge about student rental properties, (3) management problems, and (4) needed repairs.

After about two weeks of advertising the property, I ran into a friend, and I told him about the property for sale. Since he was in the market for another apartment complex, he was very interested in examining the figures. He asked me if the sellers would be interested in an exchange for a small mobile home park nearer their home office. I wasn't sure, so I told him to make an offer.

The offer was to exchange the sixty-five-unit apartment building for a fifty-space mobile home park. Since my clients had about $500,000 equity in the apartment building and my friend had only $200,000 equity in his mobile home park, I knew there would be problems.

But my friend came up with a solution: He would bring in a partner who had a smaller apartment complex of thirty units with $300,000 equity. Together they would buy out my clients' equity.

The offer was submitted and accepted by all parties.

Let's examine what kinds of benefits each party received. First of all, my clients, who happily paid me a fee of $19,000, received the following benefits:

—Rid themselves of a deteriorating problem property
—Rid themselves of an unfamiliar and poor management situation
—Acquired units closer to their home office
—Were able to start all over again.

My friend, who owned a major interest in a local management firm, received these benefits:

—He rid himself of a mobile home park he had held for years without realizing any substantial cash flow due to a depressed market situation.
—He acquired an ownership position in a unit closer to his home office.
—He could have needed repairs and maintenance done at wholesale prices.
—He increased his leverage position.

The partner who owned the thirty-unit apartment building was also eventually able to increase his leverage position.

All parties to the transaction came out with a bundle of benefits greater than the bundle of benefits they were leaving behind.

The transaction was a two-way exchange: A took what B had,

and B took what A had. Let me give you an example of a three-way exchange.

2. Three-Way Exchange.

Just before I got married some time ago, my wife let me know in no uncertain terms that she had no intention of living in the small duplex I had purchased only months before. Since I refused to pay rent, I had to find a home we could live in. I had no cash, so I had to find someone who would take my duplex in exchange for a house.

I remembered that a friend of mine was having trouble selling his house, mostly because of seasonal market fluctuations, so I approached him on an exchange. His home was worth $55,000, and he had a loan of $37,000. My duplex was worth $39,000, and I had a loan of $31,000. Here is how the equities paired up:

	House	Duplex
Value:	$55,000	$39,000
Loans:	37,000	31,000
Equity:	$18,000	$ 8,000

Since I was $10,000 short, I had to come up with something more. I proposed that he accept as part of the equity a $3,000 note which was owed to me. He accepted the note at full face value. I still had to come up with $7,000.

Can you see any solution? I took the obvious: a refinance. Since I was going to live in the house, I could qualify for a 90 percent owner-occupied loan. The loan would pay off the existing first mortgage of $37,000, pay off the $7,000 I owed the seller, and leave me with $5,500 in cash.

New loan	$49,500
Less old loan	37,000
Cash from refinance	12,500
Less $7,000 to seller	7,000
Net to me	5,500
Less closing costs	1,500
Net cash to me	$ 4,000

The exchange seemed to be working out so smoothly. But there was one hitch: The house seller did not want my duplex. Here was a case for a three-way exchange:

A wants B   B doesn't want A   C wants A   B wants C

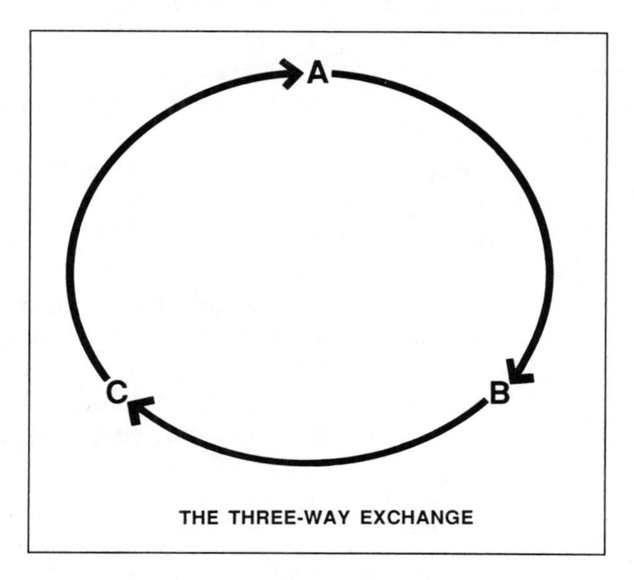

THE THREE-WAY EXCHANGE

I brought in a third party who agreed to buy the duplex from the house seller as soon as he received it from me in an exchange. The third party offered to buy the duplex from the house seller for $39,000. The $8,000 equity in the duplex would be given as a note secured by the duplex with a payment of $1,000 in six months and the rest amortized over a two-year period with payments of $100 a month and a balloon payment at the end of the two years. The seller agreed to the three-way exchange, and we signed the papers. Thirty days later I qualified for the new home mortgage of $49,500 and the exchange was consummated.

I received the house and $4,000 proceeds from a new refinance loan. The house seller received $7,000 in cash, a $3,000 note, and an $8,000 note secured against my duplex. The third party purchased a duplex with no down payment. A got B, B got C, and C got A. Everyone was happy.

3. *Lemonading.*

One of my very first exchange clients was a couple who had purchased a piece of speculative real estate years before. It was more a swindle than an investment, and they had experienced little appreciation. What's worse, the property had been up for sale for more than a year with no success. They came to me wanting to see if there wasn't some way to move the $19,000 equity in their land into something more attractive.

I came up with a quick solution by suggesting that they refinance their house and add the proceeds of $30,000 to the equity in the land; with $49,000 equity composed of land and cash, they might have a better chance of moving their problem property.

I made a trip to Phoenix to a Real Estate Exchangers' meeting, and within two days I had twenty or thirty offers to trade for the property. I quickly learned that when a little cash is involved people pay attention. Lemon plus sugar makes lemonade. Add sugar (cash) to your sour investments (lemons) and see how fast they go!

4. *Exchange Cash Generator.*

This can be an excellent solution for you. I have even heard of a real estate operator who buys up older homes with little or no down payment and then exchanges them with don't wanters for cash plus their don't wanter properties. Here's how it works:

Our man buys a home for $100,000 with a $10,000 down payment and a $90,000 mortgage. He finds someone who has a piece of land he doesn't want with an equity of $10,000. He persuades the don't wanter to give him the $10,000 piece of ground plus $10,000 in cash in exchange for the house with a $90,000 mortgage. Thus our man gets his $10,000 back and has a $10,000 piece of property as profit. And let's not forget the don't wanter. He is now the owner of a house and is much happier than when he owned the land. Benefits, benefits, benefits.

5. *Anything Goes.*

It is not always necessary to trade real estate for real estate. A few years ago I responded to an ad in the newspaper that was advertising a house for "low down." The agent told me the home had sold a few days earlier for $38,000, and the seller took an old camper as a down payment. I couldn't believe that the seller had taken just an old camper. Then I remembered my own situation with a three-acre parcel of ground: I had been willing to take almost anything as a down payment for my equity in the ground. It's amazing what a true don't wanter will do.

There are a number of things you can offer as full or partial down payments on real estate:

—Use any dead equities you may own, such as recreational lots you never use and that you shouldn't have purchased in the first place.

—Use mortgage notes that are due you. Suppose you had sold your home a few years ago and you took back a second or third mortgage of $5,000 payable at $50 a month for the next thirty years. Offer it to a don't-wanter seller. Be sure to offer it at face value. You'll benefit, too, because you'll get rid of a "thorn in the side" note you haven't been able to sell on the open market for cash without suffering a heavy discount. Double-check with your accountant on the tax angles.

—Use any furniture or personal items you no longer have any use for. Give them an assessed value and include them as part of your equity in an exchange. If the seller accepts, you will have solved two problems: clearing out your basement and reducing the amount of equity needed to complete a transaction. I recently met a man who had sold one of his investment houses taking a motorcycle as a down payment. Be creative.

6. Trading Discounted Paper.

You almost never have to discount real estate notes or mortgages when you use them in a real estate exchange with a don't wanter. This fact implies a great money-making opportunity. One group of smart investors in California buys such notes or paper from anxious people who are willing to take a substantial discount on the face value of their paper in order to raise cash. For example, suppose you were the holder of a $20,000 note second mortgage payable at $214.92 a month including 10 percent interest over fifteen years. If you wanted to sell this note for cash to an investor, you would probably not be able to get more than $13,000 cash, since the investor would want his investment to yield him at least 18 percent. These real estate investors in California buy up these notes for a discount and trade them for real estate equities at full face value. They would buy your $20,000 note for $13,000; they would then trade your same $20,000 note into a $20,000 equity in an apartment building. If they were to sell the apartment building immediately, they would realize a profit of $7,000, a 54 percent return on their investment. If you'd like to try something similar, you can arrange for a bank line of credit or partnership money to buy older mortgages at a discount. The sky is the limit.

*7. **A Bull for a Bear.***

If you are a heavy loser in the stock market and want to recoup your losses, offer your depressed stocks to a real estate seller who wants immediate cash and who will discount the value of his property. He will get cash, and you can trade your stocks for equity that is greater than the face value of the stocks you traded. If you know of someone in this situation, offer to buy his stocks for more than what they would sell for. Then find a seller who will discount the value of his property for cash. You make the trade and sell the property for cash, netting you enough money to pay off the owner of the stocks and to put a few thousand dollars in your pocket for your trouble.

Is there good money to be made in exchange transactions?

In one buying spree, my partner and I bought five houses and one ten-unit apartment building. Our investment for the $425,000 worth of real estate we purchased was about $60,000, just over 14 percent down payment. Of this $60,000 my portion of the down payment was borrowed on a six-month note at 12 percent interest; I invested no money of my own. One alternative would have been to increase the price of this portfolio of properties by $60,000 up to $485,000 and then to look for a don't wanter with an equity of $120,000 who wanted to pick up some neat, clean, professionally managed investment in exchange for his problem property (problem ownership). Since we bought all of the properties under the market price, this is one way to turn a tidy profit quickly.

Not only can you as the investor increase your equity dramatically using exchanging formulas; you can also pyramid your holdings from smaller properties into larger ones. The classic example of this is the small-fry investor who begins by buying one small investment house with the objective of making cosmetic improvements and trading his increased equity in the now improved property. He searches for someone who is interested in trading a larger property, perhaps a duplex which might have minor problems to solve, for a smaller property which is neat and clean. Once again the philosophy of exchange benefits is important here. The smaller property owner wants to increase his leverage and real estate holdings and is searching for a larger property to exchange for the smaller. The owner of the larger property wants just the opposite. He wants to come "down and out." He is looking for less leverage. He wants a smaller property because he may feel that he can better manage it. Or perhaps he feels that he could sell a smaller property for cash with less difficulty. Once the exchange is completed, the new owner of the duplex begins the same process of fixing up, improving the rental picture, cutting expenses where possible, and thereby improving the value of the property. Then he can continue the process of exchanging and pyramiding upward. Perhaps he looks for a four-unit apartment building. He may be able to handle a larger unit. His goal is to find a don't wanter of a larger property who wants to come down or who is willing to take other equities in exchange for his own. In the period of only a few short years, a dedicated exchanger might be able to pyramid a meager investment into two or three hundred apartment units. How high can you count? That's your limit.

There is one major benefit of exchanging that we have not touched upon: *tax advantage!* The IRS has given major tax advantages to real estate owners who want to exchange their properties for larger real estate properties. The section of the IRS code dealing with this is section 1031. Your accountant should be involved in any exchange you enter into because of the complexities of the code. However, let me give you a layman's explanation so that you are at least aware of the general nature of tax-free exchanges.

One of the biggest misconceptions in the minds of beginning investors concerning tax-free exchanges is that they are entitled to sell their investment property on the open market for cash without tax consequence as long as they reinvest the sale proceeds into another larger property within the following eighteen months. This is false. If you sell for cash, you will pay taxes on your gain, no matter what you do with the money. The only way to "defer" taxes is to exchange your equity for a larger piece of property. If you exchange for a smaller property, you may still have to pay taxes, and if you receive anything that is not real estate, such as cash or personal property, you may also be liable for taxes on your gain. However, if you exchange into a property of greater dollar value with a higher total mortgage amount without receiving any cash or personal property as part of the deal, you may be eligible for a tax-free exchange. You will not be required to pay taxes on your gains until you either sell the new property for cash (you could exchange again tax-free) or until you die. In this manner, a shrewd investor can defer any taxes he has on the gain in his properties for a lifetime, just as long as he follows the rules set down in section 1031 of the Internal Revenue code. Therefore, not only does his real estate shelter a portion of his personal income tax with depreciation, it also shelters his capital gains. This leaves him with more money to invest. And one of the cardinal rules of any investor is the preservation of investment capital. Now you can see why real estate is such a great investment.

Let me show you some of the ways you can use the above knowledge to your advantage. Suppose you own a small apartment building you bought several years ago for $250,000 with a small down payment. In just a few short years, the value of this property has skyrocketed. Your equity is now over $200,000. If you sell for cash you will have serious tax consequences.

Someone approaches you with a cash offer to sell. You can't accept his offer because of tax problems. How can you use this situation to your advantage? You know you can't receive cash but you *can* exchange for a larger building. Using this knowledge, you counter the cash offer with the following terms:

—The buyer will place his $200,000 cash in escrow pending the closing.

—The seller (you) will look for a larger building for sale which requires $200,000 as a down payment. You instruct the buyer of your building to buy the larger building instead with the $200,000 cash as a down payment. Then he immediately trades the new property to you for your property.

In this way, the buyer ends up with your building. You end up with a new property in a tax-free exchange. And the seller of the new property gets a sale with $200,000 down payment. The exact mechanics of the above transaction can be easily taken care of by your title company or your attorney. Don't try it without advice. You wouldn't want to do it wrong.

How do you find someone who wants to exchange? Any seller is fair game for an exchange. Include exchange items (if it is to your advantage) in every offer that you write. You will find that many sellers are already familiar with the advantages of exchanging—especially the tax advantages—and some sellers will not make a move without exchanging.

On the other hand, most sellers don't understand the mechanics of an exchange. Since a confused mind always says "No," you may find that your sellers would rather stick to conventional means of selling, such as all cash, rather than depend on an unfamiliar solution such as an exchange. You may have to do some educating.

If you are currently using a real estate agent, there is a society of real estate exchangers who deal strictly in creative real estate transactions. Such "exchangers" meet in organized groups all over the country on a regular basis to solve their clients' problems. Usually once a month—but sometimes as often as once a week—these specially trained real estate agents meet, prepare a copy of the client's property information, and pass these packets out to each real estate agent present. Then everyone offers his suggestions as to the solution of the client's problem, and generally one or more of the real estate agents present has a client who wants just such a property. If you have properties you would like to exchange through a real estate agent, contact your local Board of Realtors to find names of those persons actively engaged in exchanging. Ask for the name and telephone number of the president of the local or state exchange group. He can tell you where to go and whom to see about your property. If you become more informed and involved, ask him to invite you as his guest to the local exchange meeting. It's a real eye-opener. And a lot of fun.

CHAPTER 19

Making a Million: The Option Blueprint

When you were a child, did you ever sit on the scorching cement on a sweltering July afternoon, patiently hold a magnifying glass over a scrap of last night's newspaper, and stay motionless until the edges of the paper began to blaze? You learned that by concentrating the sun's rays into a limited area, you increased their power significantly.

The same principle applies in real estate. If you concentrate all of your energies and abilities in one limited area of real estate investment, you will increase your power significantly. One such specialty is options.

An option is the greatest form of leverage available to the real estate investor today. It is a simple agreement between the seller and the prospective buyer that says the seller will sell his property to the buyer at a fixed price in the future. In exchange for this "right to buy," the prospective buyer gives the seller an agreed-upon amount of money.

For example, if I give you $1,000 for the right to buy your duplex for $95,000 within two years, if I come up with $95,000 to pay you anytime within the two-year period you *must* sell the duplex to me, even though you may have changed your mind in the meantime.

OPTION

In consideration of $..., ...
and .... of.............................. County, State of............................,
Optionor...., grant.... to.. and...,
Optionee...., the option to purchase the hereinafter described property for the purchase price of $....................,
to be exercised by giving written notice thereof to Optionor.... at.., County of
...., State of......................................., at any time on or before...................................,
19........., at.................... o'clock .... M. If this Option is exercised, then after receiving written notice thereof,
Optionor.... will furnish Optionee.... with an abstract of title brought up to the date of exercise of the Option or a policy of title insurance in the amount of the purchase price and, upon payment of the purchase price due, will deliver to Optionee.... a good and sufficient..................................deed conveying marketable fee simple title to the hereinafter described property, free and clear of all encumbrances except as herein mentioned. The consideration paid for this Option shall........... be credited on the purchase price.

DESCRIPTION OF PROPERTY

....
....
....
....
....

ENCUMBRANCES

....
....
....

Dated at.. this..................
day of..., 19..........

....
....
Optionor....

STATE OF.. }
COUNTY OF.. } ss.

On the............................day of.., 19.........., personally appeared before me.. and.., the signers of the above and foregoing instrument, who duly acknowledged to me that they executed the same.

....
Notary Public

My Commission Expires:

Residing at...

....

FORM 119 - OPTION - KELLY CO., 55 WEST 900 SOUTH, SALT LAKE CITY, UTAH

Why would you give me an option to buy your duplex on such terms? There are three very good reasons:

1. Your property may be worth only $80,000 on today's market, and you might think its value could never increase to $95,000 in the two-year period of time, a figure that would represent 9 percent increase annually. If you planned on keeping the duplex for at least two years, taking my $1,000 option would just be gravy.
2. The $1,000 option money is not taxable until the year the option is exercised. This means that you could take my money and spend it as you wished without reporting it on your income tax statement. If I exercised the option, you would simply include the $1,000 as part of the down payment and pay the tax accordingly. If the option was not exercised, you would pay capital gains tax on the option money received. It is like receiving tax-free dollars.
3. The innate greed in each of us yearns for an outlet—and that outlet is the option. If you feel the value of your property can never increase to as high as the option price, you lose nothing by gambling on me. You are actually hoping that I succeed in paying such a price for the property. It's like having your cake and eating it too. You get to use my $1,000 for two years tax-free, and your chances of getting an outrageously high price for your property are also high. In essence, we make a bet with each other: I am betting $1,000 that your property will be worth more than $95,000 in two years. You are betting the imaginary profit that I am wrong.

So why in the world would I want to take an option to buy your property? Obviously, I don't want to gamble $1,000 of my money on an option unless I am absolutely sure that the property I am buying will be worth *more* than the option price at the end of the option. But suppose I know that your duplex is located across the street from a vacant parcel of ground which has just been rezoned commercial for a regional shopping mall. Your property might be worth twice as much as commercial office or retail space instead of a duplex. I decide it's worth a gamble. And sure enough, the mall goes in. I sell for $160,000, pay the $95,000 option price, and pocket a tidy profit.

To pull this off you must be comfortable with several assumptions:

—The property optioned is optioned at the right price; you must know the market.
—The property has potential for increase in value.

There are advantages to options besides profit. The holder of an option does not have to manage the property during the option period, nor is it necessary for him to pay taxes, insurance, or any other expenses. Since the liability of the option holder is limited to the extent of his option money, he does not have to be bothered with large debts or mortgage payments. If at the end of the option period the option holder decides not to purchase the property, he simply fails to exercise the option and loses his initial option money, but he has no legal problems that would have resulted if he had contracted to buy the property. The biggest benefit of all is that the option holder does not have to pay interest.

All in all, the option is simple, easy to use, and very profitable if it is used correctly. It requires very little money and involves very little risk. Let me share with you a success story that illustrates how the use of options can be extremely valuable to the high-leverage investor.

Stewart, a close friend of mine, decided to do some investing in real estate on his own without partners. He discovered a four-unit apartment building the owner wanted to sell for $69,000—definitely under the market price at that time. Stewart contacted the owner of the building and offered to buy his building in four months for $69,000 cash. To bind the transaction he received an option to buy the building at the agreed price. He gave the seller $2,000 option money and placed this ad in the classified section of the newspaper:

Fourplex for sale by owner
$78,000
Call Stewart 555-1234

Within three days he had a buyer who came up with cash. Stewart walked away from the transaction less than three months later with $8,000 in his pocket.

A short-term option like this can be used only if you are absolutely sure that the property optioned is substantially underpriced and if you are absolutely sure that a strong market exists that will enable you to sell quickly. Long-term options involve much less risk.

Another friend of mine did the same thing with a piece of development ground which he optioned for $1 and sold within a few weeks for a substantial profit.

In my travels to various seminars I have had conversations with several investors who spend their entire time studying the values of land in their respective areas and then paying for options on the ground or buildings which seemed to offer the greatest potential for appreciation. They do not purchase any property at all; they just option it. It is a full-time occupation and very lucrative. A very astute real estate agent in my area optioned a large tract of land from a local farmer for a rather outlandish price. I'm sure that the farmer supposed that there was zero possibility of the real estate agent's ever coming through with such a high price. The real estate agent went to the planning commission and had the property rezoned for commercial shopping space and resold the package to a developer for at least $1 million profit—on just one transaction. Ironically enough, the developer who bought the land has resold some of it for an even greater profit. Everyone made money.

Options are powerful, but they aren't easy to come by. It takes weeks or months of evaluating potential pieces of property. And it's usually difficult to convince the property owner that he should let you have an option on his property.

1. Equity for Options.

If you don't have any money to work with and you would like to use options as a tool to increase your net worth, offer a prospective property owner personal property as an option payment instead of cash. I once offered my duplex as an option payment for a large twelve-unit apartment building. If I had not come up with the cash to buy his building within six months, he could have kept my duplex. Needless to say, I hurried. If you have a recreational lot somewhere in the arid reaches of this planet that you bought while you were half-crocked, you could always offer it to a seller as an option on his property. Any equity that you have is usable as an option on another piece of property. If the seller balks at the idea of using your property as an option, convince him that you will cash him out at the end of the option period.

Shouldn't an option involve the least amount of cash possible? Not always. If it causes the seller to balk at your offer, you may be better off to raise a larger amount of cash as an initial option deposit in exchange for more lenient terms for exercising of the option. Once the seller agrees to the terms of the option, he cannot change his mind later on, so work the option to give the best leverage at the end, not the least cash at first. You should always try to structure the option so that the terms will be enticing to a new buyer if you need to sell your position to someone else during the term of the option.

What happens if when the term of the option arrives, you don't have the money to cash out the seller? You need to provide for this eventuality in the original option by negotiating a rolling option: State in the option agreement that the option can be extended for another year by the additional payment of $10,000 (or some amount agreeable to the seller). If you really want the property, it would be easier for you to come up with an additional $10,000 than to have to come up with the entire purchase price. In addition, you'll have an additional year to come up with the necessary money. Negotiate two or three such terms of extension if the seller is agreeable.

The rolling option is also used extensively in land transactions when a developer does not want to buy a large piece of ground all at once. The interest charges on a large piece of undeveloped property would eat a developer alive within a short period of time. Instead, a developer can negotiate to buy a smaller portion of the ground for cash and option the remainder of the ground at higher prices for later on. If the project does not go as well as the developer desires, he can drop the options, lose a small amount of money, and go on to another project. But if the project is a success, he can option the remaining ground as the need arises. In effect, he rolls his option from one piece of ground to the next until the entire property is purchased and developed.

There are two especially creative ideas that use the option philosophy:

2. The "Earnest Money" Option or "Offer to Purchase" Option.

Whenever you purchase a piece of property, you normally use a standard Earnest Money Receipt or Offer to Purchase signed by you and the seller to bind the transaction. The earnest money agreement establishes the terms of the sale and the completion date, which is usually thirty to sixty days in the future. If someone should come along within this thirty-to-sixty-day period and offer you more money for the property than you had committed to pay for it, is there any reason you could not sell him your interest in the earnest money agreement for a profit?

Suppose you found a twelve-unit apartment building that was priced $30,000 under the current market rate for such units. If you could find someone who wanted to buy the building from you for a $10,000 profit before the closing date, there is no reason why you could not do so. It is totally legal and honest. You have given the seller a check for earnest money that will be forfeited to the seller if you are unable to complete the transaction according to terms. If the seller gets his terms, it doesn't matter *who* ends up with the property.

Whenever you find a property that is substantially undervalued, make an offer on it subject to an earnest money agreement to perform within sixty to ninety days. Then you have two to three months to convince someone else that the property is a good buy, and you can pick up extra cash by selling your interest in an earnest money agreement.

The first time I used this technique was when I found a choice apartment building for sale offered on excellent terms and for an excellent price. I did not hesitate. I made an offer to purchase, and the sellers accepted my $500 check as earnest money. The closing date was scheduled seven weeks later. I immediately contacted a client and convinced him that the property was an excellent buy—for $10,000 more than I had agreed to buy it for. He checked with his advisers and verified my claims. When the original closing date rolled around, he gave me the money to close the transaction in my name. As soon as I legally owned the building, I sold it to my client for a nice $10,000 profit.

Note some important factors about this deal. First, I did not have the $50,000 needed for the down payment that I had agreed to pay in the earnest money agreement. But I *had* given $500 to the seller, which I would have forfeited if the deal had fallen through. You don't have to have cash in your pocket in order to tie up property. Use the earnest money option technique.

I could have avoided the hassle of closing the above transaction in my name if I had written the original Earnest Money Receipt or Offer to Purchase correctly. I had agreed to close in my name in the original offer to purchase. However, if I had written that I "or my assigns" would close, then I would have been able to let my client come in with the down payment on closing day. He would have bought the property with the written understanding that as soon as he received title to the building he would transfer the $10,000 profit to my account. This kind of transaction can be accomplished without ever having to notify either the buyer or the seller of your intentions. The seller does not have to know that you are immediately reselling his property for a profit, and the buyer does not have to know that you don't own the property he is buying (you merely control it with an earnest money option). This is best accomplished by setting up separate accounts at two different title companies. In the first title company you deposit your earnest money check and your earnest money agreement or Offer to Purchase. You give instructions to the closing officer that you will be depositing the down payment for the closing on or before the day of closing and that the money will be coming from another title company. At the second title company, you instruct your new buyer to deposit his down payment (which is enough to cover your down payment negotiated with the seller of the property and a little extra to cover the profit you wish to make on the transaction). The buyer does not need to know that you are making a quick profit. He just expects that when he deposits his down payment, you will be transferring to him the title to the property. In actuality, the closing officers of the two title companies confer on the phone about how the title is to be transferred from the seller to you to the new buyer. This is called a simultaneous closing, or a double escrow. The result of the double escrow is that the money from your new buyer is used to pay off the seller and you keep whatever profit you earned for putting the two people together.The mechanics of the double escrow are well known to the title companies in your area. If you have any questions about how this works, you might give one of these companies a call before you use the earnest money option technique.

I read about a couple in Texas who began optioning ground a few years ago and who made more than $1 million in five short years. How did they do it? They copied from the county records the names and addresses of all property owners who lived out of state. They reasoned that these people would be less likely to have kept track of the rising values of their property. They were right. They sent out form letters to hundreds of out-of-state owners, offering to buy their property for cash with a 90- to 120-day closing. A large percentage of the owners offered to sell at a price that was usually below current land values.

Once an affirmative letter was returned, the man and wife would go inspect the ground to see if it really was worth buying. If they felt that a profit was probable, they would send a $500 earnest money check to the owners and would have them sign the agreement binding the transaction. Then they would place ads in the local newspapers announcing a sale of the property. They tried to price the property just under current market prices to ensure a good response. As soon as a buyer was located for the higher-priced land, they closed the transaction, using a double escrow, and kept the difference as profit. As an example, suppose the couple found eighty acres below the market at $3,000 per acre. If the going market price was $5,000 per acre, they could tie the property up with a $500 earnest money agreement and proceed to sell the ground for $4,000 per acre. It would not take long to sell the property for cash at such a good price. Their profit would be $1,000 per acre—a total of $80,000 on one transaction. This is not impossible.

You can do the same if you can find a seller who does not realize the value of his property and who is willing to give you a longer than normal time period for closing the transaction. In one of my seminars, I discussed the use of the earnest money option, and two of my students took my techniques to heart. One father-and-son partnership began researching the county records in a sparsely populated county of Utah, and to their surprise they found hundreds of properties belonging to out-of-state landowners who had held their land for years without realizing its value. They have made thousands of dollars buying ground from out-of-state owners and selling the property in smaller pieces to in-state owners on good terms. Another law student used the same idea and took the county records which showed the out-of-state owners of improved property. He wrote thirty-five letters, received eight replies, and affirmed two offers to sell. A lady called him long-distance to tell him that she had owned a triplex for several years and wanted to sell at a price and terms which he could dictate within reason. This young student didn't have any money, but he did have a good idea, and it paid off for him.

In another example, I'm familiar with a group of real estate agents who recognized the potential of a particular piece of ground and approached the seller of the ground with an offer to buy. They requested a closing date nine months in the future, to give them time to come up with the money. The seller agreed and accepted $200 as a deposit. In the next nine months these enterprising men had the property rezoned from agricultural to multiple residential dwelling land. They took an architect in with them who drew up plans for a beautiful condominium project. With these plans, the city gave them preliminary approval for the development. Then they found a local building contractor who showed an interest in the property and sold the ground to him for $125,000 more than they had agreed to pay the original seller. They did this without ever having to own the property physically . . . they just controlled the eventual sales price with an offer to purchase. When the time rolled around to close with the original seller, the new owner, the building contractor, simply completed the transaction in the place of the real estate agents. Obviously, this is a powerful technique.

3. Lease With an Option to Purchase.

Another creative way to use the option technique to lower your down payment requirements is to use the "lease with option to purchase" technique. Let's look at an example that shows the benefit of such a technique.

While searching for property to buy, you find a man who has a house up for rent. It is a four-bedroom house located in a decent neighborhood. It is worth $100,000. The owner is trying to rent it because his home sat on the market for six months, priced at $110,000 with no takers. Since the owner had already bought a new house and had moved into it, assuming the additional mortgage payment and all other homeowner bills, he decided to put the house up for rent or lease rather than go into the hole every month to pay the $600 per month on the existing $60,000.

Obviously the owner doesn't need a lot of cash, since he has already purchased his new house and has already adjusted to making a higher mortgage payment. But he is definitely concerned about having to fork out an extra $600 a month until his old home is either leased or sold. This seller is a special kind of don't wanter. He doesn't want the hassle of managing his own property, and he wants to save himself from a negative-cash-flow situation.

Offer him a solution to his problems and create an advantage for yourself: Offer to lease his home from him for five years for $650 a month. Tell him that you will handle all maintenance and that he will never get a call from you—only a regular monthly check. In return, ask him for an option to buy his house from him in five years at a price of $125,000, which is an increase of about 5 percent a year on a $100,000 price. You should also require that at least 25 percent of the lease payment be applied to the eventual purchase price. In this case that 25 percent would amount to $9,000 and would lower your option price from $125,000 to $116,000.

Suppose that the seller decided to accept your offer of a firm price of $125,000 within five years but with no lease credit. If property values increase at an annual rate of between 5 percent and 10 percent as they have been over the past few years, then the house will be worth between $125,000 and $150,000 by the time the option is ready to be exercised. The seller can sell the house to anyone he wants to in the meantime, but the option will remain in force, and the new owner will have to honor the contract that the seller had with you.

The only investment you will have in the option is time. Once you have negotiated your option, you will have to find a renter so that you don't have to make the $650 monthly payments on the lease. As soon as you locate a renter, your only responsibility will be to make sure the renter treats the property carefully and that the property always stays rented.

As the second and third year roll around, you will be able to increase the monthly lease payments by as much as $100 a month. Every time a new renter moves in, the rent can be increased. If you have five or more "lease/option" properties, your monthly cash flow could easily be more than $500 after only two years of operation.

You're probably wondering where to find people who will lease their property with an option to buy. Think about it for a second.

RESIDENTIAL LEASE WITH OPTION TO PURCHASE

RECEIVED FROM ____

____, hereinafter referred to as Tenant,
the sum of $ ______________ (____ DOLLARS),
evidenced by ____, as a deposit which, upon acceptance of this Lease, the Owner of the premises, hereinafter referred to as Owner, shall apply said deposit as follows:

	DEPOSIT RECEIVED	BALANCE OWING PRIOR TO OCCUPANCY
Non-refundable option consideration	$ ______	$ ______
Rent for the period from ______ to ______	$ ______	$ ______
Security deposit	$ ______	$ ______
Other	$ ______	$ ______
TOTAL	$ ______	$ ______

In the event that this agreement is not accepted by the Owner or his authorized agent, **within** ________ **days,** the total deposit received shall be refunded.

Tenant hereby offers to lease from the Owner the premises situated in the City of ______________, County of ______________,
State of ______________, described as ____

and consisting of ____
upon the following TERMS and CONDITIONS:

1. **TERM:** The term hereof shall commence on ______________, 19______, and continue for a period of ______________ months thereafter.
2. **RENT:** Rent shall be $______________, per month, payable in advance, upon the ______________ day of each calendar month to Owner or his authorized agent, at the following address: ____
or at such other places as may be designated by Owner from time to time. In the event rent is not paid **within five (5) days** after due date, Tenant agrees to pay a late charge of $______________ plus interest at ______% per annum on the delinquent amount. Tenant further agrees to pay $______________ for each dishonored bank check.
3. **UTILITIES:** Tenant shall be responsible for the payment of all utilities and services, except: ____, which shall be paid by Owner.
4. **USE:** The premises shall be used as a residence with no more than ______________ adults and ______________ children, and for no other purpose, without the written prior consent of the Owner.
5. **PETS:** No pets shall be brought on the premises without the prior consent of the Owner.
6. **ORDINANCES AND STATUTES:** Tenant shall comply with all statutes, ordinances and requirements of all municipal, state and federal authorities now in force, or which may hereafter be in force, pertaining to the use of the premises.
7. **ASSIGNMENT AND SUBLETTING:** Tenant shall not assign this agreement or sublet any portion of the premises without prior written consent of the Owner which may not be unreasonably withheld.
8. **MAINTENANCE, REPAIRS, OR ALTERATIONS:** Tenant acknowledges that the premises are in good order and repair, unless otherwise indicated herein. Owner may at any time give Tenant a written inventory of furniture and furnishings on the premises and Tenant shall be deemed to have possession of all said furniture and furnishings in good condition and repair, unless he objects thereto in writing **within five (5) days after receipt** of such inventory. Tenant shall, at his own expense, and at all times, maintain the premises in a clean and sanitary manner including all equipment, appliances, furniture and furnishings therein and shall surrender the same, at termination hereof, in as good condition as received, normal wear and tear excepted. Tenant shall be responsible for damages caused by his negligence and that of his family or invitees and guests. Tenant shall not paint, paper or otherwise decorate or make alterations to the premises without the prior written consent of the Owner. Tenant shall irrigate and maintain any surrounding grounds, including lawns and shrubbery, and keep the same clear of rubbish or weeds, if such grounds are a part of the premises and are exclusively for the use of the Tenant.
9. **ENTRY AND INSPECTION:** Tenant shall permit Owner or Owner's agents to enter the premises at reasonable times and upon reasonable notice for the purpose of making necessary or convenient repairs, or to show the premises to prospective tenants, purchasers, or mortgagees.
10. **INDEMNIFICATION:** Owner shall not be liable for any damage or injury to Tenant, or any other person, or to any property, occurring on the premises or any part thereof, or in common areas thereof, unless such damage is the proximate result of the negligence or unlawful act of Owner, his agents, or his employees. Tenant agrees to hold Owner harmless from any claims for damages, no matter how caused, except for injury or damages for which Owner is legally responsible.
11. **PHYSICAL POSSESSION:** If Owner is unable to deliver possession of the premises at the commencement hereof, Owner shall not be liable for any damage caused thereby, nor shall this agreement be void or voidable, but Tenant shall not be liable for any rent until possession is delivered. Tenant may terminate this agreement if possession is not delivered **within** ________ **days** of the commencement of the term hereof.
12. **DEFAULT:** If Tenant shall fail to pay rent when due, or perform any term hereof, after not less than **three (3) days written notice** of such default given in the manner required by law, the Owner, at his option, may terminate all rights of Tenant hereunder, unless Tenant, within said time, shall cure such default. If Tenant abandons or vacates the property, while in default of the payment of rent, Owner may consider any property left on the premises to be abandoned and may dispose of the same in any manner allowed by law. In the event the Owner reasonably believes that such abandoned property has no value, it may be discarded. All property on the premises is hereby subject to a lien in favor of Owner for the payment of all sums due hereunder, to the maximum extent allowed by law.
In the event of a default by Tenant, Owner may elect to (a) continue the lease in effect and enforce all his rights and remedies hereunder, including the right to recover the rent as it becomes due, or (b) at any time, terminate all of Tenant's rights hereunder and recover from Tenant all damages he may incur by reason of the breach of the lease, including the cost of recovering the premises, and including the worth at the time of such termination, or at the time of an award if suit be instituted to enforce this provision, of the amount by which the unpaid rent for the balance of the term exceeds the amount of such rental loss which the Tenant proves could be reasonably avoided.
13. **SECURITY:** The security deposit set forth above, if any, shall secure the performance of Tenant's obligations hereunder. Owner may, but shall not be obligated to, apply all portions of said deposit on account of Tenant's obligations hereunder. Any balance remaining upon termination shall be returned to Tenant.
14. **DEPOSIT REFUNDS:** The balance of all deposits shall be refunded within two weeks from date possession is delivered to Owner or his Authorized Agent, together with a statement showing any charges made against such deposits by Owner.
15. **ATTORNEY'S FEES:** In the event that Owner is required to employ an attorney to enforce the terms and conditions of this agreement or to recover possession of the premises from Tenant, Tenant shall pay to Owner a reasonable attorney's fee whether or not a legal action is filed or a judgement is obtained.
16. **WAIVERS:** No failure of Owner to enforce any term hereof shall be deemed a waiver, nor shall any acceptance of a partial payment of rent be deemed a waiver of Owner's right to the full amount thereof.
17. **NOTICES:** Any notice which either party may or is required to give, may be given by mailing the same, postage prepaid, to Tenant at the premises or to Owner at the address shown below or at such other places as may be designated by the parties from time to time.
18. **HEIRS, ASSIGNS, SUCCESSORS:** This lease is binding upon and inures to the benefit of the heirs, assigns and successors in interest to the parties.
19. **TIME:** Time is of the essence of this agreement.
20. **HOLDING OVER:** Any holding over after expiration hereof, with the consent of Owner, shall be construed as a month-to-month tenancy in accordance with the terms hereof, as applicable. No such holding over or extension of this lease shall extend the time for the exercise of the option unless agreed upon in writing by Owner.
21. **PEST CONTROL INSPECTION:** The main building and all attached structures to be inspected by a licensed structural pest control operator prior to delivery of physical possession. Owner to pay for (1) Elimination of infestation and / or infection of wood-destroying pests or organisms, (2) For repair of damage caused by such infestation and or infection or by excessive moisture, (3) For correction of conditions which caused said damage and (4) For repair of plumbing and other leaks affecting wood members, including repair of leaking stall showers, in accordance with said structural pest control operator's report.
Owner shall not be responsible for any work recommended to correct conditions usually deemed likely to lead to infestation or infection of wood destroying pests or organisms, but where no evidence of active infestation is found with respect to such conditions.
If the inspecting structural pest control operator shall recommend further inspection of inaccessible areas, Tenant may require that said areas be inspected. If any infestation or infection shall be discovered by such inspection, the additional required work shall be paid by Owner. If no such infestation or infection is discovered, the additional cost of inspecting such inaccessible areas shall be paid by Tenant.
As soon as the same are available, copies of the report, and any certification or other proof of completion of the work shall be delivered to the agents of Tenant and Owner who are authorized to receive the same on behalf of their principals.
Funds for work to be done at Owner's expense shall be held in escrow and disbursed by escrow holder to a licensed structural pest control operator upon receipt of Notice of Work Completed, certifying that the property is free of infestation or infection.

FORM 106 (5-90) PROFESSIONAL PUBLISHING

22. OPTION: So long as Tenant is not in substantial default in the performance of any term of this lease, Tenant shall have the option to purchase the real property described herein for a PURCHASE PRICE OF $________ (________ DOLLARS), upon the following TERMS and CONDITIONS:

23. DISCLAIMER: The parties acknowledge that speculation of availability of financing, purchase costs, and lender's prepayment penalties is impossible. Therefore, the parties agree that these items shall not be conditions of performance of this agreement and the parties agree they have not relied upon any other representations or warranties by brokers, sellers, or other parties.

24. FIXTURES: All improvements, fixtures, attached floor coverings, draperies including hardware, shades, blinds, window and door screens, storm sash, combination doors, awnings, outdoor plants potted or otherwise, trees, and items permanently attached to the real property shall be included, free of liens, unless specifically excluded.

25. PERSONAL PROPERTY: The following personal property, on the premises when inspected by Tenant, shall be included in the purchase price and shall be transferred by a Warranty Bill of Sale at close of escrow.

26. ENCUMBRANCES: In addition to any encumbrances referred to above, Tenant shall take title to the property subject to: (1) Real Estate Taxes not yet due and (2) Covenants, conditions, restrictions, reservations, rights, rights of way and easements of record, if any, which do not materially affect the value or intended use of the property.

The amount of any bond or assessment which is a lien shall be ☐ paid, ☐ assumed by ________.

27. EXAMINATION OF TITLE: Fifteen (15) **days from date of exercise of this option** are allowed the Tenant to examine the title to the property and to report in writing any valid objections thereto. Any exceptions to the title which would be disclosed by examination of the records shall be deemed to have been accepted unless reported in writing **within said fifteen (15) days.** If Tenant objects to any exceptions to the title, Owner shall use all due diligence to remove such exceptions at his own expense **within sixty (60) days thereafter.** But if such exceptions cannot be removed **within the sixty (60) days allowed,** all rights and obligations hereunder may, at the election of the Tenant, terminate and end, unless he elects to purchase the property subject to such exceptions.

28. EVIDENCE OF TITLE: Evidence of Title shall be in the form of ☐ a policy of ________ title insurance, ☐ other: ________, to be paid for by ________.

29. CLOSING COSTS: Escrow fees, if any, and other closing costs shall be paid in accordance with local custom, except as otherwise provided herein.

30. CLOSE OF ESCROW: Within ________ **days from exercise of the option,** or upon removal of any exceptions to the title by the Owner, as provided above, whichever is later, both parties shall deposit with an authorized escrow holder, to be selected by the Tenant, all funds and instruments necessary to complete the sale in accordance with the terms and conditions hereof. The representations and warranties herein shall not be terminated by conveyance of the property.

31. PRORATIONS: Rents taxes, premiums on insurance acceptable to Tenant, interest and other expenses of the property to be prorated as of recordation of deed. Security deposits, advance rentals or considerations involving future lease credits shall be credited to Tenant.

32. EXPIRATION OF OPTION: This option may be exercised at any time after ________, 19____, and shall expire at midnight ________, 19____, unless exercised prior thereto. Upon expiration Owner shall be released from all obligations hereunder and all of Tenants' rights hereunder, legal or equitable, shall cease.

33. EXERCISE OF OPTION: The option shall be exercised by mailing or delivering written notice to the Owner prior to the expiration of this option and by an additional payment, on account of the purchase price, in the amount of:

$________ (________ DOLLARS)

for account of Owner to the authorized escrow holder referred to above, prior to the expiration of this option.

Notice, if mailed, shall be by certified mail, postage prepaid, to the Owner at the address set forth below, and shall be deemed to have been given upon the day following the day shown on the postmark of the envelope in which such notice is mailed.

In the event the option is exercised, the consideration paid for the option and ________ percent from the rent paid hereunder prior to the exercise of the option shall be credited upon the purchase price.

The undersigned Tenant hereby acknowledges receipt of a copy hereof.

________ Tenant's Broker Dated: ________ Time: ________

By: ________ Agent ________ Tenant

Broker's Initials: ________ Dated: ________ ________ Tenant

________ Address ________ Address

________ Phone ________ Phone

ACCEPTANCE

The undersigned Owner accepts the foregoing offer.

BROKERAGE FEE: Upon execution hereof the Owner agrees to pay to ________, The Agent in this transaction, ________% of the option consideration for securing said option plus the sum of $________ (________ DOLLARS) for leasing services rendered and authorizes Agent to deduct said sum from the deposit received from Tenant. In the event the option is exercised, the Owner agrees to pay Agent the additional sum of $________ (________ DOLLARS). This agreement shall not limit the rights of Agent provided for in any listing or other agreement which may be in effect between Owner and Agent. In the event legal action is instituted to collect this fee, or any portion thereof, the Owner agrees to pay the Agent a reasonable attorney's fee and all costs in connection with such action.

The undersigned Owner hereby acknowledges receipt of a copy hereof.

Dated: ________ Time: ________

________ Owner's Broker ________ Owner

By: ________ Agent ________ Owner

FORM 106(a) (5-90) PROFESSIONAL PUBLISHING

If you were in the same situation, what would you do? Advertise! Turn to the "Homes for Rent or Lease" section of your daily newspaper classified ads and see how many ads are there. Call every person listed in the ads and ask, "Are you interested in giving an option to buy your property if I lease your house?" Don't forget to ask if some of your monthly rental can be applied toward the eventual option price.

Most people won't be interested. Don't get discouraged. This is a numbers game. You may have to call every night for a week or more. You'll soon be able to recognize the old ads and save time. Even of the people who are interested in your offer of a lease option, only a small percentage will finally agree to let you have a long-term lease of up to five years. Of those who accept the long-term lease, only a few will agree with the option price necessary for you to make a profit. Some people will be well aware of the increasing values for local real estate, and will insist that the option price be determined by evaluating the current market value of the house (perhaps determined by appraisal) and increasing this value by 10 percent or more per year until the option date. Forget dealing with this kind of seller. You won't see a penny of profit, so why should you handle maintenance and find renters for someone else?

Even though a good lease/option property is rare, it is well worth it. What are the benefits of this lease/option wealth blueprint?

1. It lets you become a future owner of real estate now without the outlay of a large amount of cash.
2. It provides a future cash-flow situation as the market rents increase. Depending on the number of homes you have lease/optioned, you can have hundreds of dollars of positive cash flow from property you don't even own!
3. You don't have to fight the constantly increasing tax and insurance costs. Your lease should be for a constant sum for a five-year period. If you negotiate otherwise, be sure there are enough benefits in the property (such as a low option price or the ability to apply lease payments toward option price) to ensure that you will benefit in the long run.
4. Usually people who are lease/optioning their property are trying to avoid a constant mortgage payment figure. This mortgage payment will often be much lower than the property rental value. Since the mortgage is seasoned, the interest rate

on the mortgage is probably lower and the payment is much lower than a monthly payment to amortize the selling price. The difference can be $150 or more. Thus, you avoid having to charge higher rental rates that would render you less competitive.

5. You have locked in a price based on a future value. If the property is well selected, you may make much greater returns than normal, especially if the property can be converted to a different use, such as commercial or office space. The option can be sold at any time for as much as you can negotiate. It could provide a handsome cash flow to you as you sell off your options to other investors.

There are some negatives. You cannot retain any tax advantages from such optioned properties. The seller still owns the property; you have just negotiated a future sale. You will have to spend hours managing your properties and leasing them to new tenants. You will also have to be responsible for all major repairs and minor maintenance unless you specify otherwise in your lease agreement.

Here are some general guidelines to follow in the lease/option game:

1. Don't lease a property unless you can get a long enough lease to make it worth your while—preferably three to five years. Always begin with a five-year option, and don't come down unless your other benefits are great.
2. Make sure that the future option price allows you enough room to make a profit. I usually try to keep the eventual price less than 5 percent per year compounded increase. You can lower the option price by having the seller credit part of your monthly lease payment toward the eventual option price, a technique that can defray the bite of a large future option price.
3. Option only properties that are in a good neighborhood and that have potential for steady increase in value. If the neighborhood is deteriorating, you will be working for nothing. Also, choose properties that are easily maintained, such as those constructed of brick.
4. Call your local rental agency and offer to pay it a finder's fee for every property it refers you to that you eventually lease

with an option to buy. Try placing an ad in the newspaper requesting "a lease with an option to buy." Keep at it and you'll eventually get results.

Investing in real estate through options is a five-year retirement plan that is feasible and possible with determined effort. Don't be discouraged if people are not thrilled to lease their properties for five years. Start out with a few shorter-term options, and look for the kind of a don't wanter who will let you write the terms of the lease/option to suit yourself. Your knowledge and confidence will grow as you become more familiar with the option market. I'll wager that five years from now your hobby of buying with options will be a full-time one, and you'll be on your own as a free lance.

CHAPTER 20

Born-Again Property: Consider Conversions

Once you have invested in real estate property, consider increasing your return on the investment by using the method of conversion.

Everywhere you look you will see buildings that are functioning in a completely different capacity from that for which they were designed. Homes have become office buildings. Old churches that have lost their congregations have become dance schools or restaurants. Apartment buildings have become condominiums. Gas stations have become retail stores. Farmland is now prime residential and commercial ground. To convert a property is to change its use from one utility to another. This is done for three reasons:

1. A building or piece of land has outlived its originally intended use.
2. A building or piece of land has failed in its originally intended use. For instance, a gas station can't compete with the other two gas stations on the block, so it is converted into a retail store.
3. It has become economically unfeasible to operate the property as was originally intended. Maybe a farmer is not able to

return enough money from his crops, so he sells to a commercial developer, who builds a shopping mall on the site of the old farm.

Conversions provide limitless possibilities for the creative real estate investor. Look at the relative values of a typical acre of ground under different uses:

A typical acre of raw undeveloped ground (43,560 square feet) used for grazing of animals or left unused could go for as little as $1,000. This converts to a fraction of a cent per square foot—.023 cents per square foot, to be exact.

If this same property were sold as farm ground or converted to farm ground, it might sell for $2,500 per acre, or about 6 cents a square foot.

If this same land were converted to subdivision lots, it would sell for $25,000 or more per acre, or 60 cents per square foot and/or up.

If the subdivision ground could be used instead for apartment ground, the seller could reap more than $75,000 an acre in some cases.

The highest-priced ground is land used to build shopping centers and office buildings—land that sells for up to $250,000 per acre and more.

The graph below shows the relative values of each of the different types of property:

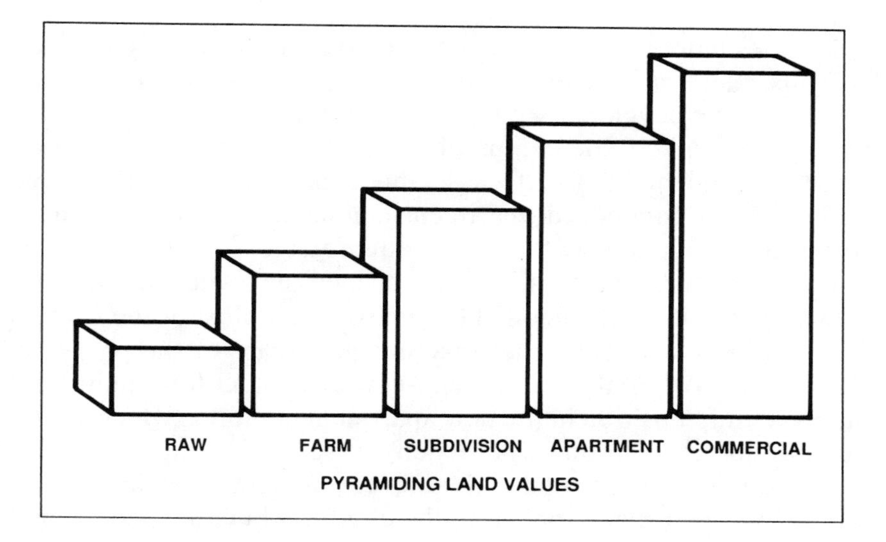

PYRAMIDING LAND VALUES

Between any two categories of ground there lies an absolutely fantastic opportunity for profit—all you need to do is convert land from one use to another.

Unfortunately, it is not easy to do in the conventional real estate market. To convert raw land to farming ground takes ingenuity and guts. Several years ago, one of my closest friends hired a full-time legal legman to file claims with the Idaho state government to homestead the vast unusable tracts of Idaho desert. Once the ground was in his name—perhaps 5,000 acres at a time that he acquired for little or nothing—he purchased one of those massive circular sprinkling systems. He filed for a well permit and proceeded to irrigate the property until it became suitable farm ground. By converting only 1,000 acres a year and at $1,000 an acre or less, he could make up to $1 million at a time. Not many people are doing this; not many people have the guts or the creativity. But it only has to happen once to put you over the hump.

Converting farm ground to subdivision ground is a little bit easier, since any ground within a two-to-five-mile limit of your town, if you live in such an area of the country, is fair game for a future subdivision. If you can buy the ground for as little as $1,000 an acre and resell it to a builder for up to $5,000 or more an acre, you will turn a tidy profit, multiplied by the number of acres you buy—although it may take a few years for the city to grow out to your land.

In cities where houses in depressed areas are abandoned for tax reasons, there may be an excellent profit opportunity for an apartment building developer who is looking for new ground to build his next project on. If you can purchase contiguous houses at a good price, you might be able to assemble a package of ground large enough for a good-sized apartment complex. The houses can be torn down, making way for a beautiful project.

I heard of two investors who approached the owners of old, run-down houses in an area zoned for apartments. Most of the owners were widows who could not take adequate care of the property; the investors offered them a brand-new apartment for a home and an ownership position in the new apartment complex, which would be built upon the ground where their houses now stood.

These two men persuaded a sufficient number of widows to go along with their plan, applied to the city for a building permit, and built a beautiful unit where the new owners of the property were able to live for the rest of their lives rent-free.

Since the land was donated to the partnership, the two developers did not have to invest any money on the front end in order to build the property. They ended up with a major ownership in the complex without any cash investment. This is a classic example of the conversion of land from one type of use to another, more profitable use.

How do you know how to take advantage of these changes? It is very simple. Just go down to your city's planning department and ask for a zoning map; the map indicates how each area is zoned. Apartments are usually zoned into one specific area, commercial space into another. Any property that is in an area zoned for different properties can be converted. For example, any house along a major artery leading into a major shopping district has potential as either an office or a shopping space. Of course, the property must be in an area that is zoned for commercial use, or you'll have to apply for a zoning change—something that is difficult and time-consuming to obtain. But if it were easy everybody would be doing it. A little hard work can pay off big.

Another potential conversion exists when one property lies directly adjacent to another zone of higher use. When an older apartment building is directly next to an office zone, for example, there is the possibility that the apartment building could be converted to offices.

Let's look more closely at some conversion possibilities.

1. Conversion of an Apartment Building to an Office Complex.

One of my first major purchases was a beautiful old twelve-unit apartment building in the center of my city of 60,000 people. It was a classic building with a fifty-year-old brick veneer and stately white balconies in an excellent location, directly across from the county courthouse. It cost me $141,000.

I kept the building for six years. It never generated much income and appreciated only modestly. I avoided spending a lot of money on it because I always wanted to convert these units to office space for my corporate headquarters. In 1981 the time came to make a major decision. The units needed at least $25,000 in repairs. It was time to ask some hard questions.

How many square feet were usable as office space on each floor? Approximately 3,000 square feet each for three floors.

Was there adequate parking for office space? Checking with the city, I learned I would need one parking space for each 500 square feet of office space. I would therefore need eighteen spaces. I had thirteen spaces already, and I could rent an additional five spaces from a neighboring office building.

Was the property zoned for the intended change? The city master plan showed that my building was in a professional office zone. The city planner indicated that there would be no problem with the proposed conversion but that I would have to submit my plans to the city council for its approval.

Was there an adequate market for office space if I didn't take up all of the space with my own operations? I called one of the county commissioners and found out that they needed extra space for some of their county offices. In fact, they had recently purchased some buildings across the street from my unit for some badly needed office space. One of the tenants in the buildings that the county bought needed a new office and asked about my rates. Others also expressed an interest. Signed leases from future tenants would give me added borrowing power at the bank.

What about costs? I hired a local architect to make a study of the kinds of improvements that would have to be made to the building; his cost estimate was $150,000 for major renovation.

What about the bank? Would it lend the money? By now I had enough clout at the bank to show the loan officers the benefits of a construction loan to convert the building.

What would it be worth after conversion? I estimated rents on similar office space would run $7 per square foot per year including utilities. If I could end up with 9,000 square feet of space at $7 per square foot, that would give me $63,000 gross income. Net income would be 60 percent of that, or $37,860. If I capitalized the net income at 7 percent, the value of the building could be $500,000 or more when complete ($37,800 ÷ .07 = 540,000). If this were the case I could turn my old, run-down $200,000 apartment building into a brand-new office building worth perhaps $500,000—with a substantially larger equity.

The diagram on page 235 shows how the building looks before and after the proposed conversion.

And what about the cash-flow picture? As an apartment building, it generated a break-even cash flow at best when you consider all the repairs needed to keep the fifty-year-old shell patched together. But I estimated that even after I had incurred $150,000 in new debt, the income from the new office building (when I made adjustments for the fact that I would be a major tenant) would be a positive cash flow.

I decided, finally, that the only logical alternative was to start the conversion process.

And so we began—and immediately ran into all kinds of unanticipated problems. Let me summarize by saying that the total bill came in at about $350,000—only a slight $200,000 miscalculation by the architect. But the extra money spent turned the project into one of the top-notch office buildings in the city. An appraisal ordered by my banker put the value at $735,000 (I had guessed low!), and based on this appraisal the bank advanced the necessary money. Since it is such a prime location and has such fine amenities, we have no trouble charging top dollar for office rent.

So in the final analysis, the conversion of this apartment building to an office building was a profitable one—although I had my doubts there for a while. The building became worth over $700,000 with loans of about $450,000.

And the nicest gift of all is when my accountant informed me

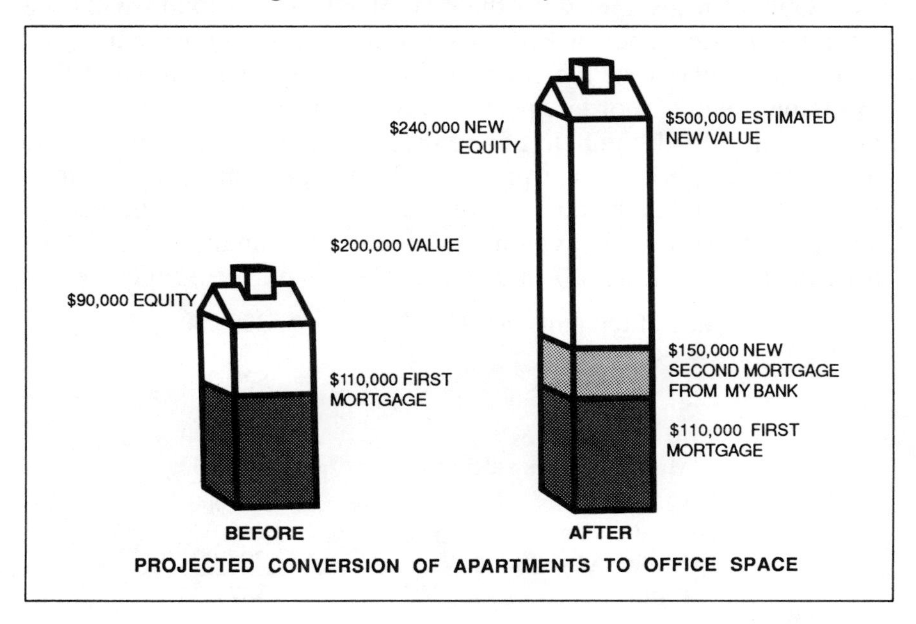

PROJECTED CONVERSION OF APARTMENTS TO OFFICE SPACE

that because of a government tax break we were able to take a 20 percent investment tax credit on the money we spent rehabilitating the building. That's 20 percent of $350,000 or $70,000 in tax savings.

So, as you see, conversions can be sweet—if you're careful.

2. Condominium Conversions.

My first positive experience with condominium conversion took place in 1978. My partner and I were able to locate a choice ten-unit building in an excellent location. Four of the units were being rented out as commercial office space. The remaining six units were apartments, each containing about 1,000 square feet of space with two bedrooms. We negotiated a purchase price of $208,000 with a down payment of $30,000 and a land sales contract of $178,000, with monthly payments of $1,524.36 until paid in full. Once we owned the building we contacted our attorney and had him prepare the necessary documents for the conversion of the ten units into ten condominiums. In essence, this would convert the individual units from a rental status to an ownership status.

In order to accomplish this, certain items had to be taken care of. First of all, the city had to give authorization for the change in use. Our attorney met with the city planners to explain what we intended to do. They asked to see our condominium documents and a new survey of the property. Once they were satisfied that the papers were in order, permission was granted to sell the individual units. With the help of a real estate company, we placed the units on the market for a price of $32,000 per unit. All the units were sold quickly because of our easy financing; we agreed to accept a $5,000 down payment and to carry the financing ourselves for the balance of the $27,000 owing. Here is our profit picture:

Sale of ten units @ $32,000	$320,000
Less:	
Commissions	$20,000
Survey	1,000
Attorneys' fees	2,500
Miscellaneous sales costs	1,500
	$(25,000)
Net sales proceeds	295,000
Less cost of building	208,000
Profit	$87,000

The interesting part of the story is yet to come. We required a down payment of $5,000 per unit with a total cash down payment for all units equally of $50,000. When we deducted our $25,000 costs of conversion (commissions, attorneys' fees, etc.) from the total down payment, we came away with $25,000 in cash. This returned to us almost all of our original down payment of $30,000. Then where is our benefit for converting the units to condominiums? As you remember, our monthly payment on the property when we bought it was $1,524.36. By selling the units as condominiums and carrying back the paper ourselves, we created a situation whereby the new owners made a total monthly payment of approximately $2,500 per month. With this money we make the payment of $1,524.36 and keep the difference of almost $1,000 a month for the next twenty-five years. In summary, we bought the building with a $30,000 down payment, sold the units as condominiums, got back $25,000 in cash at closing, and a monthly cash flow of approximately $1,000 a month for twenty-five years. We did not have to make any extensive improvements in the property—we simply sold the units "as is." The attorney did most of the work for us. The real estate company took care of the sales. All that was necessary for us to do was to come up with the idea in the first place and to delegate the details to the professionals. Profit was created because we knew that people will pay more for a condominium than they will for a rental apartment unit. If you're like me, you'll be out looking for an apartment building just waiting to be converted.

3. *Land Subdivisions.*

Another form of conversion from one use to another is converting land that has been kept vacant for farming or other reasons into a land subdivision. Your land is a prime candidate if it is near a growing metropolis. The increase in price from one use to the other is dramatic.

Let's look at a ten-acre parcel of ground that has been used for raising corn. The farmer is getting older and wants to retire; he has watched the sprawling city slowly encroach and almost completely surround his small farm. Since his livelihood has been derived in part from his land, he has resisted the offers of previous land subdividers; now, with retirement in sight, he begins to contemplate selling his property so he can enjoy the life he has always wanted.

Along comes a creative real estate investor—we'll call him Bob. Not much money jingles in his pockets, but his ideas won't stop. Since Bob has done his homework, he knows that farm ground in the country has been selling for $4,000 to $10,000 an acre; however, ground this close to the city limits has recently sold for $20,000 to $30,000 an acre. The farmer has kept close track of the higher land price sales, and he wants at least $25,000 an acre for his ground. He must have $25,000 or nothing at all.

When Bob begins to negotiate, he must have all of the facts at his fingertips. He checks with the city to determine the difficulty of obtaining building permits on any subdivision lots that would be created. Is there adequate water, sewer, and fire protection? Is the city going to cause any trouble when a final plan of the subdivision is submitted to the planning department for approval? Is the land properly surveyed? Is there a market for property in this area? What size lots can be sold and at what prices?

Bob checks with a reputable land surveying company and asks the surveyor these questions; he has most of the answers.

In the case of the ten-acre parcel, all of the signs are GO. Building lots have sold for as high as $20,000 a lot within the last three months. The surveyor draws up an inexpensive preliminary subdivision plan showing that once roads and sidewalks are accounted for, there will be about thirty lots ready for sale.

Bob is able to obtain a firm bid from a local contracting outfit (recommended by the surveyor), which has agreed to do the improvements on the property such as roads, sewer, water lines, and sidewalks. Here is the financial picture:

Cost of the land	$250,000
Cost of the improvements (at $5,000 per lot)	$150,000
Sales costs at $1,000 per lot	$ 30,000
Total costs	$430,000
Gross sales of 30 lots at $20,000	$600,000
Less total costs	$430,000
Total profits	$170,000

The profit picture is outstanding for such a small piece of ground, ten acres, for a year's work. You would also be wise to sell the lots on a wholesale basis to a local builder who needs the land for his next home subdivision. You may be able to sell the whole thirty-lot package for $17,500 per lot, avoiding sales costs, and end up with a profit of $125,000. The profit is quicker this way and does not involve advertising campaigns. Always pick the quick profit over the long-term method. Better to make a fast nickel than a slow dime.

What about financing the land in the first place? Use the subordination technique discussed earlier. The seller is going to have a tremendous tax consequence if he receives all of his $250,000 in one year. Convince him that he should accept only 25 percent of the money during the first year of sale. Thus by structuring the receipt of cash in several tax years, the tax consequences are greatly reduced. A 25 percent down payment amounts to $62,500; the rest ($187,500) should be subordinated to a construction loan which you have obtained to make improvements on the property. Since the improvements will cost about $150,000, you will need to find a bank that will give you a development loan; some will lend up to 75 percent of the value of the developed building lot.

Every year thousands of homes are being built, and land is needed desperately by growing building companies. You can fill a need by bird-dogging the land for them and reap a profit in the process!

Keep your eyes open. Make conversions like this one and the others we've discussed work for you.

CHAPTER 21

Creative Self-Unemployment: How to Retire in Five Years on a Tax-Free Income

Forty-five-minute lunch hours.

Traffic jams in the mornings—and in the afternoons.

Working twice as hard as the guy in the next office for half the pay.

Punching a time clock.

Two measly weeks of vacation in return for fifty weeks of hard labor.

The incessant clang of the alarm clock.

Hand-to-mouth existence.

Shackled.

Aren't you sick of it all?

It's time for you to say goodbye to a job you don't enjoy. Use your knowledge of real estate and your creative abilities to become financially independent. The time is right. The opportunities are there. *You* can do it. You have been successful in your real estate investment program even though you were doing it on a part-time basis. Just think what would happen if you can devote full time to it.

Declaring your financial independence by quitting your job is a lot like jumping off the edge of the world. Make sure you look before you leap—and consider the following elements:

1. Cash Flow.

As soon as your last paycheck arrives, you are on your own. Unless you have established a monthly income stream from some other source, it won't be long before you will be in trouble. As a rule, you should not quit your job until you have at least six to twelve months of living-expense money in the bank (or until you have an adequate outside monthly cash flow). Remember—quitting your job is supposed to provide you with more time to cultivate your real estate investments. If you're not financially prepared, you'll waste your time worrying about money—or scrambling for money. Don't leap until you have a parachute of some sort, even if it's only a small umbrella. Can you imagine how embarrassing it would be if you had to come crawling back to your employer—all because you didn't plan your "escape" well enough and weren't prepared to handle cash-flow problems?

We'll never know how many prospectors closed down their mines because they ran out of money when they were only days away from discovering a rich vein of gold. Don't let it happen to you. Have a one-year supply of either food or money on hand before you quit.

2. Office Space.

If you have been used to working in an office that your boss provided for you free, you will be shocked to discover just how much it costs to rent and maintain your own office space. You won't need much—perhaps a hundred square feet in a corner somewhere—but you'll need something. I work out of my home, but children, your spouse, and other family concerns can really cut into your productive working time. If you are doing your job, you will be out looking at real estate much of the time, but there will be times when you'll need a quiet place to concentrate. Do what seems best for you.

3. Time Management.

If you have trouble managing your time, you will find all kinds of excuses not to be out there hustling all day long. It takes tremendous discipline to overcome a streak of laziness or fear. Set rigid goals for yourself on a daily basis: "I'll visit ten homes or apartment buildings today. I'll present five offers today. I'll buy something today. I'll talk to ten real estate agents today. I'll read up and study today." I recently read a story about an investor who woke up one morning and decided to see just how much money he could make that day from dawn to dusk. He began his search, located a property, tied up the property with an option, sold the option to a group of investors—all within the prescribed time limit—and netted for himself over $2 million.

4. Loss of Company Benefits.

You must realize that you are probably going to leave behind a group insurance program, some kind of retirement benefits, the use of the company car, and all those other goodies that come with the corporate life. These are called "golden handcuffs," and more than one potential free lance has not answered the knock of opportunity because of them. These benefits are designed especially to keep the best employees from moving on to other jobs. They are meant to shackle you. You must recognize them for what they are: the bars that invisibly keep you a prisoner in a job that makes you unhappy.

5. Lack of Borrowing Power.

As soon as you quit your secure, steady-paying job, you are also cutting yourself off from the help of the bank. If you are planning to do any refinancing of properties or borrowing for down payments, you will be wise to do as much of it as you can *before* you quit your job. After you quit you will have to rely on partners with strong financial statements to help you until you are strong enough on your own.

Okay. So there are some disadvantages. You can counter them with adequate planning and conservative judgment if you are aware of the disadvantages and if you are determined to overcome them.

There are also some huge pluses.

1. Time.

All day long—every day, if you wish—you can be free to seek your fortune however you wish. That's the biggest plus of them all. No longer will you have to "push someone else's pencil." No more "Yes, Massa; no, Massa." You will be amazed at how quickly your net worth increases when you work full time at it. A sense of accomplishment will swell inside of you until you feel like bursting. You will be building your own empire instead of building someone else's. You will be leaving a legacy to your children. This sense of freedom was the foundation upon which our great nation was built. Fifty-six brave men signed their own death warrants when they affixed their names to the Declaration of Independence in 1776. Where would we be now if they hadn't? The freedom to spend one's time in whatever manner one wishes is sacred. Don't let someone deprive you of it.

2. Money.

The risks of self-employment are tremendous, but the rewards are well worth the trouble. When the money starts to flow, it will come in larger amounts than you had thought possible. In the meantime, hang on—by your fingernails if necessary. Stay rational. Don't make any hasty decisions.

You must realize that in order to increase your ultimate financial freedom you will have to cut back on your expenditures for a short period of time. As the chart below illustrates, when you become your own boss your standard of living sometimes has to be adjusted downward in comparison to your neighbors, the Joneses. They spend almost every dollar they earn on "butter" and have nothing worthwhile to show for it. You must learn to sacrifice immediate pleasures for the long-range satisfaction that financial independence provides. There is no other way. You either pay the price now for a short period of time (and live the rest of your life in financial independence) or you pay the price later, when you reach age sixty-five and have nothing to show for your butter life-

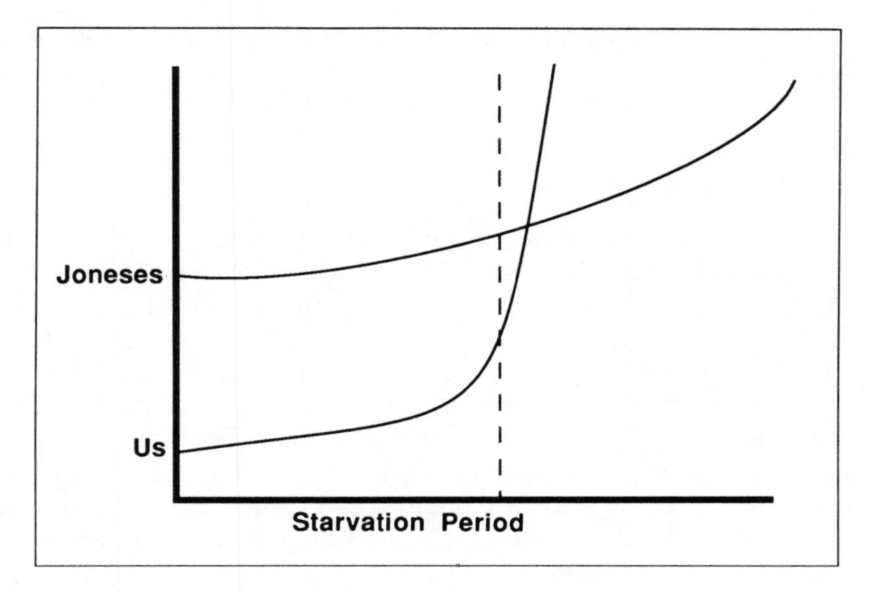

style and must rely on social security for the rest of your days. It's your choice.

Up to where the lines cross on the chart, your life-style is lower than the Joneses' because you have chosen to take a gamble and to invest full time in real estate. The "starvation period" won't last long. After the lines cross you are financially independent. The Joneses still struggle. You don't.

A ship in a harbor is safe, but that's not what ships were built for. What were *you* built for? Think about it as you drive to work tomorrow morning.

3. Security.

Security? That's right. Security for the future—security that your wise investments of today will afford you a great deal more security than the retirement program you're now paying into. Security that says your income will always keep pace with inflation. It's a solid kind of security, better than the "security" of having a steady—albeit small—income.

What can you do to make your free-lance experience successful? A successful free-lance experience, of course, is one that provides enough cash flow to meet the costs involved in living expenses and to provide the cash you want to continue in your investment program. Let's look at how you might obtain such a cash flow.

Plan #1. Buy low, sell for nothing down with high price.

This consists of finding an undervalued property that is also available for a small down payment. These kinds of properties are difficult—but not impossible—to find. They are generally those that require quite a bit of fix-up and cosmetic work. Buy the property, clean it up, and sell it for a nice profit. You might do something like this:

Two-Unit Apartment Building

PURCHASE PRICE	SALES INFORMATION
Cost: $120,000	Sales price: $142,000
Down payment: $10,000	Down payment: $12,000
Mortgage: $110,000	Mortgage: $130,000
Payable at $1,048 per month with 11 percent interest	Payable at $1,387 per month with 12.5 percent interest
Fix-up expenses: $2,000	Net to you: $12,000 cash
Total cash: $12,000	You will also receive the difference between the old and new loans: $339 a month.

This $339 cash flow comes in each month and gives you a source to help you with living expenses. You still have your $12,000 capital to invest in another project. If you "roll your money over" several times like this, you might be able to generate enough cash flow from your properties to give you the courage you need to quit your job and devote full time to your real estate ventures. As I mentioned in the previous chapter on conversions, on one project alone my partner and I were able to create a cash flow for ourselves of almost $1,000 per month by converting a small ten-unit apartment building into condominiums. We bought low and sold high and kept the profit in the form of a steady monthly cash flow.

Plan #2. Triple Net Lease.

If you are just starting out and you would like to delay buying real estate until you know the ropes, try the triple net lease approach to making steady monthly cash flow. You simply need to approach owners of apartment buildings or of office space in your area who are especially tired of managing their properties and agree with them to pay them a certain guaranteed income from their properties if they will allow you the privilege of operating their building for them.

For instance, suppose you find an elderly gentleman who has owned and operated a twelve-unit building for twenty years, owns it free and clear, and does not have the time or energy to manage his property anymore. He doesn't want to sell it, and he doesn't know management firms exist. Your main selling point would be to relieve him of his headache and give him a guaranteed, steady, hassle-free cash flow each month. If the building rents for $3,600 a month ($300 an apartment) and the expenses are running at 40 percent of the gross income—about $1,440 a month—then he normally receives about $2,200 a month net cash flow before taxes. Offer him a net $2,000 a month for a five-year lease on his apartment building. This would give you $200 a month for your efforts in the first year. In later years as rents increased and you were able to keep expenses to a minimum, you might get up to $500 a month from your lease contract.

This income will not come without some work on your part. You will have to keep the units rented at all times and take care of maintenance problems. But once you understand the building and how to run it efficiently, you can turn it over to one of the building tenants in exchange for a partial rent reduction. Then you can keep the excess income and spend your precious time on other projects.

The leasing of single-family residences with options to buy (as discussed in the chapter on options) can also provide additional monthly income. I have heard of some investors who have taken this technique seriously and have leased dozens of houses with a small monthly cash flow. A portfolio of nine or ten leased houses could possibly generate enough positive cash flow to support a modest living budget for the potential full-time investor.

Plan #3. Buy low, sell high—all cash.

In real estate, a smart investor can make as much money in one transaction as the average American makes working for fifty weeks a year (at a job he can't stand, I might add). The skill comes in recognizing which property has potential and which property does not. The more you know your real estate marketplace, the easier it will be to recognize the "once-in-a-lifetime deals" that seem to pop up about every other week. In this book I have given examples of transactions in which the buyer made tens of thousands of dollars in only *one* transaction in less than a year's time. These are not isolated examples. They are happening every day—around you, in front of your very eyes. On your way to work each morning you are driving by dozens of properties which are crying out for someone with vision and courage to buy them. The next move is yours.

Let's go through a quick example. Suppose you are working nine to five at a job you are not in love with. You agree with the principle of becoming your own boss but realize that you don't have any money saved up to make the break on your own. You begin studying and researching the real estate market to find out how it operates. At this point, you should be looking for a property that needs some minor cosmetic repair—a "sleeper" that most people have overlooked because of its condition. Suppose you locate a rundown single-family house (the worst house in the best average neighborhood) with a price tag of $100,000 and a down payment of $10,000. With a little work, you surmise that it could be placed back on the market for $130,000 with the buyer obtaining a new loan to cash you out. You tie the property up and use one of the techniques outlined in this book to come up with the cash. Then you begin to make the necessary improvements. Since you do a lot of the work yourself, the fix-up job is completed in about three months at a total cost of $5,000. At this point you have $15,000 invested in the property. You place the property back on the market, listed at $130,000, and six months later the building closes and the new buyer cashes out your equity of $40,000. You may have to return the $10,000 and the $5,000 you borrowed plus interest—but even at that you are left with at least $25,000. Not bad for a few extra hours and a part-time effort.

If you look at what you accomplished with only minimal effort, you may begin to ask yourself, "Why don't I do this full time?" Remember that you will need a cushion to start with—but isn't $25,000 in the bank enough? It should be adequate to keep you alive for a year until you locate your next property and turn it over for another profit. One cardinal rule to remember is that each time you sell a property for a profit, you should always try to buy a property to keep. Take a portion of your earnings and reinvest it in another property, which you will leave in your portfolio for long-term growth. If you follow this pattern it won't be long before your money worries will be gone forever.

Plan #4. For Property Owners Only.

If you have property that you've owned for some time, you might be lucky enough to have a cash flow from your units. If you raise rents regularly on a competitive basis, there will come a time when the building will generate a rather substantial monthly cash flow. There are two other ways to realize cash from properties you already own: refinance the property and reinvest the profit, or sell the property. But why should you sell your property if you don't have to?

Let's look at a really exciting prospect—retirement in five years with a tax-free income, without selling your property.

Of all the formulas mentioned in this book, this one has the most promise, is the easiest to accomplish, and requires the least amount of time.

This plan centers around single-family residences. Why? Because they are in the greatest supply; most people understand the methods of home purchasing because they've gone through the process at least once. And single-family residences are usually easiest to buy for the small investor. (Of course, you can work this same plan with any investment medium, but for our purposes we will discuss only single-family residences. You may apply the principles any way that will benefit you most.)

Suppose you were able to devote one full day a week—say, Saturdays—to looking for real estate investments. Since you have fifty-two Saturdays a year, you should be able to find and purchase just *one* property, one small home valued near $60,000, from a seller who is anxious to sell and will accept a $50,000 price with a $3,000 down payment. This will take some looking, but remember you have a year to find it. When you find the right property, buy it. If necessary, borrow the down payment, using one of the creative methods discussed earlier in this book. Then rent the house.

The next year, do exactly the same thing. Buy just *one* property priced at least 15 percent below market value with a small down payment. Again, rent the house; you'll have to be able to rent the house for enough money to cover mortgage payments, including taxes and insurance. The tenants will pay all utility bills and minor maintenance bills. In the first year or so the rental income will be tight, but after several years you will begin to experience a steady positive cash flow.

In the third year, do the same thing. And so on until the fifth year, when you'll own five rental houses, all rented out, with no negative cash flow. If you have chosen the property well, you should enjoy 5 to 10 percent yearly appreciation on each house.

Let's look at our equity position in five years in these five houses, assuming 10 percent growth (all figures are rounded to highest one thousand):

	House #1	**House #2**	**House #3**	**House #4**	**House #5**
Value	$97,000	$88,000	$80,000	$73,000	$66,000
Loans	$46,000	$46,000	$47,000	$47,000	$47,000
Equity	$51,000	$42,000	$33,000	$26,000	$19,000

How do you make the money? Do you sell? No. You refinance. And you attempt to find the highest possible loan on your properties. Help yourself to do just that. Paint the trim on the houses, maintain the yard, or consider new carpeting or draperies. You might even paint the interior throughout the entire house. Do as much as possible with as little money as possible. Your aim is to get the highest appraisal possible for your invested cosmetic dollar.

Then do your homework. Be prepared to convince the appraiser that the value of the house has increased steadily over the past five years. If you are able to obtain a new loan of 80 percent of the value of the appraisal, you should be able to refinance your first property for at least $75,000.

If your existing loan is $46,000, your net proceeds from the new loan will be $28,000, less loan fees, which may be as high as $2,000. So you should be able to keep at least $26,000 of the new loan, a figure that represents the equity that belongs to you and that, as such, *is not taxable*. It's my understanding that you won't have to report this income to the government as long as you don't sell the property (one good reason not to sell!).

Can you now rent the property for enough to pay the mortgage payment? A mortgage payment on a $75,000 mortgage at 13 percent interest for thirty years would amount to $820.75 plus taxes

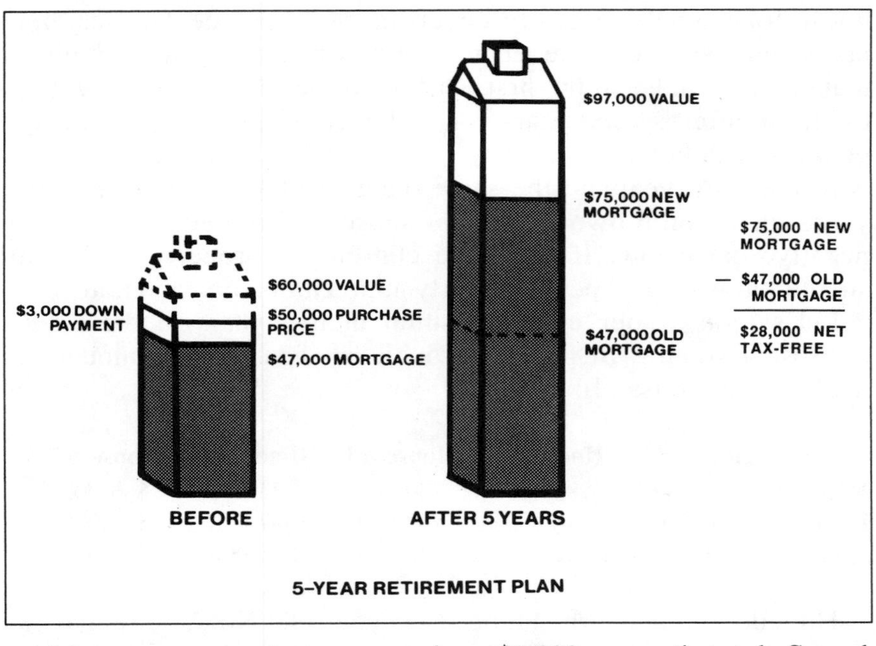

5-YEAR RETIREMENT PLAN

and insurance—perhaps as much as $1,000 a month total. Sound impossible? Remember, you're looking at rents five years down the road; they're bound to be considerably higher.

Still uncomfortable? Hold out $2,000 from your refinance profits. That will give you $166 a month for twelve months to apply toward the mortgage payment as you look to raise rents. You'll still have $25,000 left over to spend as you want to, *and it's tax-free*. Kick off your shoes and pursue a full-time real estate investment hobby. In the sixth year of your program, the second investment house is now ready for refinancing after your having experienced five full years of appreciation.

Do this with one house each year. Refinance in January, and you're set for the year.

Is your program finished after you have refinanced the fifth investment house (in the tenth year)? Of course not! Your very first house, which you refinanced (harvested) in the fifth year of your program, has now had five more years to grow a new crop. It's ready to be harvested once more. And so you start all over again. Ad infinitum.

If you want to retire with an even higher income—insurance against inflation—buy *two* houses a year. Then, at the end of five years, start refinancing *two* houses a year. It's twice the work, but it will be twice the income. And you'll still have plenty of time for your new hobbies and life-style.

Now, what if you don't think properties will appreciate at 10 percent a year for the foreseeable future? Change your strategy. Buy properties in foreclosure where you pay sometimes 60 to 70 cents on the dollar. Go the fix-up route. It's up to you. But either way, there is a viable way of retiring in ten years or less.

For those property owners who don't want to wait for five years to take advantage of the five-house retirement plan, there are ways of pulling all of the equity out of properties you own without having to sell them. Let me illustrate. Whenever you are paying mortgage payments to a private party who holds a mortgage on your property, there exists the possibility of flexibility. One of my first purchases was an older twelve-unit building which I bought with $5,000 down. As in the illustration below, I ended up with a $125,000 contract for twenty years. The underlying $100,000 portion of the contract was held by an elderly woman who sold the property years earlier, carrying back a first mortgage of $100,000 at 7 percent interest. Her sons soon realized that a 7 percent mortgage is really not a very good interest rate in these double-digit days. I approached them with an interesting proposition. I asked them how they would feel if I refinanced the property and placed a new $150,000 loan on it. Normally, the proceeds of the new loan would go to pay off all underlying indebtedness—thus paying $100,000 to the woman in cash. The sons orally agreed that if I were to place a new loan on the property, they would split the proceeds of the money their mother would receive—therefore, she would receive only $50,000 in cash and I would get the remaining $50,000 in cash. This latter amount would be lent to me at a higher interest rate and would be secured by a second trust deed on the twelve-unit building. It is easy to see the rationale behind this offer to refinance the property. The sons would thereby obtain at least half of the outstanding $100,000 debt. Their mother would be able to improve her life-style and enjoy herself more—and in addition, she would increase the interest rate on the $50,000 portion that she did not receive. Likewise, it is easy to see the rationale behind my desire to offer them this plan. I could refinance the property and thereby borrow out 100 percent of my equity and still be able to retain ownership of the property. I would walk away from the

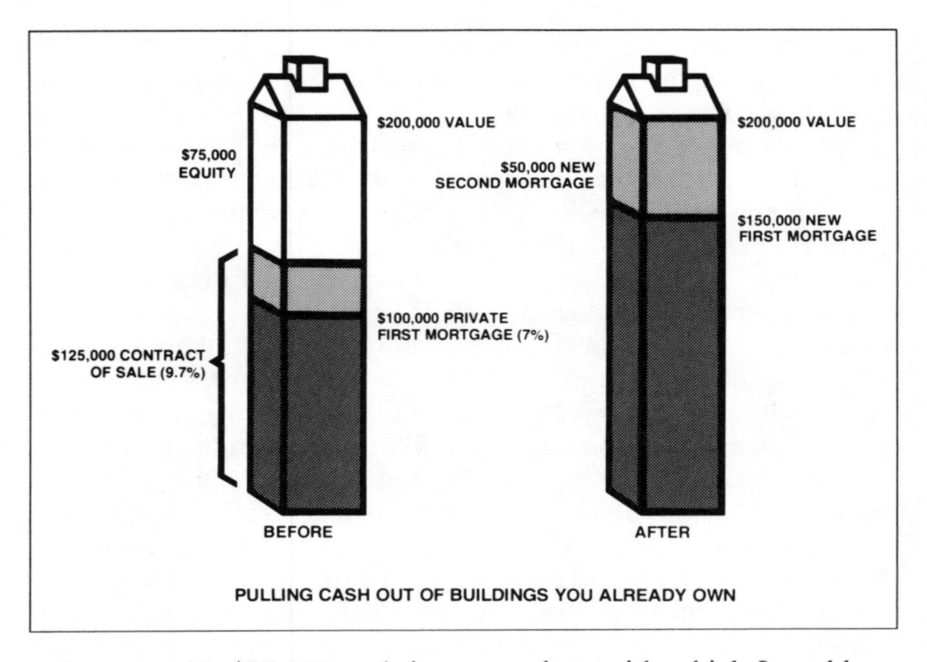

PULLING CASH OUT OF BUILDINGS YOU ALREADY OWN

refinance with $75,000 cash in my pocket, with which I could go out and buy more real estate. The only thing I would have to worry about in the above situation is negative cash flows. As it turned out, I decided to do something else, but I'm sure you can see the benefits of the above approach.

Apply these solutions; commit yourself to a life-style that will afford you ultimate freedom and security. Begin planning now for the day you will walk up to your boss with a smile on your face and a letter of resignation in your hand. Dream about it. Plan for it. Make your goal specific; mark the day on your calendar. Do these things faithfully, and you will reach your goal. You're one step closer just by deciding to do it!

Your goal might seem unusual to some, and there will undoubtedly be those who will try to deter you from your course, just as there were those who tried to talk Columbus out of sailing for the New World. Thank heaven he did. And you'll thank heaven you did. Take the road less traveled by—it *will* make all the difference!

· I'd like to thank Jack Miller and John Schaub for sharing the basic idea for the five-year retirement plan in their nationwide seminar entitled "Making It Big on Little Deals."

CHAPTER 22

Different Strokes for Different Folks: Variations on the Nothing-Down Theme

"*Chacun à son goût.*" So goes the French expression which roughly translated means "Each to his own taste," or "Different strokes for different folks." You get the idea.

Some of you reading this book won't have two nickels to rub together. That's what attracted you to the book. And that's fine. That's the way I got started. Others of you will have plenty of cash to burn and want to know what to do with it. There is plenty of room for both of these groups in the nothing-down philosophy. Let's look at each of them more carefully.

Especially for Cash-Poor Investors

Real estate is a multifaceted investment—a miracle of flexibility. It will do for you financially just about anything you want it to. If you want appreciation, tax shelter, equity buildup, or cash flow—or any combination of these—you can find a formula which will solve your needs. But you have to be specific. If you want appreciation, choose formulas which are suited for appreciation. If you want cash flow, you need to use cash-flow formulas. The mistake most investors make is using appreciation formulas when what they really need is cash flow.

Take, for example, the case of a beginning cash-poor investor. He can barely keep his nose above water, couldn't even think of handling a negative cash flow, and would be devastated by any unexpected expenditure such as a major roof repair. And despite these strikes against him, he buys big chunks of real estate hoping for the big long-term bucks when it is those short-term bucks which hold the key to his success or failure. He doesn't need $1 million in five years. He needs an extra $300 per month now. And when he has *this* problem solved, maybe he will be in the right frame of mind to think about the future.

Perhaps a better approach is for a cash-poor investor to take things one step at a time. Rather than marching out into the cold, cruel world of investments to make a quick fortune, he should look upon his real estate operations as a sort of part-time job with a goal to have his real estate activities (you'll notice I didn't say "investments") generate for him a comfortable cushion of monthly cash flow plus a few small chunks of cash to be used later on in his investment program. The primary goal is to generate cash or cash flow to enhance the financial strength and stability of the investor (I really should say "employee").

I am trying to make the distinction between "investor" and "employee" to reinforce the fact that real estate is technically not an investment . . . it is a business. And those who treat it like an active "hands-on" business generally prosper while those who treat it like a passive "armchair" investment are the ones who moan and groan the loudest about how lousy real estate is as an investment. It is lousy as an investment, but it is simply marvelous as a business. (I hope that doesn't confuse anyone.)

Therefore, let me catalog a few of the many cash-flow-generating techniques and formulas that are available. Go for the cash flow first, then build up a cash pool, and when you are ready you can go for the capital gains.

To make this a little more realistic and useful to you, let's assume that you are a cash-poor investor (who isn't?) with a steady job and fairly good credit rating (more of a rarity these days). You are living from paycheck to paycheck. You want to invest in real estate but don't dare because you don't have much margin for error. You would feel more comfortable if you had $10,000 in cash and $400 or $500 per month surplus income.

Question: How could you use your knowledge of real estate investing to help you reach your comfortable cash-flow goals within a six-month period of time?

Let's try it.

The first step is to write down our goals. Let's get the subconscious mind on our side.

Second, devise a plan. There are five major ways to squeeze cash or cash flow from real estate:

1. Buy it right and lease it out.
2. Buy it right and sell it.
3. Lease it right and sublet it.
4. Option it right and sell the option.
5. Buy discounted paper right and sell it.

The essence of all of these cash-flow-generating categories is becoming an expert in finding bargains, wholesale situations, and remarketing those bargains to the public at retail. That's what free enterprise is all about.

Let's examine each one in turn.

1. Buy it right and lease it out.

What do I mean by "buy it right"? In order for you to buy a home, for instance, and have a positive cash flow of at least $100 per month, you would need a perfect combination of the following ingredients:

—Low price
—Low interest rates on mortgages, and/or
—Deferred payments on mortgages
—High rent-to-value ratio.

What is the probability that you will find an inexpensive home that you can buy for 60 cents on the dollar with nothing down which has a low-interest-rate, long-term assumable loan? Not very great. And this probability is reduced even further if you don't live in a city with an abundance of cheap housing (sorry for those of you living in major cities like Los Angeles, Washington, D.C., Honolulu, etc.).

But this doesn't mean that it is impossible. If you have chosen to buy wholesale properties and rent them out for cash flow (and you happen to live in areas of the country where this is more feasible), then you should gear up a program which will increase the probability that you will be successful. Here are the six things I would do, if this were my formula:

1. Become an expert in foreclosures. Visit every sale.
2. Visit every savings and loan association, finance company, bank, or credit union in my area and ask to speak to the person in charge of "real estate owned" or the bank repossession department. Ask to study the bank's portfolio of repossessed properties. Look for properties in lower price ranges which could be purchased below market with below-market financing offered by the lending institution.
3. Make a thorough study of the rental market in your area. Learn what is in demand and what is not. Get a feel for what properties are renting for, what deposits are asked, etc. The more you know, the easier you will find a blind spot—that area of the market which is in short supply, making the rents higher and the properties easier to rent out.
4. Place an ad in the paper in the "Real Estate Wanted" section of the classified advertising, stating that you are in the market to buy property at full price but on the condition of extremely flexible financing. Don't be disappointed if you have very few calls. You need to advertise. How can you catch fish if you don't have your bait in the water?
5. Do a thorough study of prices in your city. How can you know what is wholesale if you don't know what retail is?
6. Volume is the key. I'm sure that you would have to sift through a hundred properties before you found one that even came close to your needs. All sources of properties should be combed. Multiple listing service (MLS) books, real estate agent contracts, reading ads in the newspaper and generally circulating in the right circles (apartment owners associations, local investment groups, or exchange groups).

2. Buy it right and sell it.

Once you have found a bargain property, you may decide not to rent it out for cash flow. You may choose to sell it. And if you sell it you have two choices. You can sell it for a higher retail price and pocket the cash as your profit. Or you may decide to sell for full price with a small or no down payment and retain your profit in the form of a note with monthly cash flow coming in to you over a period of years. There is no secret to this.

But if I had decided to make the buying and selling of real estate for cash-flow profit, I would be sure to do the following:

1. Read Wade Cook's book *How to Build a Real Estate Money Machine*. It is a classic on the subject and is available in major bookstores.
2. Search out five of the top experts in your marketplace who are entrepreneurs in this area. Take them to lunch. Find out what their "cookie cutter" strategy is.
3. Develop a list of investors to whom you can sell your properties. You may wish to start with real estate agents who deal with investor clients who are looking for good deals. Get in the habit of finding excellent buys which you can tie up for a few dollars and remarket to these investors for a small cash profit. The better the deal and the lower your markup, the faster you will be able to turn over your properties. And turnover is critical.
4. Advertise in the paper. You may even wish to include a clause in your purchase agreements that will give you ample time to market your properties before you close.
5. Set aside a fixed time each week for searching for new properties.

A footnote to this approach: Check with your attorney or accountant concerning local regulations on "investor" versus "dealer" status. Make sure your activities accord with local regulations and give you the greatest tax benefits.

3. Lease it right and sublet it.

Many beginning investors shun this approach because it doesn't involve ownership. But ownership is not what is critical. *Control* is critical. And when you have a lease on a property, you control it . . . at least partially. For instance, let's suppose you locate a beautiful three-bedroom home which is available for lease for $750 per month, but is worth perhaps $1,000 per month on the open market. The seller is desperate to get it rented out because of the monthly payment. He agrees to accept just enough to cover his mortgage payment of $750 if you will agree to a long-term lease of three years with the right to renew for two extra years. He is thrilled to have the headache taken care of. You proceed to find a new tenant and sublet the property to him—for $950 per month. Notice that you don't charge full market rent. You charge less than market to attract a solid tenant who has an incentive to move in and stay there. The positive cash flow accrues to you for the management trouble.

You can make this even more attractive by asking the seller of the property for a lease with an option to buy. By negotiating a good future purchase price, you can increase your profits. But the key to this formula is the cash flow. In essence, you are in business to find property which is underrented and your job is to rerent it for a profit.

If this formula interests you, you would do well to take the following steps:

1. Visit every rental property firm in your area. Establish relationships with these companies. They are looking for good rentals for their customers, who usually pay a fee for the service. You will need a ready source of renters for a fast rental of your units.
2. Become thoroughly familiar with the rental customs of your area. What are the best areas of town? Will people pay more for a furnished apartment? Are one-bedrooms more in demand than three-bedrooms?
3. Join the local Apartment Owners' Association. Learn all you can about tenant laws and rights. You will need to walk a thin line from time to time.
4. Study carefully the "Houses and Apartments for Rent" columns of the classified section of your local paper. Call on the new ads daily. If this is going to be your part-time job, you'd better be the best there is.

4. Option it right and sell your option.

In the chapter on options, I talk about a $30,000 profit I made on the sale of an option on a tract of ground. To recap briefly, I found an excellent piece of property which was owned by a major church. The church's board members had been trying to sell but had not generated the kind of offers they wanted. I was informed that for $2,500 option money they would give me the right to buy this four-acre parcel in one year for $200,000. It was in a prime location, I knew the area well, and I felt that the price was low. I brought in a partner to put up the $2,500 cash (nothing down to me, of course) and sold the parcel about nine months later to a developer for $275,000. The sellers received a better offer than they were able to generate by themselves, and I was able to split a $75,000 profit among my partners.

What made this profit possible? Of course, my knowledge of the value of property, my decision to act, and my ability to find a suitable buyer. If you want to make money in options, you should be prepared to comb the market for super bargains, have the money to tie up the properties you find, and be prepared to market the property you control up until the final bell. Options are a relatively open field, and not much has been written about them. If you know of a good book that deals with the subject in depth, drop me a line. I would like to read it.

5. Buy discounted paper right and sell it.

I feel that the field of discounted mortgages is the greatest opportunity for creating wealth in a real-estate-related field of any that I have studied. Billions of dollars of owner-carried-back financing has been created in the past ten years. That means that we will see a good portion of this paper flooding onto the discounted paper market in this coming decade.

How do you make money in discounted mortgages? The same way you make it in real estate. You hunt for bargains and don't wanters. You negotiate for profit. For example, suppose you find a holder of a note with a face value of $10,000 with monthly payments of $143 per month at 12 percent interest. It is completely amortized over a ten-year period of time. He decides that he wants cash instead of this steady income stream. How much cash would you be willing to pay him for his note? The marketplace would pay him about 65 cents on the dollar . . . or about $6,500. This would yield the investor in the note about 24 percent on his invested dollars. Not bad, eh? Yes, but what if you don't have the $6,500 in cash to buy this gem? Well, what do you think all of those money market fund investors are doing with their money these days now that rates are down from their highs of 17 percent to around 10 percent or less? Do you think some of them would flee the safety, security, and liquidity of money market funds if you offered them 20 percent on their money? You tell them that for $7,400 you will sell them your interest in a note which will yield them over 20 percent per year for the next ten years. Not too bad! Well, if you bought (or optioned) the note for $6,500 and sold it for $7,400 . . . that means $900 in your pocket without having to risk or invest a lot of your money. I think you are getting the drift. For more information, see the chapter on discounted mortgages in my second book, *Creating Wealth*.

I just wanted to give you a taste and tell you how excited I am personally about this area.

As a summary, then, we had a goal to make $10,000 plus a monthly income of $400–500 within a six-month period of time. How would I go about this, now that we have reviewed the many areas of potential cash flow?

I would go immediately to a lease-option formula, placing emphasis on generating cash flow. I would attempt to find two houses in the lower price ranges that I could lease and sublet out for immediate cash flow. This would take two to three months.

Next, and perhaps simultaneously, I would look for bargain properties which could be bought and immediately rented out for cash flow. I would want to buy at a wholesale price to build up an immediate equity position to borrow against later. I would concentrate on finding one such property in a six-month period of time.

I would want to find, purchase, and resell three or four bargain properties purchased at least 20 percent below market and sold within a short period of time thereafter. Two of them would be sold for nothing down at 90 percent of the value, with the profit being carried back in the form of a note with monthly payments.

For instance, suppose I found a house valued at $100,000 which could be bought using nothing-down techniques for $80,000. I would resell it for $90,000 (below market) with fantastic terms, retaining my profit in the form of a $10,000 second mortgage or interest in a wraparound. The payments on this note could feasibly be $200 or more per month. It would take the full six months to comfortably accomplish this, but the $200 per month minimum cash flow would be very helpful. The other two bargain properties I would buy and sell in order to generate a $5,000 cash profit each.

I feel comfortable that following a general program like this would comfortably yield you $10,000 in cash as well as $400–500 in monthly positive cash flow.

I hope this is helpful to those of you who have heretofore kept out of the real estate market because of those negative-cash-flow fears.

Especially for Investors Who Can Get Their Hands on $50,000 or More

Suppose you could get your hands on $50,000—what would you do with it? Let's just dream for a moment. Let's forget about where we are going to get this huge chunk of cash and start thinking about what you could do with it.

First of all, are there not thousands of bargains in your city right now? You should be nodding your head in the affirmative.

Okay, if there are so many bargains, what should you be doing about it? Answer: If your goal is to create wealth for yourself and your family, you should be buying properties with both hands.

Will these bargains begin to dry up in the next few months? *Yes* and *no*. There will always be bargains just as there will always be don't wanters. Even in the best of times there will be bargains. They will just be harder to find and will require faster action.

Let me tell you what I would do with $50,000 if my goal was to triple my money within twelve months.

My first task would be to have a large poster printed up which would read:

I will carefully invest my $50,000 so that on ________________
________________, I will have my $50,000 back plus $100,000 equity in several pieces of prime real estate.

Robert G. Allen

Signed this first day of

______________________.

I would tape this poster to the ceiling above my bed so that it would be a constant reminder as I went to bed and as I got up in the morning.

Second, I would get my money ready and liquid. Now, this is the hard part for a lot of people. Very few of us have $50,000 cash sitting in our money market funds. Many more of us have a lot of equity which we can borrow against. Some others have taken the time over the years to build up lines of credit with their local bankers. If you have followed my advice in my books, you should be doing your banking with at least two or three banks. The managers of each of these banks should be nurtured to a point where they feel comfortable in lending you a minimum of $5,000 on your signature alone. This could be the first $10,000 or $15,000 of your $50,000 amount. By obtaining a MasterCard or Visa from each of these banks with a minimum borrowing balance of $1,500 to $2,000, you could provide for an emergency source of cash if necessary. These credit card lines should be left open just in case you have a quick need for cash during your twelve-month investment blitz.

Current appraisals should be done (as cheaply as possible) on any of the properties you intend on using as collateral for obtaining necessary investment funds. I would recommend that you never borrow against any property you own and use the funds for investment purposes unless you do one of two things: Either set aside enough money from the borrowing to make the payments on your new loan for at least twelve months, or be sure that you can handle the payments on the new loan from your current sources of income with the assumption that you may not generate a single dollar of income from your real estate investments for at least twelve months.

And in both cases you had better be prepared to work like heck to make sure that you are covered. Many of you have net worths which allow you to borrow against your equities to generate investment capital. Should you refinance your properties with new first mortgages or get a second mortgage instead? If you have low-interest-rate mortgages which you would like to keep intact, your alternative will probably be to visit with your banker and have him set you up on a line of credit using your properties as collateral. The rate will probably be cheaper than using a local finance company . . . and you can structure your line of credit to meet your needs. Those who have not taken the time to build up relationships with bankers may have to resort to more expensive alternatives, such as one of the local finance companies or savings and loan associations. This takes time to set up, and you should allow at least a month, sometimes two, to shop for what you really want.

For those who have neither cash nor the ability to borrow from conventional sources, the problem of raising $50,000 begins to get a bit sticky. As the old saying goes, you can borrow money only when you don't need it. The obvious alternative to cash-poor investors is to stick with the pure nothing-down techniques or to bring in partners who have the financial strength you need. To a beginning investor, the goal of raising $50,000 from unknown partners seems both unrealistic and overwhelming. But as someone once said, "There's no such thing as an unrealistic goal. There's only an unrealistic time frame." So don't be discouraged by the task. Start finding bargain properties while simultaneously looking for partners to help you finance them. After you have proved your bargain-finding ability to a partner or two—and have made them handsome profits—you won't have to worry about partners again. They'll come out of the woodwork to participate in the profit. Lower your sights to buying one or two excellent properties per year until you know what you are doing and then you can raise your goals and lower your time frames.

The third step is to establish a strategy. With a twelve-month goal to create $100,000 in equity, you're not going to be planning on any appreciation. You're going to have to be buying at wholesale. The strategy then would consist of buying properties where every $1 you invest buys you $2 in hard equity. For instance, you may want to look for only one property. It could be an eight-unit apartment building worth at least $400,000, but which could be bought for $300,000 with your $50,000 down to assume the underlying $250,000 existing loan. In the above case, you would be looking for a property which could be bought for 75 cents on the dollar . . . a wholesale buy. And it may take you a full year to find such a deal. But if you set your sights on such a goal and go for it, I have no doubt that you will reach it. You'll notice that I always like to buy such wholesale buys at least 20 to 25 percent below the current market value. Why? Remember our goal? We wanted to turn our $50,000 cash into $100,000 hard equity and still end up at the end of the year with our original investment cash back in our pockets—so that we can repay our loans to our bankers or partners. If we always buy at 20 to 25 percent below market, we have enough leeway to refinance our properties at the end of the first year so that the new loans will return our original investment funds to us.

For example, a graduate of my seminar recently told me of one of his interesting purchases. He persuaded his father to become a partner with him in his real estate investments. His father's role was to provide the cash or the ability to borrow the cash to buy wholesale properties. The graduate was to provide the time and expertise in finding these wholesale opportunities.

Their first investment was a group of three small houses located in a Sunbelt city. The seller was advertising in the newspaper. He wasn't interested in any creative financing. He wanted all cash but would be flexible in price. The three houses, two two-bedroom units and one one-bedroom unit, were in good condition in an older area of town. The young graduate persisted with this seller, and they finally agreed upon a cash price of $30,000 for all three properties. (I know this sounds like a 1960s price, but this happened in the '80s.) The graduate's father arranged for his banker to refinance the properties for $35,000, because the bank appraisal came in at $45,000 . . . a 78 percent loan-to-value ratio. Since the three properties have a gross income of $850 per month, there is a conservative $100 to $150 per month positive cash flow. And the best part is that there really was no need for a cash down payment on the part of the father. Only the ability to get a new loan. In fact, the two happy investors pocketed over $4,000 cash from their first venture, since the new loan was higher than their purchase price. They ended up with $4,000 cash plus $10,000 in hard equity in three positive-cash-flow properties. Now, they only have to do this five more times to be close to reaching their $100,000 goal. I think you get the picture.

Once you get a clear strategy mapped out, the fourth step is to start fishing for the bargains. It would be a good idea to have your hook in several ponds so that you assure yourself of the best selection of bargains. Put an ad in the paper, advertising in the "Real Estate Wanted" section that you have $50,000 cash that is looking for a home in a property that can be purchased at 75 percent of current appraisal. Drop in at ten or fifteen real estate offices and leave them your card. Tell them that you know that such bargains come along rarely, but that you are ready and financially able to close immediately on the right property. A few years ago just such a strategy netted me an excellent bargain property . . . and guess who the seller was. You guessed it: one of the real estate agents I had talked to that week. Scour the newspapers for those distressed-seller clues. Call your banks and savings and loan associations. Check and see if they have repossessed any properties lately which might fit into your plans.

Once the word gets out, the bargains will start coming to you.

What are you waiting for?
Good luck and God bless.

CHAPTER 23

How to Overcome the Ten Biggest Roadblocks to Your Investment Success

What are the roadblocks to investment success? This was a question which nagged at my brother, Richard, who helped me organize this material into seminar format. He designed a barrier analysis questionnaire for the thousands of our seminar graduates nationwide. I thought you might be interested in knowing what the top ten barriers are. Here they are in order of greatest concern:

1. Negative cash flows and balloons
2. Lack of capital resources
3. Tax and estate aspects
4. Lack of time
5. Difficulty getting partners
6. Lack of equity resources
7. Lack of specific goals
8. Difficulty finding don't wanters
9. Difficulty in negotiation
10. Ignorance of creative acquisition techniques

Since there seems to be such concern about how to overcome these barriers, I would like to take you through an analysis of each of these barriers and show you how I solve these problems.

But before I do, let me tell you my attitude toward barrier analysis. Those of you who are inordinately concerned with the barriers confronting you are not thinking creatively. In a real sense, almost all of these top ten barriers are merely figments of our imagination—they are simply excuses that we create to give us an "out" for not doing what we know we have to do. As far as I am concerned, there are no barriers. *None*. In my mind, there are no barriers which stand in the way of my buying real estate. I have no excuses. When I look at myself in the mirror every morning I can truly say to myself that the only person standing in the way of my ultimate success is myself. That may sound harsh, but it is true. Now, with that in mind, let's talk about some solutions.

1. Negative Cash Flows and Balloons.

Interestingly enough, the major reasons people give when they become don't wanters, according to our analysis, are just these two—negative cash flows and balloons. In other words, the greatest barriers to getting into real estate and the greatest reasons for getting out of real estate are the same. So what do you do about it? First of all, be very careful when you buy. Don't buy without doing analysis first, and be able to afford your negatives if you are buying a property with reverse cash flow.

In order to be conservative, I also recommend the following rules:

a. *Never* buy a property which has a balloon mortgage of less than five years unless the price is *at least* 10 percent below market the day you buy it. Just don't buy it unless you are planning on reselling the property quickly for a short-term profit and are certain that you can find a buyer. If you are buying for the long run, you want to avoid balloons. In this way you train yourself not to speculate.

b. *Never* buy a property which has a high negative cash flow unless the price is *at least* 10 percent below market the day you buy it. Force yourself to get out of the speculators' fever and think rationally about every property you buy. If the seller will not cut his price, then ask for more flexible terms. Ask the seller to carry second and third mortgages with *no monthly payments* and zero interest for a period of time. Will a seller accept such terms? Sometimes yes, most often no. But we keep on asking, unafraid of rejection, until we find exactly what we need. Unfortunately, there is a dilemma we all face in buying property. Sometimes, in order to avoid negative cash flows (or to buy creatively), we need to create balloon mortgages. There are tradeoffs that each of us needs to analyze when buying. Would I rather have a negative cash flow and avoid balloons? Or would I rather have no negative cash flows and negotiate for seller carry-back notes or mortgages with short-term balloons? This is a decision that you must make for yourself.

c. Whenever you do agree to a balloon mortgage, no matter how far in the future, you should always negotiate for a twelve-month extension beyond the balloon due date just in case you can't solve the problem in time. You agree to pay a nonrefundable fee of $500 to $1,000 for the privilege of extending. This gives you twelve extra months of breathing room and can sometimes make the difference between success and failure.

For those of you who can't afford negative cash flows and who want to avoid balloon mortgages also, there is another solution. Sell half interest in your properties either to an investor partner or to the tenant who plans on living long-term in the property. A partner is easy to find to cover the negatives if a nothing-down deal is offered. In one of the recent seminars I taught, a student stood up and offered to take over up to a $450 monthly negative in exchange for half of the ownership of the property. Advertise in the paper. Your ad might look something like this:

NOTHING DOWN

Need partner to pay $250 per month negative cash flow on my excellent investment property in exchange for ½ ownership and no management hassles.

It is better to own half of something than all of nothing.

Of course, the ultimate way to avoid negative cash flows *and* balloons at the same time is to buy wholesale. Nothing down doesn't always mean that there is no cash involved in the transaction. It means that the cash doesn't have to be yours. You should be looking for partners with lots of cash (or if you are blessed with fat bank accounts, so much the better). These partners will use their cash, with your urging, to invest in the rare property which is sold 20 to 40 percent below market . . . but which requires immediate, large chunks of cash. The seller doesn't want to carry paper; he wants cash and is willing to discount for the privilege of getting it fast. In these instances you can assume low-interest-rate mortgages with low monthly payments—and, of course, no balloon payments. How you handle your partner and the repayment of his invested cash depends on your relationship. You may decide to just sell the property and claim the profit and move on to the next deal. Or you may refinance the property, pay back your partner, and keep for the long haul.

2. *Lack of Capital Resources.*

Most Americans are confused on this issue. They think that they need to have money in order to make money. Not so. They only need to know how to find the money. But what is even more important is that they learn how to find bargain properties. Then, once they have found an excellent bargain property, they can concentrate on how to bring in the necessary financial resources to solve the problem. This might mean using their own cash or that of a partner.

You should know that the motto of all creative investors should be *"If I don't have it, somebody else does."* This is the essence of leverage: using other people's strengths. By combining one person's strengths with another's weaknesses you can create a winning team. If you don't have the capital assets to get the ball rolling, you must look for those who do have the assets but don't have the time or the expertise to use them. I am reminded of a story of one of our very successful graduates who works with a wealthy attorney in buying properties. In the beginning this student had no money or assets. He approached an attorney who had both money and expertise in the foreclosure area but no time to invest in looking for property. They worked together marvelously because each could not live without the other.

So the major solution to the problem of capital assets is to borrow some, either from your friendly banker or from a partner. Remember, if you don't have what you need, someone else does.

And you can probably convince that person in a win/win way to lend you what you need in exchange for some of the benefits of real estate.

3. Tax and Estate Aspects.

Why these are a barrier, I do not know. Real estate is the only legitimate tax shelter left. I am not an accountant and can therefore not give specific advice on tax matters, but I can suggest that you do as I do—hire a competent accountant and tax planner. It is not cheap, but they save you thousands in the long run. If you are worried about paying too much taxes, the simple answer is: Buy as much property to depreciate as you can.

As for estate matters, I recommend that you align yourself with a competent estate attorney. He can help you arrange your affairs so that you can sleep at night knowing that your family is well taken care of.

How do you find these competent professionals? I find that word of mouth is the best advertiser. Ask around. Who does your work? Is he good? How much does he charge? Usually the more they charge, the better they are. Pay twice as much and get it done right the first time.

4. Lack of Time.

I can just hear you saying, "I'm so busy at my job I don't have time to look for property." Yes, most people are so busy earning a living that they don't have any time to make any real money. But each of us has the same twenty-four hours to live each day. Why is it that some of us are far more productive than others? Is it luck? Is it brains? No, I think it's just that the most successful people have developed their own unique system for managing their time more efficiently. They are in the habit of a daily routine, and as the saying goes, "Routine brings perfection within the grasp of mediocrity." In other words, even a mediocre person with a modest daily self-improvement routine will outperform a disorganized genius ninety-nine times out of a hundred.

The first step in organizing time is to set goals. Then, set priorities on your activities so that the most important tasks get done first. Most of us spend our time on the least important activities because they are easy to accomplish and give us a good feeling as we cross them off our to-do list. It is much more important to work on difficult but important tasks, because these move us toward our long-range goals.

The next step is to set aside a regular time, if possible just before you go to bed, when you review the activities for the upcoming day and block out times for their accomplishment. During the night your subconscious mind can be processing the information while you sleep. Having done this, when you wake up you will be miles ahead of the competition.

Then, arise an hour earlier in the morning than you usually do. This is important. The average person gets up at the last minute, gets ready, eats breakfast on the run, and arrives at his or her work in total chaos. What a way to prepare for the day. You need to be different. Get up a bit early. In the quiet, peaceful hours of the morning, before anyone else is up, take thirty to sixty minutes to read books and articles which are related to your long-term goals. One by one, as the lights come on in your neighbors' houses, and the world starts to groan into activity, you will feel a sense of power in knowing that you are different. Normal people don't do such things . . . that is why they are normal. But you, you are special. You have the courage to change your life a bit at a time. Slowly, day by day, you are growing. Great things are not accomplished in a day but are the result of small sacrifices taken regularly over a long period of time. Close your eyes, take a deep breath, and realize that you have overcome yourself. Meditate, pray, or just give thanks for another day to discover the purpose of your life. Open your eyes and you're ready to take whatever the world has to dish out.

Using just these simple steps, anyone should be able to budget two to five hours a week for property acquisition. It should be a regular time. Involve your family, whether your spouse or children. Delegate the finding of excellent buys to creative real estate agents. There are many real estate agents in your area who would be happy to find property for you and handle many of the details which take so much of your time. Look for those who have taken the Nothing Down seminar or who have read *Nothing Down*. Recently, I've introduced an incredibly successful hands-on real estate training seminar. It's called WealthTraining and it's fantastic. Call 1-800-345-3648 for more information about it. It's nice if the real estate agents you use already speak the language of creative financing. Use them. The commission is well earned.

I think I can say that no one is too busy to buy real estate successfully.

5. *Difficulty Getting Partners.*

How do you find partners? The chapter in this book on partners discusses several sources. Relatives. Friends and business associates. And the seller himself. I feel that the problem that many of you are having is not in finding potential partners but in getting up the courage to ask a partner to join with you in investing in the best investment in the world. What has always worked for me is to work backward. Find the deal first. Locate the property that has enormous benefits that you know you will have no trouble discussing with a partner. Once you have found the great deal, your desire to own it will force you to find a partner to help you accomplish your goal. I have often asked seminar graduates the following question: "If I could find you a great property that could be bought with nothing down, no negative cash flow, and no management hassles, would you let me use your credit to obtain a new loan and give me 50 percent of the deal?" I always have no problem finding a taker. The answer, then, is not to wait to find a partner (if this is what is stopping you) but to get out there in the marketplace and find a property that any partner would be happy to own with you.

Once you have the "bird in the hand," you can begin by calling your friends and explaining the deal to them. Always ask them if they know of someone who might be interested in a great deal. Then if they aren't interested they can bow out gracefully by giving you a referral. Then you can tell the referral that you were "sent" by someone. Approach the well-to-do people in your neighborhood or in your social and church groups. Don't be embarrassed. If the deal is really all that good you'll be doing both of you a favor by mentioning it. If your sources are exhausted in acquaintances, you might try contacting real estate offices looking for solid-money partners. Try accountants and attorneys who represent the most wealthy clients. It takes imagination and courage, but the fruits are sweet.

6. Lack of Equity Resources.

I think this falls under the category of partners. Remember our motto: "If I don't have it, somebody else does." And that somebody may be sitting next to you at this very moment. Have you asked?

7. Lack of Specific Goals.

Everyone should have the goal of buying at least one property per year. That's a minimum goal. But there are some who can't seem to get up the courage to set even a minimum goal. Are you one of those fence-sitters? Go back to the chapter on goals and reread it. At the end of the chapter is a goal-setting form for you to fill out and commit to. Set your goals! Put them in writing! Display them in a prominent place in your home and read them daily! And then let your subconscious mind work out the best way for your goals to become a reality.

8. Difficulty Finding Don't Wanters.

This can be a sticky problem, but there are easy solutions. One fellow wrote recently that he had called thirty-seven people without any positive results, and he was a bit discouraged. Remember that we all have feasts and famines—and you may be in a famine for a while. I have them all of the time. I think that the best way of finding don't wanters is in the following order:

a. Place your own ad in the paper. Have you thought about a billboard? Maybe ten of you should go together and rent a space and share the leads. It's a thought.

b. You need to let people know that you are in the market. Have you visited ten real estate offices lately and told them that you are in the market? Until you have, you can't gripe about a dearth of don't wanters. It takes time.

c. Deal with people who understand don't wanters—like exchangers around the country. Is there a local exchange group which meets regularly? Reread the chapter on exchanging.

d. Use the multiple-listing book. Go into your local real estate office and ask to study a copy of the MLS book. It is not illegal for you to ask. Look for the clues in the remarks section of each advertised property. Try to determine how flexible the seller might be. Work with a good, flexible real estate agent to help you in this process.

e. The newspaper is an excellent source of don't wanters. Learn how to recognize the clues which lead to nothing-down deals. Write me at Challenge Systems, Inc., 5931 Priestly Drive, Carlsbad, CA 92008 and ask for a free report entitled "Learning to Read Ads Like an Expert." It is a gold mine of information.

Finding don't wanters is like prospecting for gold. It is not easy but it is well worth the effort. Put your feelers out. Ask and ye shall receive.

9. Difficulty in Negotiation.

There are two good chapters in this book on negotiation. Reread them. But as you do, I want you to notice something. You will notice that I don't mention the win/win philosophy anywhere. In fact, it may seem to you that I am not looking out for the best interests of the seller when I negotiate. Not so. The best and most satisfying negotiations to both parties are those in which we try to understand the needs of the seller . . . and then try to structure our offers to meet these needs. It is only when we understand the seller's problem and try to help him that the trust that is vital in creative transactions is built. We are not trying to create adversaries in our negotiations, we are trying to build friendships! And how could you take advantage of a friend? You can't! You try to put yourself in the shoes of the seller. You ask yourself, "How can he win by this offer?" And then you practice, practice, practice.

10. Ignorance of Creative Acquisition Techniques.

There are literally thousands of techniques for putting together buyers and sellers in creative ways. Rather than muddle your mind I would have you concentrate on the most basic and useful techniques. My book describes over forty creative financing techniques.

Somehow, I feel that the reason that many of my graduates feel a barrier here is that they want to understand everything perfectly before they *act*. And this is nothing more than the age-old problem of procrastination—in different clothing. You will learn how to use the techniques by trying them out, not by studying them.

In discussing his best-selling book *In Search of Excellence*, Tom Peters said that the best strategy for success is this: *Ready, fire, aim.* (As opposed to the usual *Ready, aim, fire.*) He likes to try things out and then fine-tune his aim. Most Americans, on the other hand, are ready and aiming but they never pull the trigger.

Some people know what to do. Others do what they know. I hope that these ten barriers are not stopping you from doing what you know that you must do.

CHAPTER 24

What Do You Do When You Become the Don't Wanter?

From the tone of this book, it would seem that "don't wanter" is a put-down . . . a bad word, perhaps. Well, if that is the way you feel about it, I think that you have missed the point. And this is the point: *We all become don't wanters sooner or later!* That's right. Sooner or later, if you are in the marketplace buying (as you should be), you are bound to buy a lemon. That is the nature of risk. You should see some of the property I have bought over the years! In reality, you win some (most) and you lose some (a few). You have to have the attitude "I knew it would happen—sooner or later I had to slip up and buy a property I had no business buying."

Now what do you do when you end up with a bad situation? (Notice I didn't say "bad property." There are no bad properties, just bad ownerships, according to A. D. Kessler.) What you do determines your success or failure. Let me give you a few principles to follow when this inevitable problem arises.

1. Do your homework before you buy.

An ounce of prevention is worth a pound of cure. Be careful of negative cash flow and balloons. If you follow just this one bit of advice it will eliminate most of the don't wanteritis down the road.

2. Diversify heavily into real estate.

What I mean, of course, is to buy several properties. This reduces the risk to your overall portfolio if one of your properties should have problems. That is one reason I like single-family houses. Buy several smaller properties rather than a few large ones because if one of your properties should cause you trouble, it represents only a minor portion of your entire portfolio and you can dump it without ruining your program. On the other hand, suppose you owned a large fifty-unit apartment building and the neighborhood deteriorated (or rent controls were introduced). You would be left holding a huge white elephant with not much marketability. If you own ten properties and one of them goes sour, you can sell the bad apple and concentrate on the rest without losing much sleep.

3. Cut your losses and run with your winners.

This is an old stock market adage which holds true in real estate also. The tendency of the neophyte investor is to hold on to his precious real estate, troubles and all, either hoping for a miracle or burying his head into the sand of neglect. I see so much of this . . . and those of you who specialize in foreclosures can agree with me that people are emotional and irrational when it comes to unloading a problem property. I recommend, "Get rid of your bad situations!" They only drag you down emotionally. Salvage as much as you can and get out. You can't be positive and aggressive and creative when you are being eaten alive by a don't-wanter property. Learn from your mistakes, determine never to make the same mistake again, and get back out in the marketplace with renewed wisdom and confidence.

4. Be creative in disposing of your properties.

Let's suppose that you are examining your portfolio of properties and find one that never really measured up to your expectations. It was just wishful thinking from the start. It has a negative cash flow because your projections were too optimistic. It is a headache at best. In retrospect, you would have done better to have never laid eyes on it. It's time to cut your losses.

Some more details:

Purchase price:	$100,000	
Loans:	$100,000	(You had a balloon come due and had to refinance with a short-term, high-interest rate loan. Closing costs and deferred interest ate up most of the appreciated equity.)
Appraisal:	$110,000	
Fair price:	$105,000	
Fair equity:	$ 5,000	
Payments:	$ 1,000	monthly
Rents:	$ 800	monthly
Minimum negative:	$ 200	monthly
Location: marginal		
Appreciation potential: marginal		

Diagnosis: Get rid of this turkey!

Seven-Step Property Disposal Plan

1. Get an appraisal on the property.

Get a local appraiser to do a realistic appraisal on your property. You need to get a feeling for what your property is worth. If the appraisal is more than you expected, you can use this in your marketing efforts. If the appraisal is much lower than you expected, you can either adjust your expectations or get a second opinion from another appraiser. Try to get the best written appraisal possible.

2. Decide what you want from the sale of your property.

Depending on the circumstances, you may just want to get rid of this property at all costs and as soon as possible—the true don't wanter—or you may wish to test the market for the best price and terms with no specific time pressures. In either case, you need to be realistic about what you expect to get. If you are a don't wanter, don't let pride get in the way. Be as flexible as you can. The more flexible you can be, the easier it will be to sell. Don't be afraid to sell with nothing down as long as you protect yourself with solid buyers and additional collateral. In our case study, the property is a turkey that we want to move quickly. The questions in your mind should be: "How can I structure the sale of this property so that the buyer gets a good deal and I come out okay?" Think creative finance. Can I accept a monthly payment instead of cash? Can I sell the paper I carry at a discount for cash? Can I trade the paper I carry to another don't wanter in the next twelve months and thereby move through the paper to a better property? Am I willing to pay someone to take this property off my hands? Am I willing to accept a loss in order to move this property quickly?

Come to terms with what your bottom line is—that is, what you need and not what you want. Be realistic.

In our example, we have decided that a fair price will be $105,000 with a $5,000 equity. We decide that we will accept anything from $5,000 in cash to a free and clear Toyota. We want out.

3. Write an ad that reflects your flexibility.

You need to attract buyers . . . fast. The more buyers attracted to your ad, the more likely you are to find a taker. You have a lot of competition. Differentiate yourself from all of the other sellers in the market. The best way to attract buyers is to let them know that they are going to get a good deal. That is where the appraisal comes in. Your ad should hopefully indicate that the buyer is getting a good deal as far as either the price or terms are concerned. Such as: "You make 5k the day you move in. Professional appraisal 110k. Your price only 105k." Or: "Don't let a bank charge you 13% when I need only 10%." Or: "Nothing Down." Or: "I don't need cash. Have you got a car to trade for my house?" Or: "No qualifying" (in the case of an assumable FHA or VA loan). Or: "I want out! I don't need cash. Make me a creative offer."

A few years ago, in selling my own personal residence, I decided to use a nothing-down technique. I knew that it would take months to sell in the soft market at that time, so I sold it with nothing down and an eighteen-month balloon payment—which, incidentally, was paid on time. Sellers of property around my home were not as flexible as I was. They held out for cash, and as a result they sat on their properties for over a year, all the time making mortgage payments and subjecting themselves to many more months of the emotional stress that goes with selling a house.

Writing the ad is very important. Try to make it stand out from the rest. Put a box around it. I saw one ad in a Salt Lake City paper a while ago which stood out like a sore thumb. It read, "I'm down. Kick me!" Now that's flexibility!

Start to run your ad in the local paper.

4. Prepare a flyer on your property with pertinent details and a picture.

Indicate all of the benefits that the buyer will be acquiring by buying your property. Make one flyer for investors and another for prospective home buyers. Pass the flyer out at all meetings of any local investor clubs. It's like farming. You've got to plant a lot of seeds.

5. Talk to everyone you know who might be in the market for a bargain property.

Talk to the tenants you have in your other properties. Talk to people at work. If you have employees, let them have first crack. I sold one of my single-family houses recently to one of my employees. Of course, it was nothing down. But I was happy to do it. It might have been difficult for him to qualify for a new loan, and he was very grateful. The prime candidate for an investment house is someone living in an apartment or a mobile home. Leave flyers at some of the apartment complexes showing the residents just how easy it will be for them to afford your property.

6. If the numbers permit, involve a creative real estate agent.

In our example, it will be difficult to involve a real estate agent because the fee will be at least $6,000, and after closing costs you get nothing. Also, the real estate agent's fee often has to be paid in cash, so this negates some of the creative financing you are trying so hard to make available to your buyer. But in many circumstances, real estate agents can be invaluable. The local multiple-listing book is a great tool and exposes your property to every real estate agent in your city—a marketing strength which can't be overlooked.

If you have room to include a real estate agent, you should at least search out a creative one. I like to deal with those real estate agents who have been educated in creative financing through my own year-long WealthTraining* or one of the other excellent courses available. Call up your local Board of Realtors and ask for the names of any real estate agents who are involved in exchanging in your city. As I explained in the chapter on exchanging, there are groups in most major cities in the United States. The best way I know for getting rid of unwanted property is to contact a local exchanger, list your property with him or her (paying a commission, of course), and let the exchanger present your property at a local marketing meeting. These creative exchangers are well versed in the benefits theory and have experience in moving don't-wanter properties. The *Creative Real Estate* magazine is published by A. D. Kessler from Rancho Santa Fe, California. A subscription to the magazine costs $72 per year or $99 for three years, but if you send $6 to Drawer "L," Rancho Santa Fe, CA 92067 and ask for a recent issue you'll be sent one.

Once you have found a worthy real estate agent, work with him or her to write creative ads in the newspaper as well as writing grabbing details for the multiple-listing book. Most listings do not indicate such flexibility. Make sure that your listing stands out. I have often agreed to pay a 7 percent commission instead of a 6 percent commission and have indicated so in large bold letters in the listing in order to attract the attention of more real estate agents to my listing in the MLS book.

* Write me at Challenge Systems, Inc., 5931 Priestly Dr., Carlsbad, CA 92008, or call 1-800-345-3648.

7. If the above steps don't produce results, change your ads, meet more people, or get more flexible or creative until you do get some results.

If you are willing to be more flexible, you may consider running the following ad in your paper:

> I'll pay you $2,000 to move into my house!

Using our case study as an example, you would offer to sell the house for $110,000—the full appraised price. The buyer assumes the underlying loan. And you carry back a $10,000 second mortgage with negotiated payments, and the buyer gets $2,000 from you at closing as a buying bonus. Check out the buyer thoroughly, of course. Your money and your property are at risk, but this just might flush out a qualified buyer.

If you are suffering from an unbearable negative cash flow, perhaps you can solve your don't-wanter problem without selling your property at all. Maybe you should sell only half of it. This is what you call "syndicating the negative." (Wasn't there a song about this . . . "accentuate the positive, eliminate the negative"?) Do you think that you would have any trouble selling one-half ownership in a property for nothing down if you required your partner to pay *all* of the negative cash flow? The answer, as you should have guessed, is *absolutely not!* There are thousands of buyers out there who would love to join with you in partnership for a share of the benefits. In essence, you make the down payment and they make the monthly payments. It's a win/win partnership.

As a final solution you can do what one innovative builder did recently to rid himself of his don't-wanter properties. I quote directly from *Time* magazine:

> HOUSE FOR SALE, $100
> Larry Austgen, 31, of South Holland, Ill., is a contractor by trade, but a gambler by nature. Two years ago, Austgen built his first speculative house in suburban Chicago's posh Plum Valley: a luxury 2,400-sq.-ft. brick home guaranteed, he thought, to have the buyers lining up. Wrong. By the time it was built in August 1979, soaring mortgage rates and a souring real estate market had made a lemon of Austgen's plum. The house, appraised by realtors at $147,000, sat unsold for more than 18 months. Then Austgen had a

> sporting proposition: Why not let others take a chance on the house? He talked the South Holland Jaycees into raffling it off for $100 a ticket, of which $15 would go to charity. A minimum of 1,650 tickets (but no more than 1,800) had to be sold or the money would be refunded.
>
> The drawing is not until June 6, but Austgen is sure no refunds will be needed. The prospect of getting the house for only $100 has people snapping up three and four tickets apiece. The Jaycees are delighted. Charity is served. And Austgen stands to gain at least $140,250.

Now that is what I call creative. Remember, the odds are that you will be a don't wanter yourself someday. When that happens, don't despair. It's only a small barrier. Cross over it and be on your way to financial independence. There is no other way.

CHAPTER 25

Home Buyers—for Private Use Only

Maybe you're not interested in buying hundreds of thousands of dollars' worth of real estate. You realize that the excitement of investing is keen and that the returns are incredible, but, well, it's just not for you. You just want to buy a house, something you can live in happily and that you can afford easily. Great! The techniques described in this book still apply to you, because they can help you invest in that house even if you don't have a large down payment in the bank. And even if you do have cash, the creative techniques described here may help you to locate and negotiate a better deal.

Maybe you've been discouraged about trying to buy a house. There are two major problems that affect many young Americans today: Many are unable to qualify for a loan (because their incomes are too low or because their credit rating is poor), and many are unable to pay the required down payment. These problems are real. The goal and dream of the last generation was to pay off the mortgage. The goal and dream of this generation is just to *get* a mortgage.

But that ever-elusive creature called a mortgage can be yours even if your income is low and your credit rating isn't quite up to snuff. Your greatest asset is the knowledge that you can buy a house without even involving the bank. You can buy directly from the seller, and you can have the seller carry the loan himself on a land contract, a contract of sale, or a wraparound mortgage. There are many sellers who will agree to do just that—some to avoid tax problems, others to create a monthly cash flow during retirement—so you should be out there looking for that new house!

Let's look at a good program to follow. Before we begin, one word of advice: Your best bet as you begin your search will be to deal with competent real estate agents who know all of the ins and outs, and if they're trustworthy they can help you in countless ways. So let's see how you should go about finding your new house.

You may not be in a position financially to buy your dream house right now. But the home you are about to buy can be a steppingstone to a bigger and better house somewhere down the road. Don't let your pride get in the way. Each step you take, just like each step you take up a mountain, will bring you closer to your destination. Each time you buy a smaller house you will be building up equity for that larger ideal house. Move through several houses, possibly making several thousand dollars in profits on each move, until you are able to invest in your dream house—free and clear. It's well worth it.

If you have absolutely no down payment to work with, find a real estate agent who is willing to receive his commission from the sale in the form of a note. Many won't agree to do that; if you can't find one who is willing to help, try to learn as much about real estate as you can, and go it on your own!

If you don't have a real estate agent, you'll have to do a lot of searching yourself. Try to find a don't wanter—someone who will be flexible in the terms of the sale, someone who will agree to carry a loan instead of insisting on a large cash down payment. Especially look for people who are managing properties from out of state; they're usually the ones who are weary of the management hassle and will agree to your terms.

Don't despair. Finding the right combination—a don't wanter, a property that suits your needs perfectly, and terms that fit your budget—takes time. Don't give up; the house you are looking for may be just around the corner. Keep looking until you find it.

If you find a good bargain with a seller who is willing to be flexible but who insists on *some* cash as a down payment, and if you don't have that cash, consider bringing in a partner. Your partner provides the cash down payment. You agree to make the mortgage payments, keep the property in top condition, and even make improvements while you live there. Then, when you sell the house, you'll split any profit with your partner. Convincing a partner that his investment is safe may take some effective talking, but you'll probably be able to show him a respectable return on his investment. Use all of your knowledge of real estate to persuade him to help with the cash outlay.

You might try the earnest money option: Find a property that's a good bargain, tie it up with an Earnest Money Receipt, find another buyer immediately, and resell the property for a profit. There—you've earned your down payment!

If you belong to a credit union, you might consider borrowing the down payment. This might mean that your payments are higher until you repay the loan, but it is better than waiting to save for a down payment—something that usually never happens! You might have to hang on by your fingernails until you get that loan paid off —but if you find the right property your purchase will pay you many times over.

Look for properties on which the seller is delinquent two or three mortgage payments. These sellers are often flexible in their terms.

Search for a house that is up for lease; persuade the seller to give you an option to buy within a certain period of time. This technique locks the price in *now* and gives you the opportunity later (if you have negotiated a hard bargain) to sell the home for a price well above the option price. Again, you've just earned a down payment for the next purchase!

As a last resort, find an individual with a strong financial statement who is willing to cosign on your loan.

Any of these techniques can be used to come up with the down payment. You also ought to be aware of special programs available to home buyers.

The FHA (Federal Housing Authority) guarantees loans for people who don't have large down payments. Under FHA loans, which can be obtained through most banks and savings and loan associations in this country, you verify that you qualify for a low-down-payment loan. Depending on the price of the home, you could obtain a loan with a down payment as low as 3 percent. The interest rate is generally lower than it is when borrowing with any other arrangement. There are a few disadvantages: The loans take longer to obtain, and the appraisals are usually low (something that can cause problems at closing).

The Veterans Administration also sponsors a program for veterans; if you've served in the armed forces, you can buy a home with no down payment. You will have to be prepared to pay closing costs, however.

Local savings and loan associations often make special offers to home buyers; a qualified buyer can often buy a home for as little as 5 percent down. It's worth your time to check around your area and see if any such programs are available.

And many state and local governments have become involved in solving their housing crises by offering tax-free bonds to generate funds for low-interest-rate loans to low-income people. These funds often go begging because few people know about the various government programs.

So quit gazing in despair at the empty columns in your savings passbook. There is a house out there just waiting for you to move in the sofa, dust off the mantel, and mow the front lawn. Take a good look at this book again. We've talked in terms of large investments, but the principles are universal. They apply to you too. And they'll work for you. Study them again, and a few months from now you might be pruning your own fruit trees while your spouse drinks lemonade on your own back porch.

CHAPTER 26

Fear: The Ugliest Four-Letter Word

As you near the end of this book and prepare to begin investing in real estate, there's something you must come to grips with: fear.

In these pages I've stressed the advantages of creating a highly leveraged position, of purchasing the most real estate possible with the least cash possible. I've shown you how to invest in real estate with little or none of your own money. This kind of program works, but it does require that you live under a mountain of staggering debt. Unfortunately, that can be scary. It can breed fear. And fear is the ugliest four-letter word.

Fear can stop you cold. It can clutch at all your good resolves and send you, trembling, to hide from your goals. It can keep you trapped in a job that you hate or in one that is getting you nowhere.

There are eight reasons why people don't achieve success, reasons why people don't reach their goals. All those reasons stem from fear. Let's look at them, and what to do about them.

1. A Confused Mind Always Says No!

If you are confused about how you are going to be able to accomplish your goals, you won't accomplish them. Fear and confusion are the exact opposite of faith and confidence. Without faith and confidence you have a less than one in ten chance of reaching your goals. You can't reach them because you don't think you can.

Get your thinking straight. Think your program through. Reduce your goals to single components that will seem more realistic. Read more, study more, and then get out there and get your feet wet.

2. *The Paralysis of Analysis.*

When a child is afraid of the dark, he usually thinks some scaly monster is hiding under the bed, ready to grab him and strangle him. The only solution is to turn on the light and get the child to look under the bed.

There's an adult counterpart, but it doesn't work as well. It says that if you're afraid, read up. A certain amount of reading is good, because it helps eliminate confusion. But don't get paralyzed. In other words, don't read *too* much. Get out and do something.

3. *Procrastination.*

If you keep putting it off, you'll never get anywhere. Don't laugh. Procrastination is not funny. It can get you into hot water. What's worse, it can get you nowhere. Fast.

Ask yourself, "What are the consequences of my inaction?" Every day you are growing poorer—because of inflation—when every day you could be growing richer—because of real estate investment.

Go on, chart it out if you have to. Draw a literal picture of how much buying power you're losing now. Then draw a literal picture of how much money you could be earning through an investment, even a small one, in real estate. Then get your act together; get out and do something.

4. *The Conservative Investor.*

I ran across a friend one day who was lamenting his financial situation; seems he couldn't quite decide on "the right investment."

"I wish I had your guts," he sighed.

It doesn't take guts. It takes brains. Real estate is a *smart* investment.

Don't worry about "gambling" on real estate investments. The worst gamble of all is to be conservative and to talk yourself out of investing at all. It is foolishness to play a "waiting game," looking for the right investment.

5. Fear That the Economy Will Fail.

When Boeing laid off thousands of employees in Seattle some years ago, someone placed a billboard along a thoroughfare that read, "Will the last person to leave Seattle please turn off the lights?" The banks had such problems with delinquent mortgage payments on homes and apartments that they foreclosed buildings right and left and offered them to any investor who could come along and pay even the mortgage payments with no down payments. Seattle rebounded. Homes and apartments are full again. And those investors became very rich people.

But for the benefit of any pessimists reading this book, I'll say this: What do you lose if there is a crash?

Nothing.

That's all you had when you began. That's all you invested into each building you purchased along the way. You bought with nothing or very little down.

Most important, you gained experience. So what if there's a crash? You've lost nothing. And when things pick up again, you've got the experience, the know-how, to take advantage of low prices and great availability.

Then you've got everything to gain.

So get out there and do it! Don't be like Chicken Little, fretting about the barnyard and announcing, "The sky is falling!" You might be right—but you might be wrong. There may be a 25 percent chance that there will be a crash, but there's a 100 percent chance that you'll never reach your financial goals if you let fear paralyze you. It's simply a matter of placing your bet on the most likely thing.

6. Head-in-the-Sand Syndrome.

People who are afraid to do anything do nothing. And so they get nowhere, which is really where they wanted to be in the first place. They'd rather stand around all day with their heads in the sand. It's more comfortable that way. They don't have to think much. Enough said.

7. Fear of Asking for What You Want.

Some people are afraid of asking for a bank loan. Afraid of making an offer on a piece of property. Afraid of buying the unknown. Afraid of talking to sellers. Afraid of asking for what they want.

Try this: Walk up to a friend. Ask him to raise his right hand high into the air. Then ask him to touch the tip of his left ear with the forefinger of his outstretched hand.

He'll do it. It's amazing what people will do if you ask them.

Remember this: You'll never know until you ask. The worst thing that can happen is that someone will say no. That never hurt anyone. The best thing that can happen? The sky is the limit. You've got the world to gain and nothing to lose.

Get out there and do it!

8. Fear of Being Wealthy.

Sounds absurd, doesn't it? Replace that fear with a fear of being poor. You can become wealthy with as much or as little effort as it takes to be poor. Remember that financial bondage is *not* fun.

You've got the knowledge. Do your homework; set up your goals, find some good properties, negotiate, buy. Every time you go through that process you come one step closer to financial independence. You become a little more secure. You've got what it takes. The only thing that can hold you back now is fear. And you're a much better person than that.

I challenge you to quit stalling your financial freedom until it is everlastingly too late. I challenge you to commit yourself to buying at least *one* property each year until you reach your financial goal. Others have done it. So can you.

Go out and do it!

THE RELUCTANT INVESTOR

I hesitate to make a list
Of all the countless deals I've missed;

Nothing Down for the '90s

Bonanzas that were in my grip—
I watched them through my fingers slip;
The windfalls which I should have bought
Were lost because I overthought;
I thought of this, I thought of that,
I could have sworn I smelled a rat,
And while I thought things over twice
Another grabbed them at the price.
It seems I always hesitate,
Then make my mind up much too late.
A very cautious man am I
And that is why I never buy.

When tracks rose high on Sixth and Third,
The prices asked, I felt absurd;
Those blockfronts—bleak and black with soot—
Were priced at thirty bucks a foot!
I wouldn't even make a bid,
But others did—yes, others did!
When Tucson was cheap desert land,
I could have had a heap of sand;
When Phoenix was the place to buy,
I thought the climate was too dry;
"Invest in Dallas—that's the spot!"
My sixth sense warned me I should not.
A very prudent man am I
And that is why I never buy.

How Nassau and how Suffolk grew!
North Jersey! Staten Island too!
When others culled those sprawling farms
And welcomed deals with open arms . . .
A corner here, ten acres there,
Compounding values year by year,
I chose to think and as I thought,
They bought the deals I should have bought.
The golden chances I had then
Are lost and will not come again.
Today I cannot be enticed
For everything's so overpriced.
The deals of yesteryear are dead;
The market's soft—and so's my head.

Last night I had a fearful dream,
I know I wakened with a scream:

FEAR: THE UGLIEST FOUR-LETTER WORD

Some Indians approached my bed—
For trinkets on the barrelhead
(In dollar bills worth twenty-four
And nothing less and nothing more)
They'd sell Manhattan Isle to me.
The most I'd go was twenty-three.
The redmen scowled: "Not on a bet!"
And sold to Peter Minuit.

At times a teardrop drowns my eye
For deals I had, but did not buy;
And now life's saddest words I pen—
"IF ONLY I'D INVESTED THEN!"

—Donald M. Weill

· When he is not writing light verse, Don Weill is a broker and Senior Vice President of Helmsley-Noyes Company, Inc. The above poem was reprinted from the book *"The Reluctant Investor and Other Light Verse,"* which can be purchased through the author, c/o Helmsley-Noyes Company, Inc., 20 Broad Street, New York, New York 10005.

CHAPTER 27

WealthStrategy 2000: The Fastest, Safest Way to Financial Freedom Before the Year 2000

"To be who we are, and to become who we are capable of becoming, is the only end of life."

—Robert Louis Stevenson

As my friend Bill Martin says, "In ten years you will have arrived. The question is, where?"

Where will *you* be by the year 2000? Will you arrive in style? I know you're hoping for the best. But hope isn't enough, is it? You've got to make a plan, build it upon a solid foundation and stick with it on your way to a brighter, more prosperous millenium. (That's right, in less than ten years we'll be entering a brand new millenium.) Wouldn't it be nice to step into the new era financially free? It's possible. Now that you've read this book, there are seven distinct steps you need to take to put all that you've learned into successful action. I call these seven steps ***WealthStrategy 2000.***

Step 1. Build on a Solid Foundation

Since you'll be growing rapidly and taking calculated risks in the years ahead, you need to sink your roots deep in preparation for the squalls and storms ahead. Imagine a flat, level site upon which to build your wealth skyscraper. The stronger the foundation, the more enduring your monument. A strong foundation consists of six components—six scarce resources which each of us has to learn how to manage:

Body
Brain
Being
Time
People
Money

In this life, our task is to gain mastery over these six scarce resources. All great failures stem from mismanaging one or more of these resources. All great successes are the result of wisely mastering these resources. Let's discuss each of these essentials briefly.

Body. Do you have a regular exercise program? A significantly large percentage of the top executives of Fortune 500 companies take time out of their busy schedules for regular, prudent exercise. They can't afford not to. It helps them think more clearly and creatively, and work longer and more productive hours while keeping themselves healthier and happier. Is this one of their secrets to success? I think so.

Brain. Do you make time for regular intellectual exercise? Do you have a regular study program? Do you set aside a regular time for reviewing your game plan? Are you a positive thinker? Do you monitor your self-talk during the day? Notice how often your internal self-talk is negative. Consciously practice replacing your negative self-talk with a more positive voice. Remember what we discussed in chapter 3 about Neurobics. Do it daily.

Being is your character. Your character is made up of the principles which guide your life. Television has inaccurately stereotyped American businesspeople as greedy, shallow, and unprincipled. In my experience, just the opposite is true. Most businesspeople are decent, hardworking, and motivated by the highest of the traditional American values.

Unfortunately, however, there are some who will do almost anything to "get rich quick." They are motivated by a different set of values. In the lists below, I show the distinction between the principles of the get-rich-quick myth and the principles of what I call "Real Wealth." In my opinion, the shortest and safest passage to prosperity is through the principles of Real Wealth.

GET RICH QUICK	REAL WEALTH
Having	Being
Capital	Character
Possessions	Purpose
Power	Love
Fear	Faith
Compromise	Integrity
Obsession	Balance
Mediocrity	Excellence
Imitation	Intuition

In addition to values, Being is also about purpose—who you are as a person and what you hope to achieve. (See chapter 3.) Are you an entrepreneur? Do you love the challenge and risk of business? Do you enjoy controlling your own destiny? Are you willing to put up with the insecurity of being your own boss? Do you have the talent and intuition for business? Do you love to negotiate? Are you enthusiastic about real estate investments? Would you like to eventually be a full-time investor? If not, maybe real estate isn't for you. Think about it.

Time. Are you organized? How well do you control your time? Are you focused enough to withstand the allure of instant gratification? Are you organized enough to find ten extra hours a week to devote to your real estate game plan? Can you consistently do this week in and week out?

People. Real estate is not just a business of numbers and buildings. It's a business of solving people's problems. If people trust you easily, the world is your blank check. The more clearly you understand this, the more powerful you will become. Also, does your family support you? Do you have supportive friends? The stronger your support network, the safer your journey to the top.

Money. An assault up the money mountain will require that you become relatively stable financially. The more stable you are before you mount your assault on the money mountain, the better. Read the following questions and notice which ones hit you in the pit of the stomach. Become determined to strengthen yourself in your areas of weakness:

—Do you have a steady, stable job?
—Do you have access to transportation?
—How good are you at managing your money?
—Are you under severe financial pressure?
—Can you handle more pressure or should you get your financial act together first?
—Are you adequately insured?
—Do you maintain orderly checking and savings accounts?
—Can you save?
—Do you have a "rainy day" account?
—Have you prepared a complete financial statement?
—How is your credit?
—Do you live by the guns-and-butter theory? (See page 24.)

Where do we learn how to juggle these six resources? Not in school or university. It's just assumed that we'll learn them in the school of hard knocks. If you are strong and balanced in the above six areas of your life, life won't knock you as hard.

This is your foundation. Build it strong.

Step 2. Establish a Long-Term Intention

With a strong foundation in place, you're ready to set your long-term intention. What are you going to want in the year 2000? The truth is, most of what you want won't change much in the next ten years. You'll still want a strong foundation—health, personal growth, great relationships, intellectual stimulation, and the satisfaction of being involved in many fulfilling and financially rewarding projects.

As long as you're balanced, fulfilled, generous to people less fortunate—and humble enough to give credit to your Higher

Power—they why shouldn't you be making a ton of money? (Have you ever wondered just how much money there is in a ton? How much is 2000 pounds of money? Suppose it takes 500 one-dollar bills to equal one pound of weight. Then 2000 pounds of dollar bills would equal a cool one million dollars!)

Let's get outrageous. Is it unrealistic to expect that you could be earning a "ton of money"—a million dollars a year—by the year 2000? Why not? Hundreds of corporate executives earn that now. And what about the thousands of "on purpose" professional athletes, doctors, lawyers, and entrepreneurs? If it's possible for them today, why not for you by the year 2000?

Well, how do you do that? As my friend Zig Ziglar says, "You can have anything *you* want in life if you'll just help enough *other* people get what *they* want." The only way to earn a ton of money is to provide a ton of excellent professional service. You've got to be good. Darn good. But you've got ten years to accomplish that million-dollar goal.

So with balance, growth, satisfaction, humility, and the ability to earn a ton of money in our long-range sights, what's next?

Step 3. Establish a Short-Term Game Plan

The very next step is to divide your long-term intention into short-term, bite-sized morsels. What is realistic for you in the next twelve months? If you're a novice, you'll be lucky to buy one property and profit from it. And that's after many hours of study, market research, and assiduous application.

You could do much better but, as I said, let's be realistic. I don't want to get your hopes so high that you'll be discouraged in the first few months. So set your sights a bit lower. Hunker down for the long haul. Believe me, it will be well worth it. In order to increase the probability of beginner's luck, here is what I expect from you in the first year:

—Twelve months of practical, prudent, profitable practice
—Yielding from one to four completed transactions
—Targeted to existing, small residential properties one to four units in size

—Priced in the bottom quartile of the market
—No more than fifty miles from your own home.

In completing these one to four transactions, there are two broad approaches you will choose from:

1. QuickTurn approach.
2. Portfolio-Builder approach

With the Portfolio approach, you focus on buying properties wholesale, renting them out, and holding them for cash flow and long-term appreciation. Each year you'll add more properties to your growing portfolio of investments. The key to this strategy is learning how to manage properties for maximum cash flow with minimum hassle.

With a QuickTurn approach, you focus on rapid turnover of your properties for short-term profit. The key to this strategy is learning how to market properties for maximum profit in the shortest amount of time with the minimum of investment.

Either strategy can be excellent, but it depends on your target city, the neighborhood in that city, and your own personal preferences. However, during your first year in this business, no matter where you live, you should focus your attention on the QuickTurn strategy. Even in markets that are declining, the QuickTurn approach can be extremely profitable. Your goal should be to QuickTurn at least one and as many as four properties in order to generate immediate profit.

Thereafter, I would recommend that you broaden out to accumulate select, choice projects for long-term cash flow and appreciation. Eventually, you will balance your activities between short-term profit taking and long-term accumulating. The ratio of QuickTurn vs. Portfolio building will depend on you.

Now all of this leads us to a discussion of individual cities and where to invest in those cities for maximum profit during good times and bad.

Step 4. Create Your Own Treasure Map

As Diane Ravitch said, "The person who understands 'how' will always have a job. The person who understands 'why' will always be his boss." First, let's understand why your property is going to make you so much money, and then I'll show you exactly how to pull it off. Glance at the charts in the Appendix (page 325). They graphically show the trends of real estate prices in the top twenty-four cities in the country. The figures in the black columns represent actual real estate prices for single-family homes based on data gathered from the U.S. government's Annual Housing Survey. The figures in the gray columns are averages for the intervening years estimated from the actual figures shown in the black columns. See if your city is represented. Notice how the median price of a house in those cities fluctuated, stagnated, or shot upward during various years.

These charts reflect average city prices, but within each city, price ranges and rates of growth differ dramatically from neighborhood to neighborhood. Why? Let's take a rough stab at the basics of why properties go up or down, and then you can be clear on why, where, when, and how you're going to buy your next profitable piece of property.

A quick lesson in economics. It all boils down to two words that affect your entire future: supply and demand. Entire books have been written on the subject, but when it's all said and done you have basically three great forces which substantially affect supply and demand:

—Economic forces
—Social forces
—Political forces.

How do economic forces affect supply and demand? If jobs are prevalent and interest rates are relatively low, homes are in demand. If unemployment rises and/or interest rates rise, demand shuts down. People sit on the sidelines. As soon as the economy picks up and/or interest rates decline, demand also picks up again —and the upward trend continues.

As for political forces which affect supply and demand, I will give you one fine example. In many California cities, city governments try to slow growth and limit building permits. This directly affects supply. If the supply doesn't meet growing demand, more and more buyers compete for a dwindling number of properties. This forces prices upward unnaturally, and savvy real estate investors reap huge profits as they did in San Diego and Los Angeles in the late 1980s.

What social forces affect supply and demand? Let me give you one example: the rate of divorce. As families split up, the splintering groups each need adequate housing. If more families stayed together, there would be less demand for housing.

With these things in mind, pick a city—any city. Pick a city where you will most likely do the bulk of your investing over the next ten years. Perhaps it's the city where you now reside or a city you are planning to move to. Now, ask yourself these questions:

—What economic, political, and/or social forces might affect demand for real estate in my target city?
—How might foreign competition affect local industries and thereby affect the rate of job creation?
—What political forces might cause interest rates to rise thereby lowering demand for housing in my city?
—What world-wide social trends might affect the supply and demand for property in my city?

Suppose you live in Flint, Michigan, and work at the GM plant. You own a home. Life is good. You decide to invest in a lot of real estate to provide security for the future. But you ignore what the Japanese are doing to the car market. People stop buying GM and —poof—you're out of work. Along with everyone else in town. No one buys property. No one can sell property. No one can afford to rent your property. The bank has got you in their gun sights and it's only a matter of time before they pull the trigger. This is what happens in a one-industry town affected by some foreign decision-maker. The same thing happened in Texas, Oklahoma, and Colorado when the oil industry took a nose dive.

When major industries sneeze, whole regions of the country catch pneumonia. During almost the entire decade of the 1980s, we saw unprecedented economic stability and growth. But what if the economy takes a breather? Economic growth will slow. Unemployment will rise. Money will tighten up. Optimism will wane. People will tighten their belts. Demand will shut down. Home buying will slow dramatically. Will you be able to continue to rent your property in such a climate? What about the dramatic changes in our defense budgets in the coming decade? Is your city dependent on the defense industry? How will the world-wide ecology movement affect land development? What if inflation comes back? What will that do to interest rates? These are questions you need to ask yourself. You can't go on blindly assuming that things will continue forever as they are now. They won't. So before you go whole hog into your buying program, you had better evaluate the ten-year forecast on industry and business in your target city. Spend some time at the Chamber of Commerce and other municipal agencies which project future growth.

Obviously trends will be much more in your favor if you are living in a city with a diversified industrial base, excellent future job-creation potential and a mild good climate. But that description doesn't fit many cities in the country. Even if your city is exactly the opposite, the potential for profit is tremendous depending on your strategy.

So in order to help you fine tune your individual strategy, I would like you to make a rough, "stab-in-the-dark" guess at the ten-year economic prospects for your target city:

Green light = excellent prospects for solid growth
Yellow light = iffy, could go either way
Red light = most likely declining economic activity

Is your target city red, yellow, or green?

If it's red, there's not much reason to be accumulating property. Property values, because of waning demand, will be stagnant, and their charts will look like the past ten years in Portland, New Orleans, Dallas, or Phoenix—pretty much flat. There are only two reasons to build a portfolio in a red city:

—You're fairly certain that demand will dramatically increase in the foreseeable future, or
—Your strategy is to build solid long-term cash flows by buying larger apartment buildings.

Otherwise, you should stick to QuickTurn projects where you can buy substantially below market and take as long as you need to sell. More on this later.

If you give your target city a yellow rating, this indicates some caution. Sometimes a city experiences a deep economic slump the way Houston did in the late 1980s. Houston civic leaders were forced to attract new industry to broaden their economic base. By 1990 Houston was less dependent on the oil industry, and the prospects for real estate investment grew brighter. Sensing this, many WealthTraining graduates moved their investment activities to Houston where between 1988 and 1990 they were able to buy foreclosed single-family homes from banks at unheard-of prices. They stockpiled these properties and are now being handsomely rewarded for their foresight and patience. Houston is on the rebound, and prices are rapidly firming up.

If your target city is rated green, like San Diego or Seattle, you'll probably discover that because of high demand, bargain finding is difficult. At the same time, building a portfolio is also difficult because prices are rapidly escalating and sellers are rarely flexible. Still, the long-term prospects are excellent. Rents will most likely continue to increase, and there will always be a market for your property. Either strategy—QuickTurn or Portfolio building—is viable. You'll understand more in a moment when we study WealthTraks.

Now, that you've color coded your target city, I want you to get a map of your city and its outlying suburbs. You're going to begin color coding every area of your target city. For example, on my wall I have an excellent photo of my city, San Diego, taken by satellite from 450 miles above the earth. It shows the growth patterns clearly while giving me the big picture of the neighborhoods in which I'll be investing. (If you want a space shot of your city, call Spaceshots at 1-800-272-2779 and they'll send you a free catalog. These poster-size photos cost less than $20 and are a great conversation piece.)

Now with this map, I want you to do some more in-depth sleuthing. Check with the local Board of Realtors and try to make growth projections of the various major areas in and around your target city. You might even color various territories in green, yellow, or red, depending on your rough guess about what might happen to property values in those neighborhoods. As you do this, let the following questions roll around in your mind:

—Will anyone want to own a property in this neighborhood in ten years?

—Why would anyone want to rent in this neighborhood?
—Will these become green and yellow zones or red zones?

By the end of this process, you'll be choosing several target neighborhoods or territories in your target city. You have created your own TreasureMap. The more informed you are on what is going on in your target territory, the better. Speculators are too lazy to do this kind of homework. They always end up paying too much for property in the wrong areas. You'll build your business on superior information, superior strategy, and superior execution.

With this piece of the puzzle complete, let's choose a WealthTrak.

Step 5. Choose Your WealthTrak

Let's review what you've done so far:

—You've strengthened your wealth foundation
—You've determined your long-term intention
—You've established a one-year, short-term game plan
—You've chosen a target city and created your TreasureMap of the target territory.

Now you're ready to choose a specific WealthTrak. Whether you're accumulating or quickturning, each of the following WealthTraks is a way to create rapid equity in property.

Suppose you've found a property worth $100,000. The seller is flexible. How can you profit from it? There are at least five ways to profit from it quickly:

—You can rehab or fix it up
—You can convert it to a higher and better use
—You can creatively remarket it using excellent terms
—You can resell it into a rapidly appreciating marketplace
—You can buy it wholesale and remarket it at retail.

Some quick numbers for example.

Rehab WealthTrak. You buy a property for $90,000, add $10,000 in cosmetic fix-up, add a bedroom or remodel the kitchen. Then you resell for $130,000. Profit: $30,000 less carrying and closing costs.

Conversion WealthTrak. You buy a property for $90,000 and convert it from a single-family home to offices. Attorneys' fees and rehab come to $25,000. After you re-rent to commercial tenants, you remarket the project to an investor for $175,000. The time frame is longer, costs are higher, and there is greater risk and red tape. But the profit makes it worthwhile. Profit $60,000 less carrying costs.

Creative Remarketing WealthTrak. Buy a property for $90,000 on good terms and immediately resell it for $120,000 for little or no money down with the buyer paying you your profit in the form of monthly payments on a second mortgage note secured by the property. Convert your note to cash by selling it at a discount for $10,000 cash.

Appreciation WealthTrak. Buy a property for $100,000 on the front end of a fast-paced market. Return it to the market after minor cosmetic and landscaping improvements of $2,500. Resell it for $125,000. Your profit is $22,500 less closing and carrying costs.

Wholesale WealthTrak. Instead of buying properties at full market price, you shop for bargains. The faster the market pace, the fewer the bargains, but cash can always find a good deal. (Use OPM—other people's money—for your purchases so it's always nothing down to you.) You find an excellent buy from the foreclosure portfolio of a struggling S & L. It hasn't sold to other speculators because of extensive deferred maintenance. You pay $60,000 cash which you draw from your established bank line of credit. You determine that it will take less than $20,000 to bring the property to pristine perfection. You subcontract out the work and supervise the project while you are looking for other deals. The work takes four months and you put the property back on the market for $135,000. It sells for $125,000 and you pocket $45,000 less carrying costs.

Get the picture?

Review the WealthTraks. Which one strikes you? Which one causes you to say to yourself, "Now that's me!" This is an important clue. Next, get your hands on as much information about your chosen WealthTrak as you can. Read books. Listen to tapes. Visit local investment clubs. Ask questions. Find the people in your city who are using your targeted WealthTrak. Take them to lunch. Pick their brains if possible. If they're tight-lipped, you can do some fairly simple detective work to learn how they're doing it. You can learn what kind of ads they run in the paper to find their deals. You can check at the county courthouse to uncover what they pay for their properties. You can question their employees to learn insider secrets. Research. Research. Research.

That brings us to the next step.

Step 6. Closely Monitor Your Target Territory

Now that you've chosen your special WealthTrak, it's time to analyze your target territory even further. Some neighborhoods are more conducive to fix-up, appreciation, or wholesale bargains. The key to a QuickTurn strategy is to sell into a stable or strong market. If the market in your targeted neighborhood is stagnant or weak, you'll have difficulty turning a fast profit. You may be forced to change your strategy to stockpile properties until a spurt of demand forces prices upward. Be careful. If you don't have staying power, you'll bleed to death.

Since the localized demand cycle is so critical, I encourage you to do even more homework. Take the pulse of your target area frequently. Notice the cycles of real estate demand. Become a regular visitor at your local Board of Realtors. Pore over as much data as it has. Here are some questions for which you should try to find consistent answers:

—How many properties exist in your target price range?
—How many of these properties are currently on the market?
—What is the average number of days these properties remain on the market before selling? (Clue: the longer the selling time, the slower the market.)
—How does this average selling time compare to previous years?
—What are the leading indicators of when the market is beginning to slow down?
—What is the current rate of appreciation of properties in your target price range and target territory?

—How does this compare to recent years? Why the difference?
—During which months do properties sell faster?

The reason you need this information is to be able to anticipate periods of rapid appreciation and to be able to forecast periods of stagnation and slow growth. You wouldn't want to be stockpiling properties at the top of a market. By the same token, you shouldn't try to QuickTurn properties in a severe downturn. Each of these mistakes could cost you precious time and money.

With this input, it's time for the final step.

Step 7. Implement Your WealthCycle

You've laid a firm foundation. You've established a long-term intention and a short-term game plan. In your game plan, you've targeted a city, a territory in that city, and a specific target property. You've chosen a WealthTrak to specialize in. All there is to do now is to implement your WealthCycle. The WealthCycle consists of three skills which you will repeat over and over again in your investments. The three essential skills are:

Finding. You must develop an increasingly sophisticated system for generating leads for the properties you buy. The greater the competition, the more need for a finding system.

Funding. In the 1980s, the game consisted of finding highly motivated sellers and negotiating creative terms. In the 1990s, the game is becoming much more sophisticated. If you want to be a player for the 1990s, I recommend that you spend generous amounts of time locating partners to fund your many projects. Cash will be king. Your nothing-down strategy will be to use OPM. Sooner or later, you're going to have to become a professional fund raiser.

Farming. This is my term for profiting from your purchases. If you are a portfolio builder, your main focus will be on landlording —managing your properties for maximum cash flow and appreciation. If you become a QuickTurn specialist, you'll have to develop special techniques for rapidly marketing your projects during good times and bad.

First you find, then you fund, and finally you farm. Each project requires that you complete each of the three stages of this WealthCycle. Each stage is important. The more times you complete this same WealthCycle, the wealthier you become.

Making a Ton of Money

Complete enough WealthCycles and it's very possible for you to earn literally a ton of money before the year 2000. Let me show you how.

In your first year, you'll complete the WealthCycle at least once and hopefully four times. If each turn of the WealthCycle generates $10,000 in profit, it's entirely possible to earn between $25,000 and $50,000 in first-year profits.

Not bad for a novice!

As you begin your second year, you can either increase the number of revolutions of your WealthCycle—turn over more properties—or you can try to generate more profit per turn, generating $25,000 or more on each property. This could earn you between $50,000 and $100,000 in your second full year of your real estate investment profession. I have seen this happen many times with those who attend our WealthTraining classes nationwide. (Call 1-800-345-3648 for more information about WealthTraining.)

In the third year, you can continue to "make it big on little deals" as my friend and colleague John Schaub taught me, or you may choose to challenge yourself with higher-level activities by branching out into development, new construction, larger apartment complexes, industrial or commercial projects, and mobile home parks. Each area will require an entirely different approach and will be accompanied by new risks and rewards. That's the beauty of real estate. It's so varied and exciting, you can literally choose the area that fulfills you the most.

In the fourth and fifth years, you should continue to turn several projects for quick profit while adding several projects to your portfolio for long-term appreciation. Even so, it's not unreasonable for you to be earning $200,000 to $300,000 per year. It's all a function of your superior information, strategy, and hard work.

With current QuickTurn projects providing chunks of cash and accumulated properties providing increasing cash flows, a million-dollar-a-year income is entirely possible by the year 2000.

A stretch? Yes. But within reach? Absolutely!

Some Final Thoughts on the Decade of the 1990s

What will be the best opportunity and worst challenge of the 1990s? Actually, the answer is the same to both questions.

Without doubt, the savings and loan crisis of the late 1980s and early 1990s is *the story of the decade!* In the next five years, America's defunct savings and loan associations are going to dump 250 billion dollars' worth ($250,000,000,000!) of foreclosed real estate on America's real estate markets. That's the equivalent of two and a half million $100,000 houses. The ramifications are staggering. If not done carefully, it will dramatically affect the supply of real estate in many cities, thereby adversely affecting the volatility of normal real estate markets. It will create many millionaires—as well as a lot of losers.

For you as an investor in real estate, the 1990s will present an unprecedented opportunity. This opportunity is so exciting that I've called it "The Ultimate WealthTrak." If you're willing and able to take advantage of the sale of foreclosed S&L properties, there is no doubt in my mind that it could be your ticket to financial freedom. Let's briefly discuss why.

The Ultimate WealthTrak

Guess who's the largest don't wanter in the world?

Uncle Sam!

In order to bail out the failing savings and loan industry, the United States Government has ended up with tens of thousands of foreclosed properties from coast to coast. The government entity created to liquidate all of this property is called the Resolution Trust Corporation (RTC). You're going to hear a lot about the RTC in coming years.

The RTC, a division of the Federal Home Loan Bank Board (FHLBB), publishes an indispensable 3,000-page document titled "Real Estate Asset Inventory" which lists over 30,000 repossessed properties available for immediate sale. Updated every six months, this definitive guide consists of separate volumes, each devoted to a specific type of real estate: residential properties, commercial properties, and land.

Properties listed in the RTC manual are sold "as is" and range in price from $5,000 to $4,000,000. Located all over the United States, some are ready to move into, some need minor repair, and still others require a major overhaul. Originally these properties could not be sold for less than 90 percent of their assessed value. But all that is changing, and the prospect of fire-sale bargains is greater than ever.

That's the good news for real estate investors. But just because this opportunity exists doesn't mean it will be easy to take advantage of. Like all real opportunities, this one is camouflaged in a lot of confusion and red tape. We are in uncharted waters with the whole S&L mess. Dealing in this environment of confusion and uncertainty will be frustrating. But I firmly believe that if you persist and become an expert in helping Uncle Sam solve this gargantuan problem, you could reap enormous profits.

For a moment, I want you to imagine yourself walking down a congested downtown street. Standing on the street corner is a guy dressed like a clown handing out $100 bills. Do you stroll past this character with disbelief and convince yourself that the money has got to be fake and the clown has fallen off the deep end? Or is your response to walk over to the clown, take the bill, then check the validity of the currency at the bank?

The government is like that crazy clown and the RTC's "Real Estate Asset Inventory" is literally a map to the downtown corner where money is being handed out. The publication is available from the RTC for a $50 fee or may be available at your local public library.

Resolution Trust Corporation
Asset and Real Estate Division
550 17th Street, N.W.
Washington, D.C. 20429
1-800-431-0600

(Recently, this same information has become available for your IBM-compatible or Macintosh personal computer. The service is called RTCNet. The start-up kit is currently $39.95 with a monthly fee of $16 plus 41 cents a minute. It features information on 38,000 RTC properties, news, and an electronic bulletin board. You can call 1-800-RTC-2990 for more information.)

So exactly what are you going to find in the RTC publications? An entire book of the RTC series has been devoted to foreclosed single-family residential properties. There are more listings of available single-family residential properties than any other type of property. There are also listings for duplexes, triplexes, quads, mobile homes, multifamily dwellings, condominiums, residential lots, etc.

The commercial property manual has the following sections: (a) Office Buildings, (b) Retail, (c) Hotel/Motel, (d) Recreation, (e) Industrial, (f) Restaurants, (g) Special Commercial (e.g., doctor suites, self-storage facilities, etc.). For the investor who wishes to explore alternate and lucrative forms of property investments, the commercial manual lists some great opportunities and offers unique suggestions for this sort of investment.

There is even a ''Special Significance'' section which identifies properties having national, cultural, recreational, or scientific value. Many people are unaware that the government offers many grants (not requiring pay-back) and low interest loans for the acquisition and/or repair of properties with ''Special Significance.'' Finding out about these grants is sometimes like looking for a needle in a haystack, but you could start by calling your local city, state, and federal housing authorities.

Every listing in the RTC manual includes the property's street, city, and state address, the size of the structure (sq. ft.) or lot, a construction classification (e.g., stucco, brick, etc.), zoning, total number of rooms, the number of bedrooms and bathrooms, the number of units for multiple dwelling properties, and the number of floors for commercial buildings. Commercial properties state the age of the structure. The age of residential dwellings, however, is not given. For residential properties, a property condition classification is reported. Properties are rated as Good, Fair, Poor, or To Be Determined (TBD). Of course, all of this information will have to be verified by you.

When properties are listed with the RTC, an REO (Real Estate

Owned) number is assigned by the RTC. This number is your "Golden Key." When you inquire about any property appearing in the RTC manuals, whether directly with the RTC or with a broker or a lending institution, you will always be asked the REO number before any discussion can occur.

The RTC attempts to list all available properties with local real estate brokers. Where a broker has been assigned to handle an REO, the broker's name or brokerage firm name is printed in the manual. The property you are inquiring about may no longer be available, but there will undoubtedly be other more current offerings. Dig deeper.

When you wish to inquire about a property and no broker is assigned, then you must deal directly with the lending institution. The "Marketing Contact Index" located in the back of each RTC manual is a numeric list of REO numbers. The name, address, and telephone number of the lending institution is listed. It constitutes a complete guide to institutions with REOs. If an institution has one REO property, then it must have others.

Remember, since the "Real Estate Asset Inventory" is only published biannually, many hot properties never make it into the RTC manuals. Those that do are sometimes sold very quickly. But with just a little more digging, you may find the property that's just right for you.

In addition to providing biannual listings of government properties, the RTC offers seminars in ten cities nationwide (Dallas; Houston; Denver; Kansas City, Mo.; Miami; Anaheim, Ca.; New Orleans; Washington, D.C.; Phoenix; and Philadelphia). The seminar, entitled "How to Work with the RTC" is sponsored by the RTC and is divided into two sessions: Session A, "How to Purchase a Savings Association," and Session B, "Asset Management and Disposition." The seminar includes topics such as:

—Determining the nature and location of assets available for sale
—Availability of financing for asset purchases
—Marketing techniques
—Use of the private sector in marketing assets
—Negotiating the sale of assets
—Determining list prices for the REO

—Bulk purchases of assets
—Policies for responding to offers
—Special provisions for low income housing.

The fee for each one-day seminar is currently $220. The full seminar fee is payable at the time of registration and covers the cost for the seminar program, continental breakfast, lunch, coffee breaks, and program materials. (Remember, the manuals alone cost $50.) You may register by mail or phone, and early registration is recommended. For more information, write or phone

RTC Seminars
P.O. Box 539003
Grand Prairie, TX 75053
1-800-431-0600 (TX)
1-800-782-6326 (PA)

If you're willing to invest the time and prepare yourself, the savings and loan crisis could be your special ticket to the top. Suppose you become aware that your city has planned to rezone certain neighborhoods for a redevelopment project. By checking your RTC listings you discover that there are several RTC properties located in this same area. By stockpiling properties for future development, you could substantially increase your net worth in a matter of a few years. These are just a few of the possible scenarios available to the creative investor. But obviously, any property listed by the RTC should meet all the criteria we have discussed in this book. Even if Uncle Sam doesn't want it, you may not want it either. The RTC publication will help you locate desirable properties. Thereafter, all the same rules and strategies apply before you buy.

If you decide that this is your WealthTrak, I would highly recommend that you attend the RTC Seminar. You could also contact me at 1-800-345-3648 in Carlsbad, California, for a free in-depth report and update on "The Ultimate WealthTrak."

Whatever path you take, I know you are serious about your financial future and I have a feeling that you and I will meet someday. I'll enjoy hearing about your success. Until then, keep in touch and let me know of any new real estate opportunities you come across.

Robert Allen
5931 Priestly Drive
Carlsbad, CA 92008

Have a great life! And happy hunting.

CHAPTER 28

An Open Letter to Readers of *Nothing Down*

Over the years I've received thousands of letters from readers of *Nothing Down*. Most of them admitted they were skeptical at first. The nothing-down strategy seemed impossible. It just couldn't be done, they thought—until they went out and did it. Some of these letters were published in previous editions of *Nothing Down*. They are truly case studies in success. Here I'd like to present another success story in a letter written not to me but to you and all the readers of this book. I hope it will inspire you as it has inspired me.

Hi. My name is David Gilmore. I live in Madison, Mississippi, with my wife Teresa. Sometimes when you read a book like *Nothing Down,* you wonder if it can really work for you. Anyway, that's what I thought the first time I read it. Then I started putting Robert Allen's strategies to work and my doubts disappeared. That's why I'm writing you this letter about my experiences. Don't be a doubter. *Nothing Down* strategies can work for you, too. I hope my story proves it.

Teresa and I bought our first home in 1980, the year after we were married. That year I also started my own carpet cleaning and janitorial services business. We were living in a small apartment and money was tight, but we always dreamed of owning our own home. The home we found was 900 square feet listed at $29,500. The interior was in pretty bad shape, but I convinced Teresa that we could fix it up. We offered $27,500 and it was accepted. Actually, it turned out to be our first nothing-down deal—and this was long before I heard of Robert Allen. I assumed the seller's FHA loan of $25,000 and borrowed $3,000 from a local bank. The extra $500 was for repairs. My father and two brothers helped me spruce the house up, and within two weeks we had a home we could be proud of—our first real estate deal! That got me interested in real estate investing. I had several successful uncles who had "made it" building houses in subdivisions. I wondered if I could "make it," too.

In December 1982, guess what Teresa got me for Christmas? A book by Robert Allen entitled *Nothing Down*. I read it immediately and found the techniques and concepts easy to understand. I used to think that since I hadn't gone to college, I would end up being a janitor for the rest of my life. But this all changed after I read *Nothing Down*. I knew I had the drive and desire to succeed. I set myself a goal to increase my business volume to $100,000 and to purchase one rental property.

A few months later, my dad told me about a lady he knew at church who had a property to sell—a mobile home situated in a residential section of town. After her husband had died, leaving her some insurance money, she had moved to a nearby city. She sold her mobile home to a couple who had defaulted on their loan. The unit had been roughed up pretty badly and left vacant. She was extremely anxious to unload it. When I called to ask about it, I was so nervous I could barely hold the phone. She asked me to pick her up so she could show it to me. Even though she lived twenty miles away, I gladly agreed. After inspecting the property, I could see it had potential. When it came time to negotiate, I remembered one rule I learned from *Nothing Down:* "The first person to mention a number loses." I asked what the previous buyers had paid for the property. She told me $10,000. Then I asked what the previous owners had owed when they had defaulted. It was $5,000 at 9 percent interest. I told her that I was just getting started in real estate and that I wasn't in a position to offer her a down payment, but I could, instead, cut the lawn, trim the shrubs, fix the leak in the roof, repair the carpet, paint the unit, and haul away all the debris. I asked her if I could assume the $5,000 loan and continue making the same payments. I held my breath waiting for her answer. I was shocked when she said yes. It was too easy. Two weeks later we closed on the deal. It was fantastic! I owned my first investment property.

I did the repairs on the mobile home myself and kept the total expenses below $250. My monthly payment was $126.88. I rented it two weeks later for $225 per month. Five months later I sold it to the tenant for $14,625. My buyer obtained financing through a local bank. I paid the note—which made the previous owner very happy—and after closing costs, I realized a cash profit of $8,488.60! (I even paid my dad a small finder's fee.) As small as this deal seems today, at that time it was one of the highlights of my life. Teresa was so proud of me. We now had a nest egg to continue our investing. I was twenty-two years old and I knew I was on my way.

This transaction gave me great confidence in myself. I now began to concentrate on my other goal: building up my cleaning business. By September of that year I had thirteen part-time employees. I stopped doing the work myself and concentrated on sales, and Teresa and I handled administration.

That fall, one of my employees came to me with a problem. He had heard me talk a lot about real estate and thought I might be able to help him. His house was about to be foreclosed. He had moved out three months earlier and was four payments behind. He didn't want any money for his equity, but he knew it would be bad to have a foreclosure on his record. There was an existing VA loan of $13,000 at 8.5 percent. It was the worst looking house on the street—750 square feet, covered in vines and badly in need of paint. Still, I figured it to be worth at least $20,000. I agreed to bring his payments current and assume his loan. It cost me about $1,300. After cleaning the house up, I rented it out for $225 a month with a $65 a month positive cash flow. Two months later the city called me to buy an easement down one side of my lot for a drainage ditch. I gladly accepted their offer of $1,375. I had my down payment back!

The money from my first two real estate transactions helped expand my cleaning business. Although I didn't reach my business goal that year, I came close—$93,254.23. Of that, I realized $28,500 personally. I calculated with my business and real estate assets our net worth was over $50,000. Not bad for a young couple just starting out.

With this success I decided to set some new goals:

—To buy a million dollars' worth of property
—To eventually own a beautiful new home in a nice area
—To open up another cleaning company in another state
—To have my cleaning business gross $1,000,000 in sales, and
—To buy a Cadillac Eldorado with a mobile telephone.

On February 7, 1984, my mother gave me another real estate book by Robert Allen—*Creating Wealth.* It was a very practical birthday present. I could understand and follow his ideas, and what's more, the ideas were working for me. I decided that fix-up was my real estate "cookie cutter." In fact, two days after my birthday I closed on my third investment property. A few weeks earlier I had located the worst looking home in a nearby neighborhood. The neighbors told me that it had been vacant for three years. They absolutely hated the eyesore. After some detective work, I found the owners. They had inherited the home and were anxious for an offer. Average prices in the area were between $35,000 and $40,000. Because it was in such bad shape, I offered $15,000 with a $250 down payment and the balance to be paid in six months after I fixed it up. If it didn't sell in six months, the sellers agreed to extend the note until it sold. My closing costs were $150 in attorneys' fees. I brought my father in as a partner because I didn't have the cash to fix up the house. The fix-up took sixty days and cost $4,000. The house sold a few months later for a profit of $11,314.10, which I split with my dad. Hey, I was getting to like this.

It was time for Teresa and me to find a better house for ourselves. It wasn't long before I spotted this ad:

3 br., 2 ba. home, fenced,
central heat & air, needs
minor repair, lease pur.
or owner, fin. avail.
Call Tom.

The house was 1,500 square feet, needed an exterior paint job and new carpets, and was priced at $55,000. It had been vacant for two months and was pretty musty, but we had an open mind because we now knew what a bit of cosmetic fix-up could do. Tom, the owner, had a high-paying job and didn't need a lot of cash. He was my kind of guy. It was a time of tight financing and high interest rates. I decided to give him a very creative offer:

Price: $53,500
Down Payment: 0
Buyer to clean seller's personal home as earnest money.
Buyer to assume FHA loan of $34,000 at $347/mo.
Seller to carry 2nd mtg. of $19,500 at 13 percent with no payments for one year, then monthly payments of $200 for the next five years, and then payments of $275/mo. for the next twenty years.
Seller to put in new vinyl floor coverings and provide paint for interior and exterior.

He accepted it! We sold the home we were living in—our first house—made a $6,000 profit and moved into our new fixed-up home. We decided that a new home called for new cars, so I bought a new Chevy Mini Blazer, and Teresa got a beautiful new Camaro. As I learned from *Nothing Down,* this was "butter," but we deserved it!

We decided to take a breather and settle into our new home and life-style. I scaled back the size of my cleaning company because overhead had gotten out of hand. I realized that a large volume of sales didn't always mean a lot more money in the pocket. Sometimes it just meant more headaches. My breather didn't last long. One Sunday afternoon while driving around with Teresa, I spotted a new FSBO (For Sale by Owner) sign. I called, and the owner, Greg, sounded flexible. It was a two-bedroom, one-bath house in a nice neighborhood, rented to a tenant for $295 a month. The asking price was $27,000. I made an offer to buy the house:

Price: $25,000
Down Payment: $1,000
Buyer to assume existing FHA mortgage of $11,000
Seller to carry a 2nd mtg. of $13,000
Payments on both loans totaled $300 per month.

It was a break-even deal. The home was appraised for $32,500. We had made an instant $7,500 in equity! Note: I bought this home with my brother as a partner, and we still own it. The loans will be paid off in 1996, and then all of the positive cash flow will be ours for life. It will be great for retirement. Also, two years after we bought this house, Greg called and offered to discount his now $12,000 note for only $7,000 if we would do it immediately. I asked Greg why he wanted the money. He said he'd been investing in properties for several years and owned six houses. I asked him if he'd ever read *Nothing Down*. "Yes," he replied, "I've read both of Robert Allen's books. I've held my properties for five years now, and I'm liquidating and taking my profit." I accepted his offer. I went to a local bank and got a second mortgage for $7,000. Just like in *Creating Wealth,* it was win/win.

Before the end of 1984, I bought two more properties with combined equity profits of almost $20,000. This was getting to be fun! I tallied up our two years of investment activity and discovered we had purchased seven properties totaling almost a quarter of a million dollars! I was beginning to feel like a bona fide investor.

I only bought three properties in 1985. I fixed up and sold two of them for a combined profit of $13,000. The other one I bought $10,000 below market value with $1,000 down, then rented it out with over $100 a month positive cash flow. The balance of my time was spent operating my successful cleaning business and focusing on the other goal I had set for myself—to open up another cleaning business in another state. My opportunity came in February 1985 on a skiing trip with my wife, her high school friend, and her friend's husband, Jeff. They were from Memphis, Tennessee, 185 miles north. We had a wonderful time, and Jeff and I became great friends. To make a long story short, in October 1985, Jeff and I opened Memphis Building Maintenance with $1,000 cash, some used equipment, and Jeff's truck. Another goal was achieved, and soon this company would be generating enormous cash flow. It was time to buy that Cadillac Eldorado. I traded in the Chevy on a beautiful shiny black Eldorado in November 1985.

I spent 1986 building my businesses. I only had time to buy one property. It was a new duplex apartment building. The sign on the front lawn read:

For Sale by Owner. Must Sell.
Nothing Down. Assume $610.00 per mo.

I couldn't pass that up. I assumed the existing loan balance of $62,000 and added it to my portfolio. Does it get any better than this? By the end of 1986 I had purchased eleven investment properties with a combined total value of $423,925. But 1987 was going to be even better!

My first property in 1987 was a fixer-upper which I bought, fixed up, and sold in four weeks—and made a nice $3,000 profit. In August, a friend of mine told me about a group of three properties that he and his family had inherited in a nearby city. It consisted of a small store and gas station, a nice 1,600-square-foot home, and a vacant lot. It had been appraised for $68,500 and had been on the market for two years with no takers. I asked my friend if he would take $30,000 cash. They had a family meeting and decided that since the properties were vacant and were deteriorating, it was time to sell. There was only one problem. I didn't have $30,000 in cash. I needed a partner. I told my neighbor about my predicament, and he told a friend of his who happened to be a Realtor in the city where these properties were located. His friend immediately wanted in. The three of us went to the local bank and borrowed the entire $30,000 two weeks later. We cleaned up the properties and put them back on the market at a reduced price. With some of the profits from this deal I bought Teresa a white Cadillac Seville.

Late in 1987 I found a copy of *The Challenge* by Robert Allen in a local bookstore. I bought it to see what my real estate mentor was up to and read it over the next three evenings. In the book there was an 800 number which I called for information about a six-day seminar held in San Diego, California, taught by Robert Allen himself. I told Teresa we had to go, and she agreed. We attended the Challenge seminar together in December 1987.

Two very important things happened at that seminar. First, I signed the papers to sell Memphis Building Maintenance. It now had gross sales of $270,000 in less than two years of operation. Jeff and I received a wonderful offer to sell and decided to take it. I signed the closing documents via Federal Express while in California. Also during 1987 I had bought a roofing company with nothing down and built it up to a total sales volume of $750,000 in one year without even driving one nail. My combined businesses had achieved gross sales of $1,520,000. I had reached another goal. But I was getting burned out from all the pressure. The Challenge seminar helped me deal with that. In fact, it changed my life. I learned about the importance of balance and purpose. I realized that true wealth comes from within. *I* am my wealth!

After the seminar I was a new man. In 1988 I bought twelve properties and netted over $50,000 in equities, almost $20,000 in cash plus several hundred dollars a month in positive cash flow. By the end of 1988, I added up the combined total value of the twenty-seven properties I either owned or had bought and sold, and it came to $1,201,000. I had accomplished another one of my goals!

In 1989 I slowed down and bought two properties which I fixed and sold for a combined profit of just under $20,000. In 1990 I have already purchased two properties. I tied the first one up on the phone. The numbers on the property were so good I didn't even have to see it to know I couldn't lose. It was a three-bedroom, one-bath home of 1,325 square feet. I offered $19,000 with $1,000 down and to assume the existing FHA loan of $18,000 at 9 percent interest with payments of $264 per month. I closed on the home a week later. Fix-up costs will be about $3,500, and when done it will be worth almost $40,000. Not bad for a month's work.

Today's date is June 4, 1990. At 10:00 A.M. today, I closed on my thirty-third investment property. It's a nice brick commercial office building about a mile from my home. Purchase price: $55,000. Cash down payment: $0. (That's the way I like it!) The sellers agreed to a note for twenty years at 10 percent with payments of $533.77. The rents will be far in excess of that. I estimate that the value is over $80,000. This stuff really works!

So how have I done in the past seven years since I read *Nothing Down*? I have used the techniques I learned to build several thriving businesses. I have achieved financial success. Teresa and I live in a wonderful home in a great neighborhood. My relationship with Teresa is fantastic—she is my strength. In addition, I've almost finished writing my own book about how to start a cleaning business from scratch: *Clean Success* by David Gilmore. I'm doing everything I set out to do and more. I'm not a millionaire yet. But I'm close. Anyway, that's not as important to me now as it used to be. I'm living like a millionaire and loving it. And I'm not even thirty yet. Just think what I'll be able to accomplish in the next ten years!

Any final advice? All I can say is, if a high school graduate from Mississippi can do all this then so can you. I'm not saying it was easy. There were some bumps along the road. I got real discouraged in 1986 and 1987 when I was working really hard and spinning my wheels. But I got it back together again.

So go for your dreams. I know you can do it.

Your friend,
David Gilmore
Madison, Mississippi

APPENDIX

Real Estate Prices of Single-Family Homes

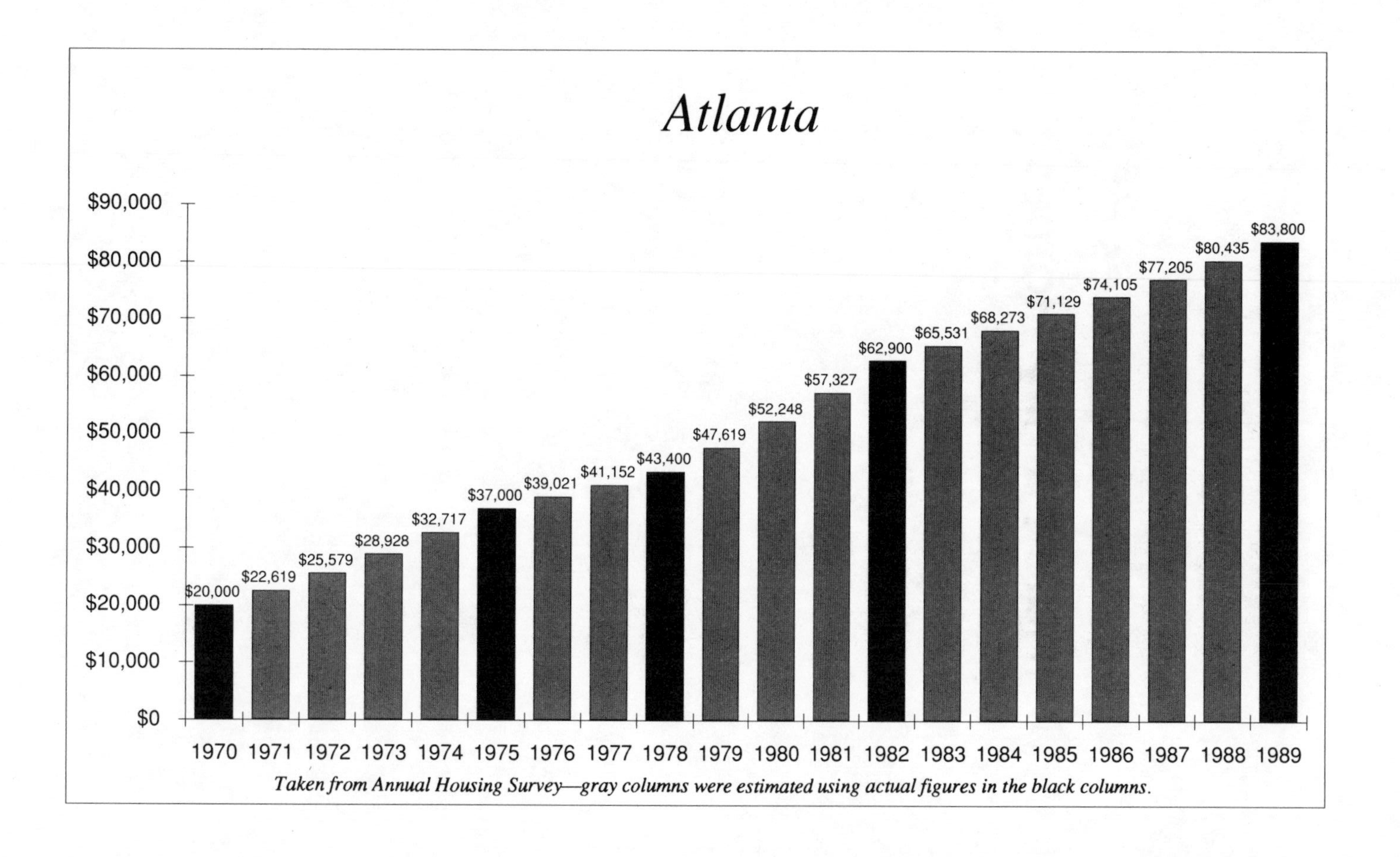

Taken from Annual Housing Survey—gray columns were estimated using actual figures in the black columns.

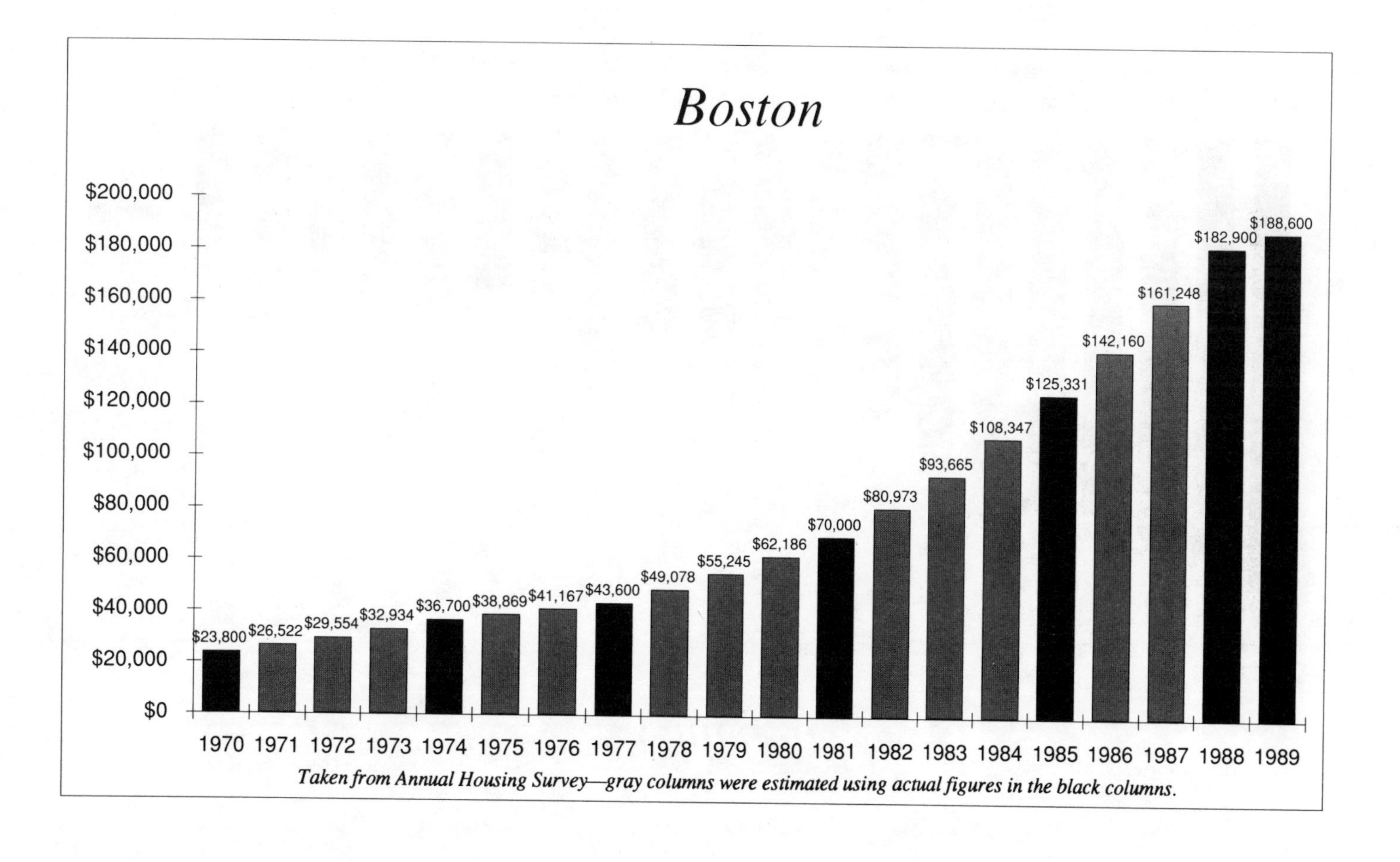

Taken from Annual Housing Survey—gray columns were estimated using actual figures in the black columns.

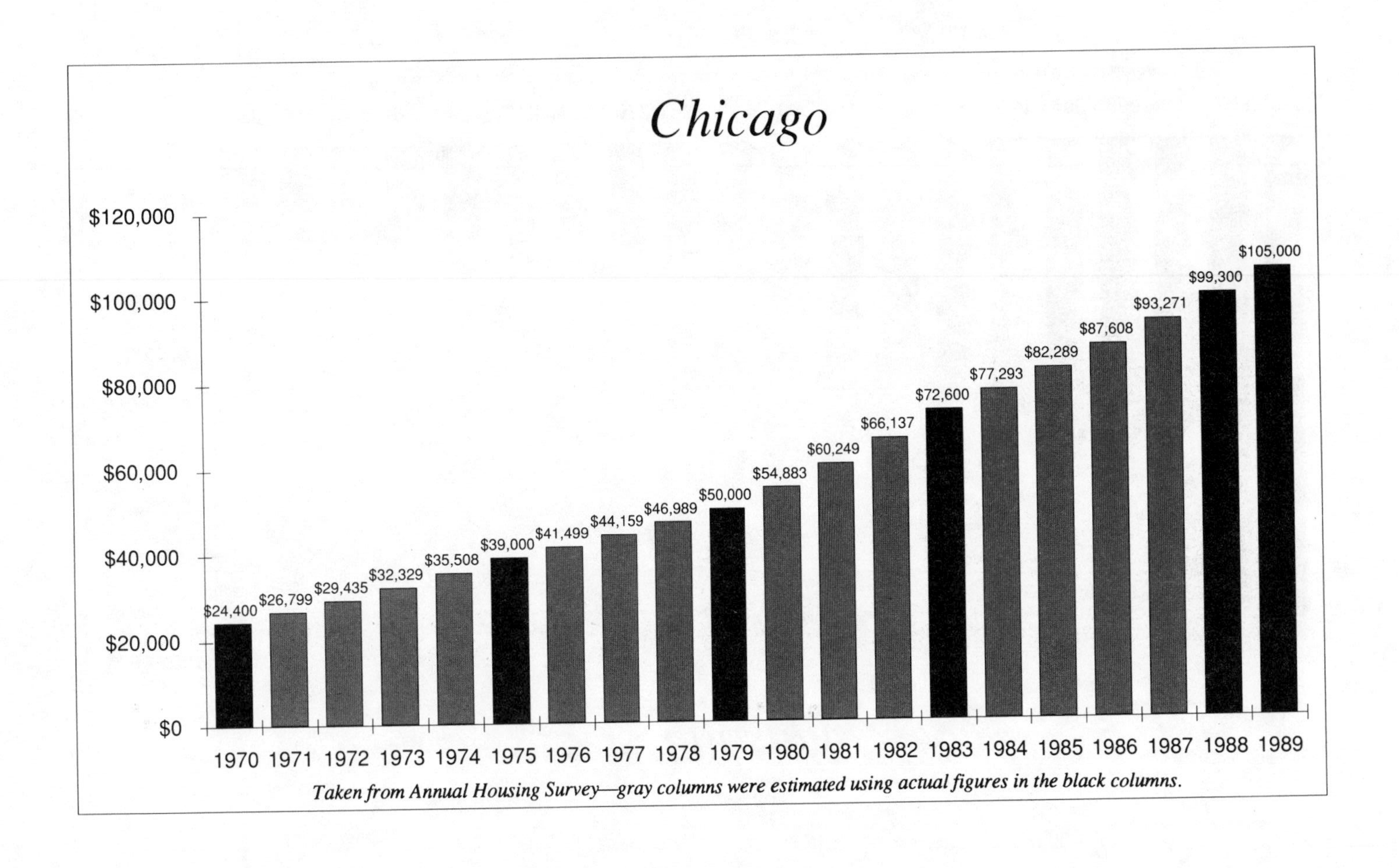

Taken from Annual Housing Survey—gray columns were estimated using actual figures in the black columns.

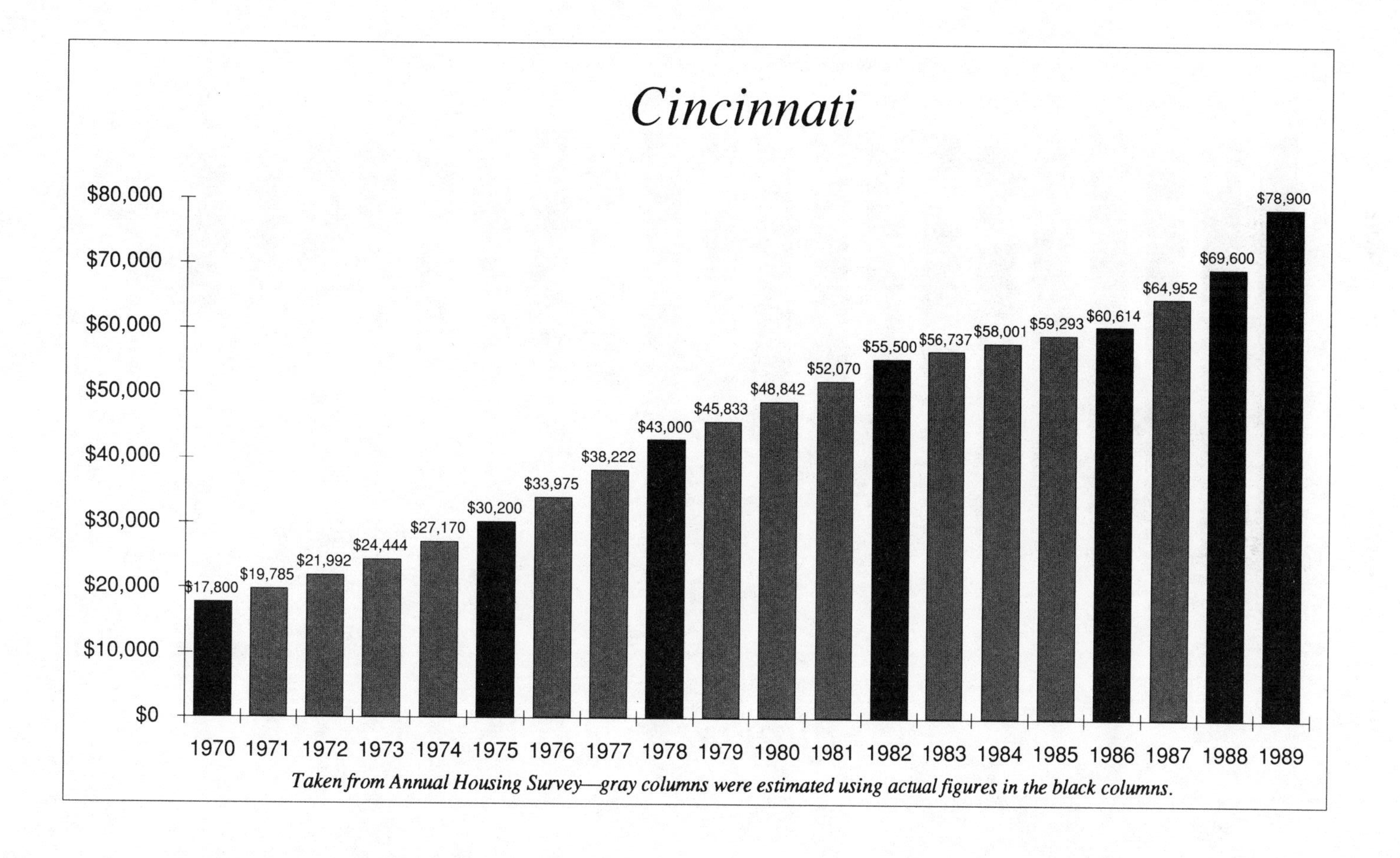

Taken from Annual Housing Survey—gray columns were estimated using actual figures in the black columns.

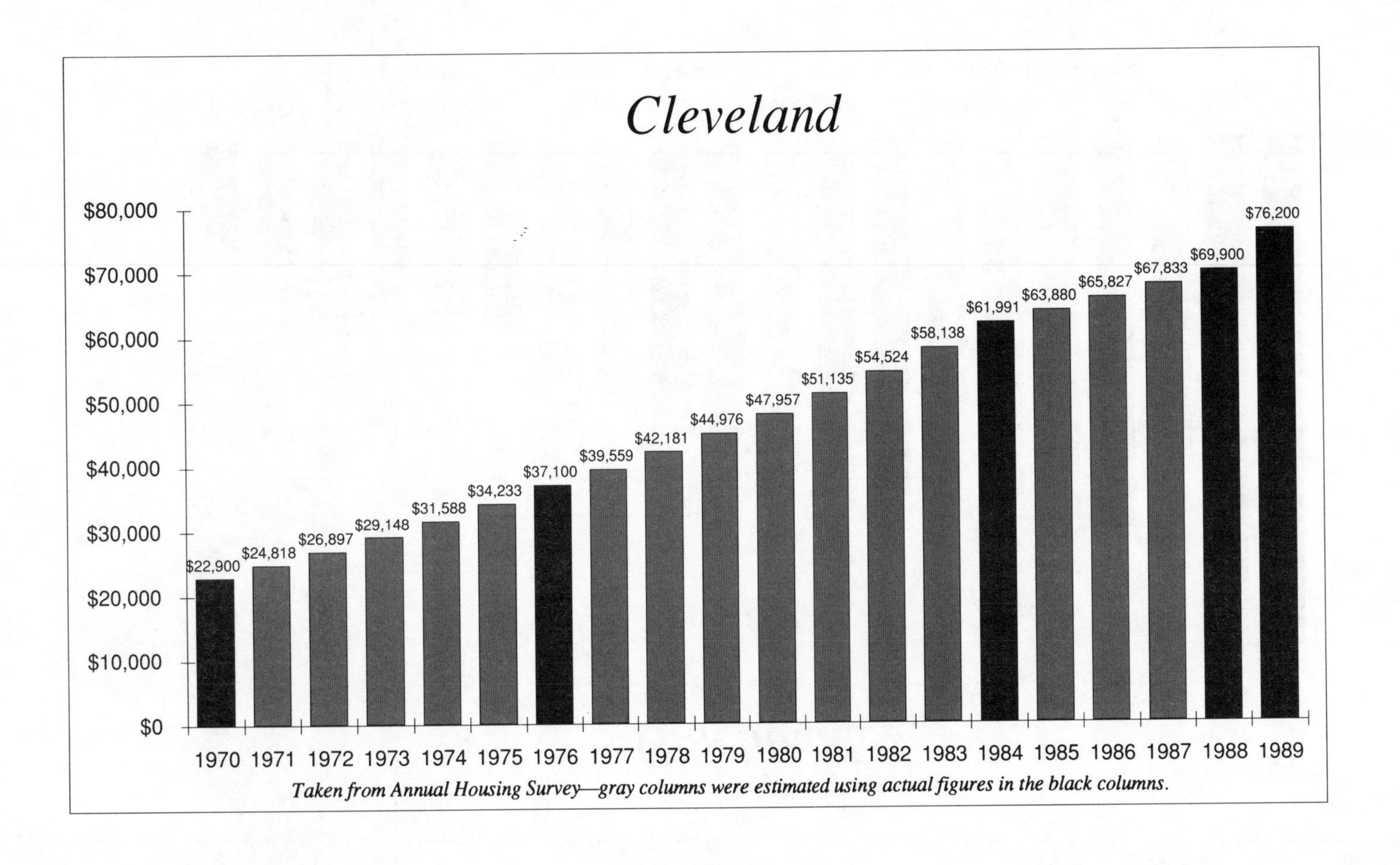

Taken from Annual Housing Survey—gray columns were estimated using actual figures in the black columns.

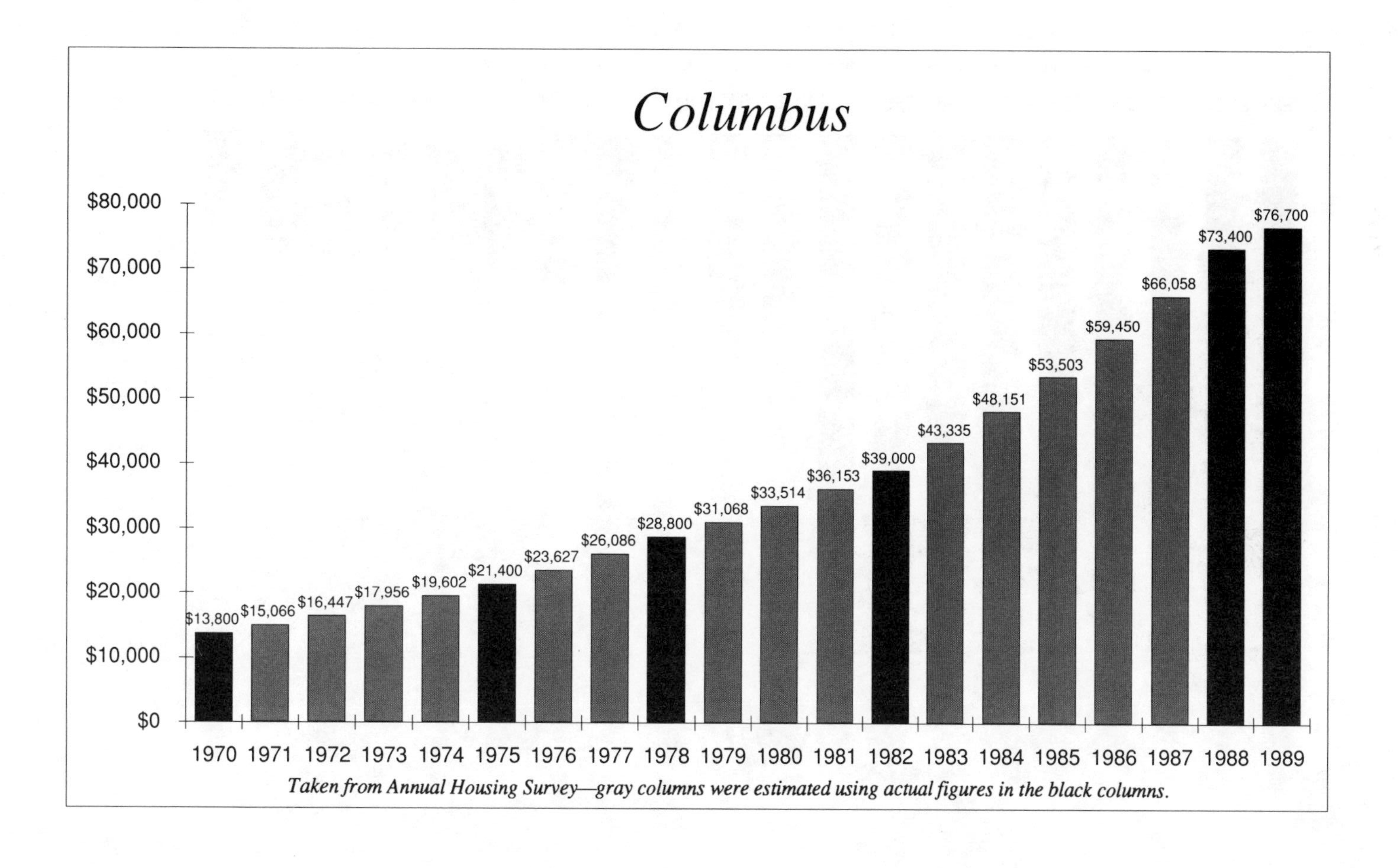

Taken from Annual Housing Survey—gray columns were estimated using actual figures in the black columns.

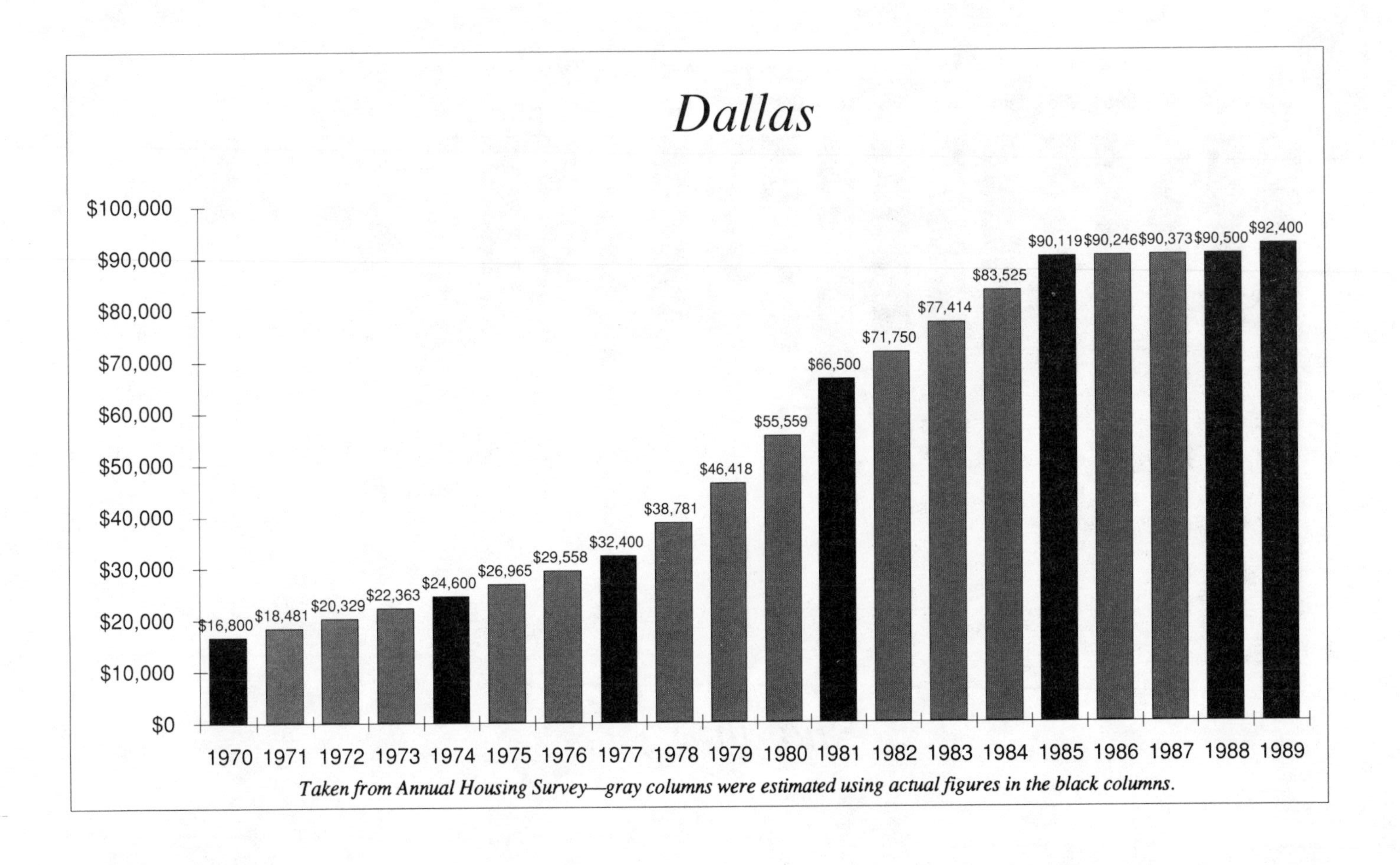

Taken from Annual Housing Survey—gray columns were estimated using actual figures in the black columns.

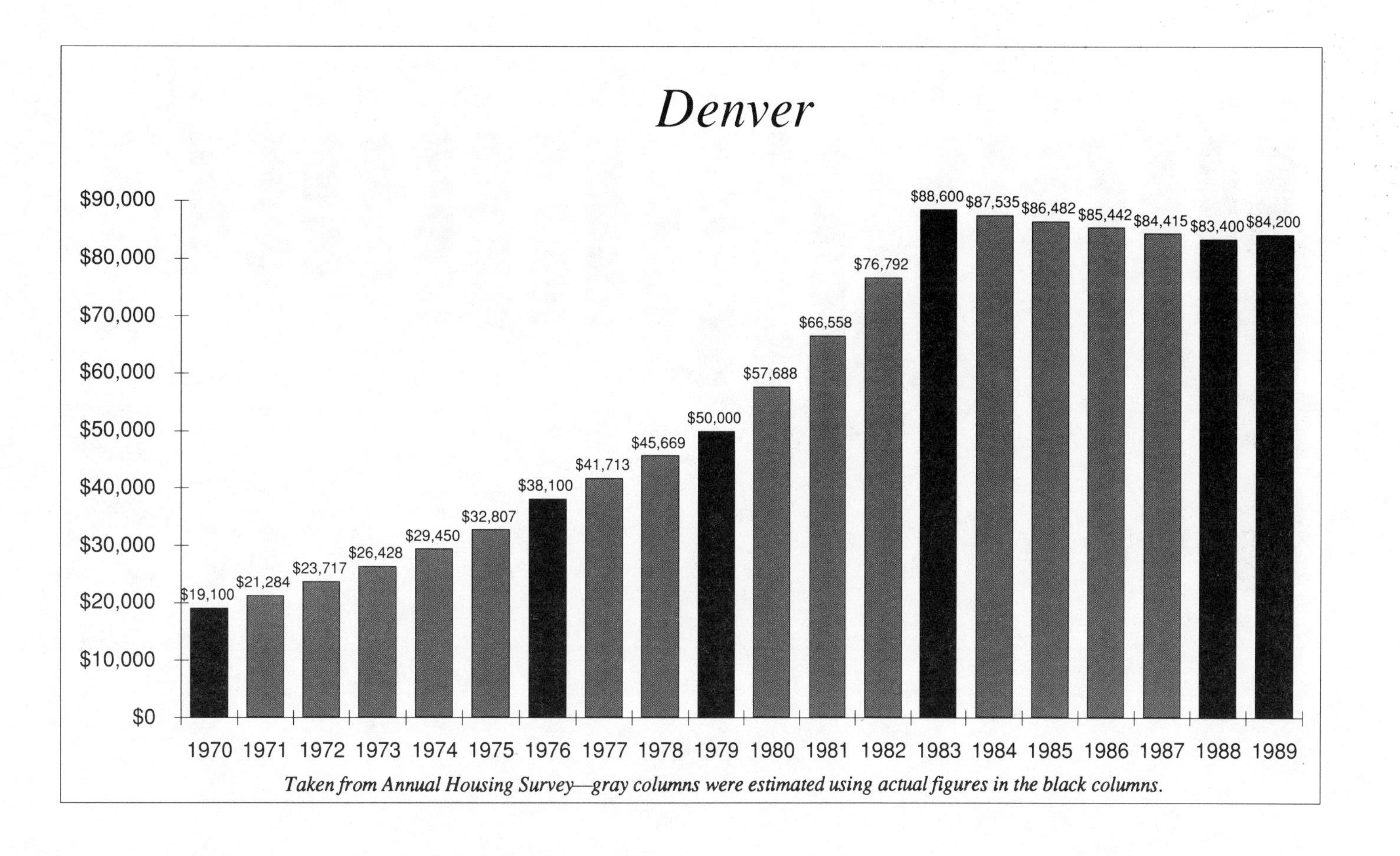

Taken from Annual Housing Survey—gray columns were estimated using actual figures in the black columns.

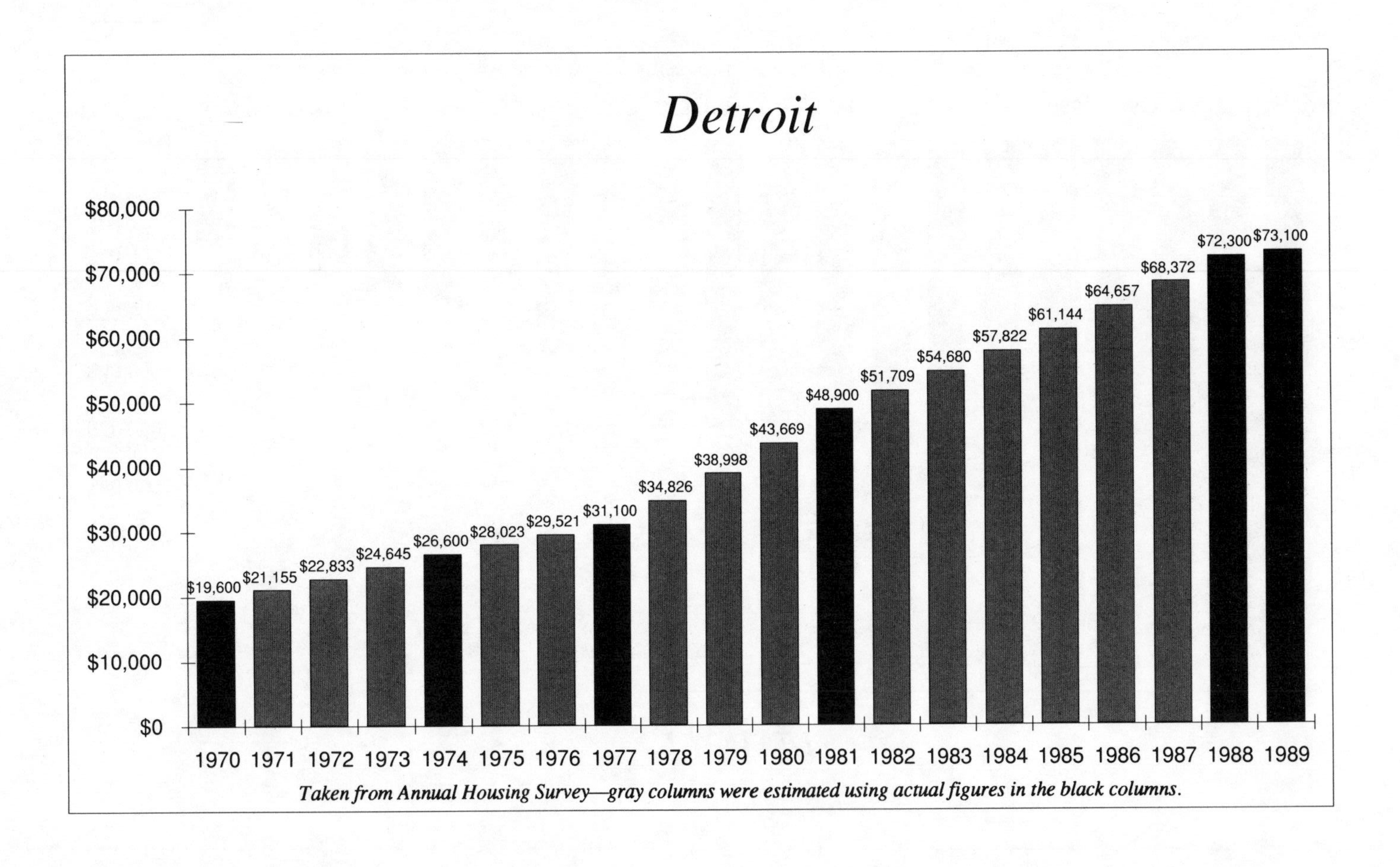

Taken from Annual Housing Survey—gray columns were estimated using actual figures in the black columns.

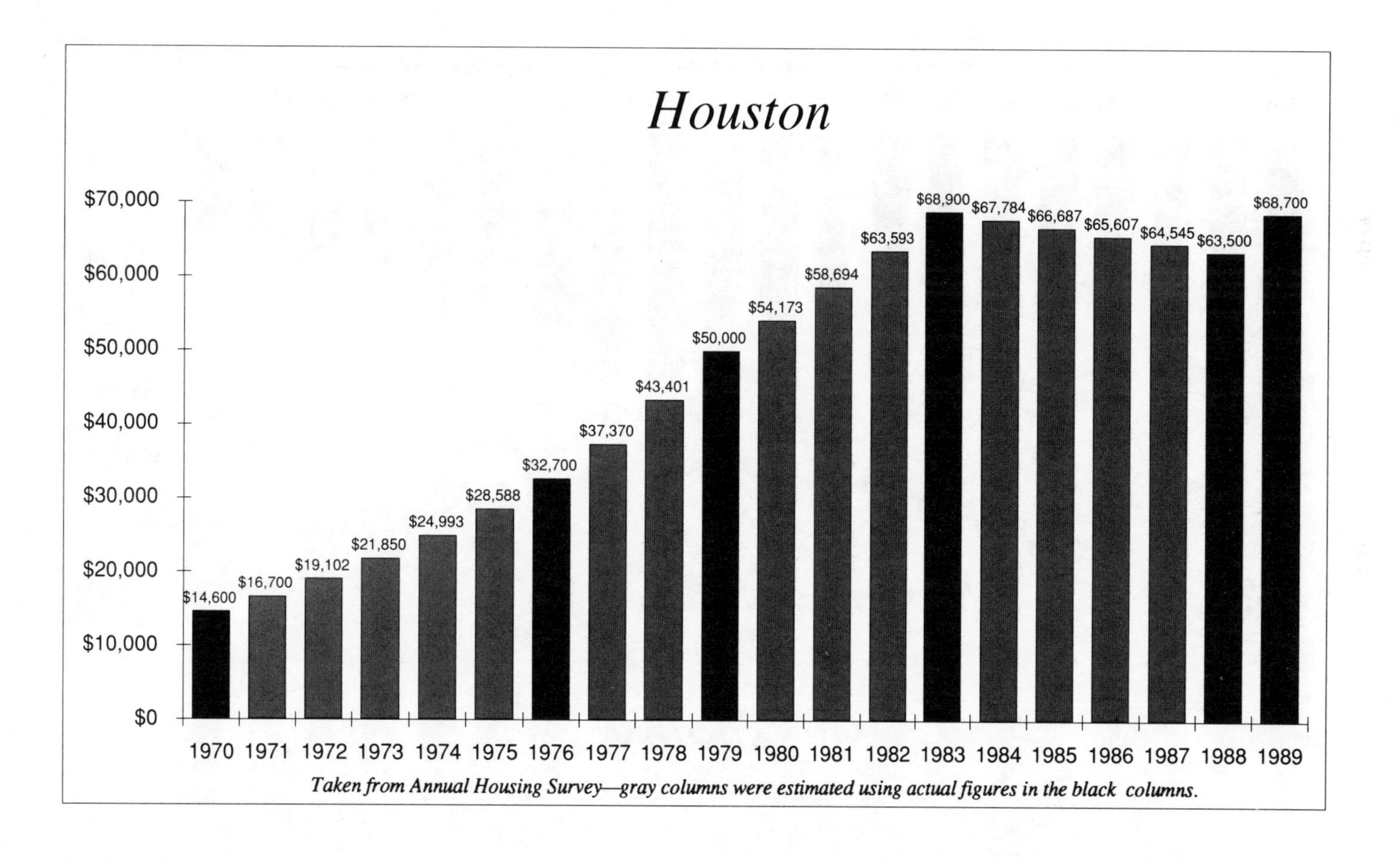

Taken from Annual Housing Survey—gray columns were estimated using actual figures in the black columns.

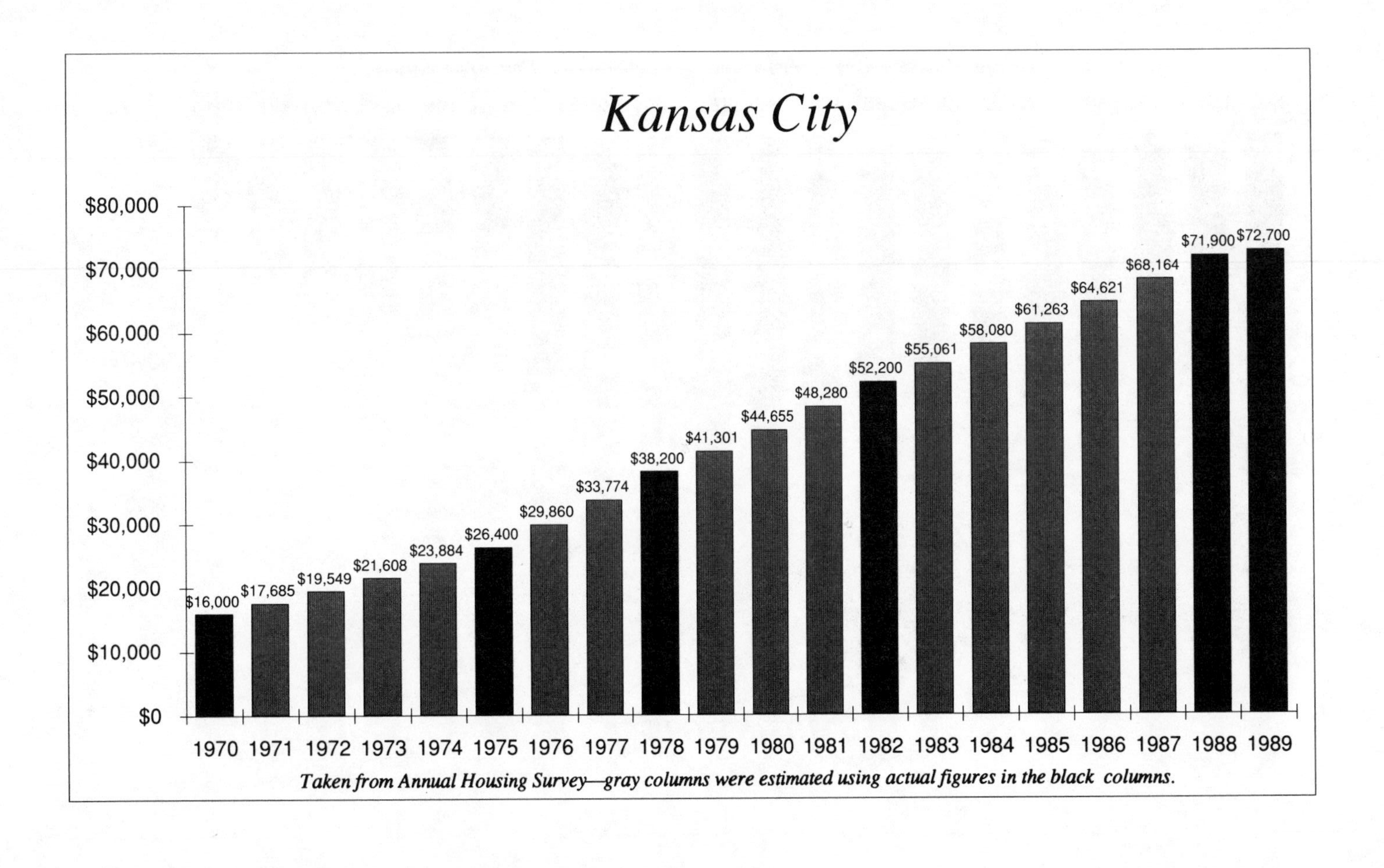

Taken from Annual Housing Survey—gray columns were estimated using actual figures in the black columns.

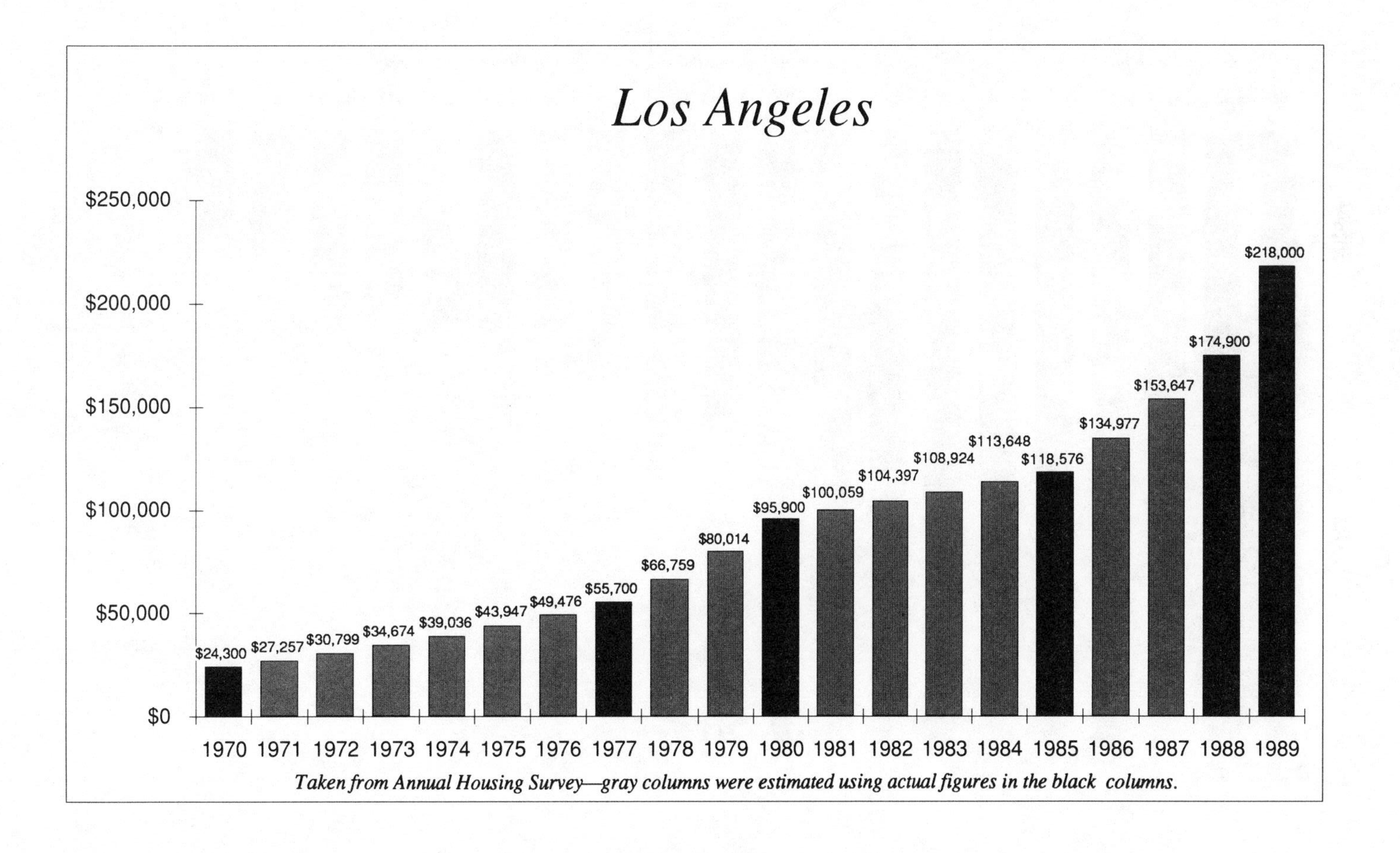

Taken from Annual Housing Survey—gray columns were estimated using actual figures in the black columns.

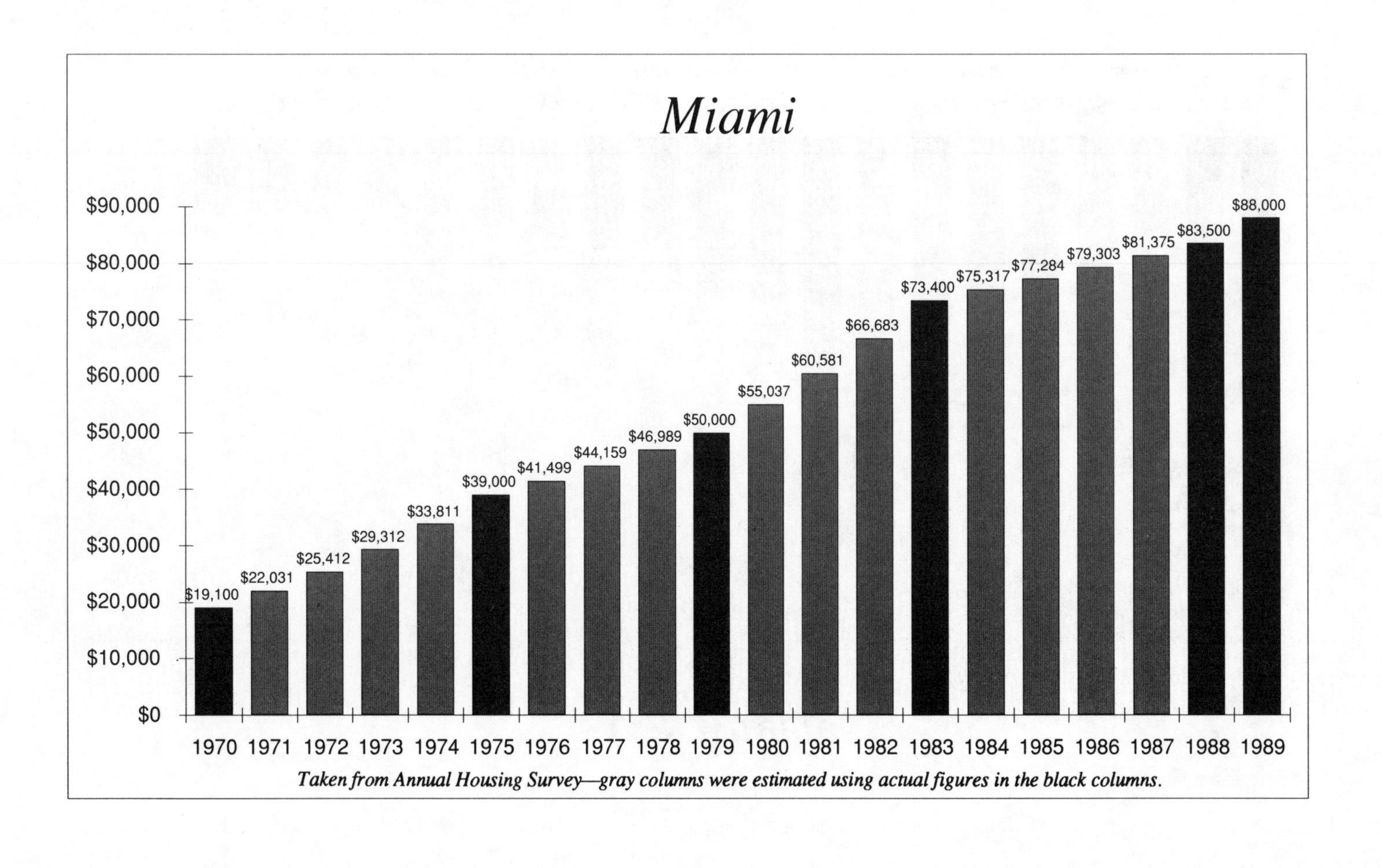

Taken from Annual Housing Survey—gray columns were estimated using actual figures in the black columns.

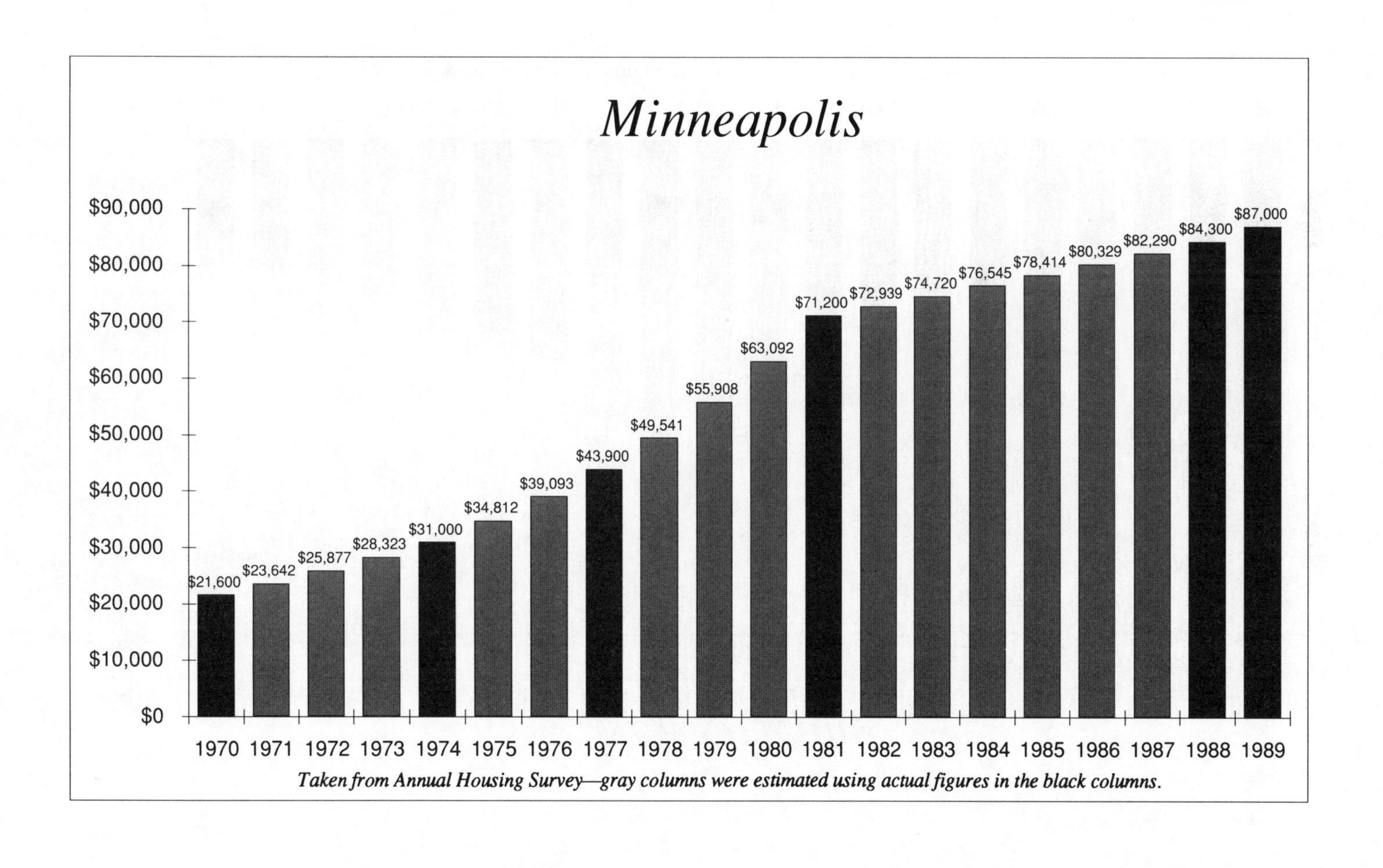

Taken from Annual Housing Survey—gray columns were estimated using actual figures in the black columns.

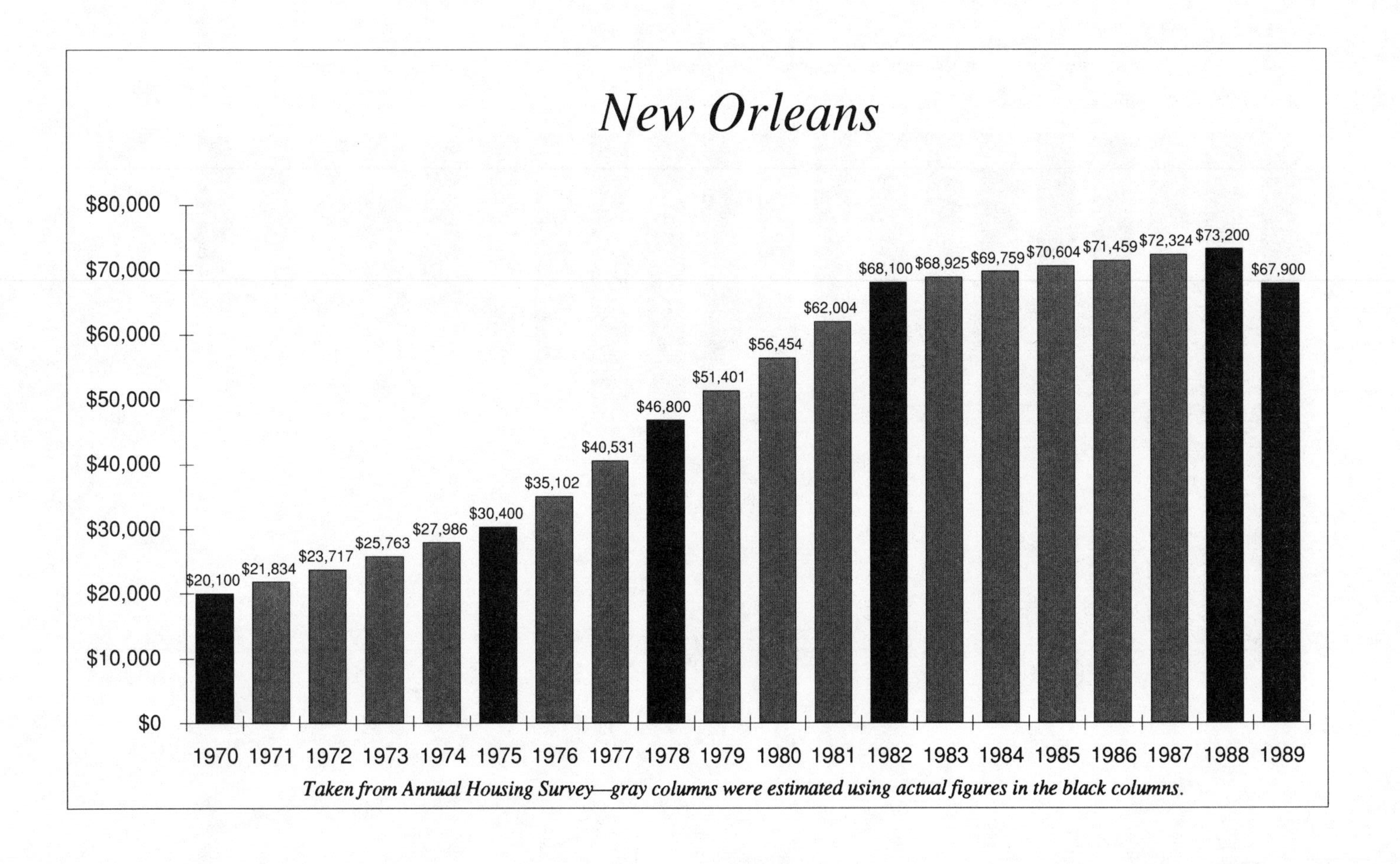
New Orleans
$80,000
$70,000
$60,000
$50,000
$40,000
$30,000
$20,000
$10,000
$0
$20,100
$21,834
$23,717
$25,763
$27,986
$30,400
$35,102
$40,531
$46,800
$51,401
$56,454
$62,004
$68,100
$68,925
$69,759
$70,604
$71,459
$72,324
$73,200
$67,900
1970 1971 1972 1973 1974 1975 1976 1977 1978 1979 1980 1981 1982 1983 1984 1985 1986 1987 1988 1989
Taken from Annual Housing Survey—gray columns were estimated using actual figures in the black columns.

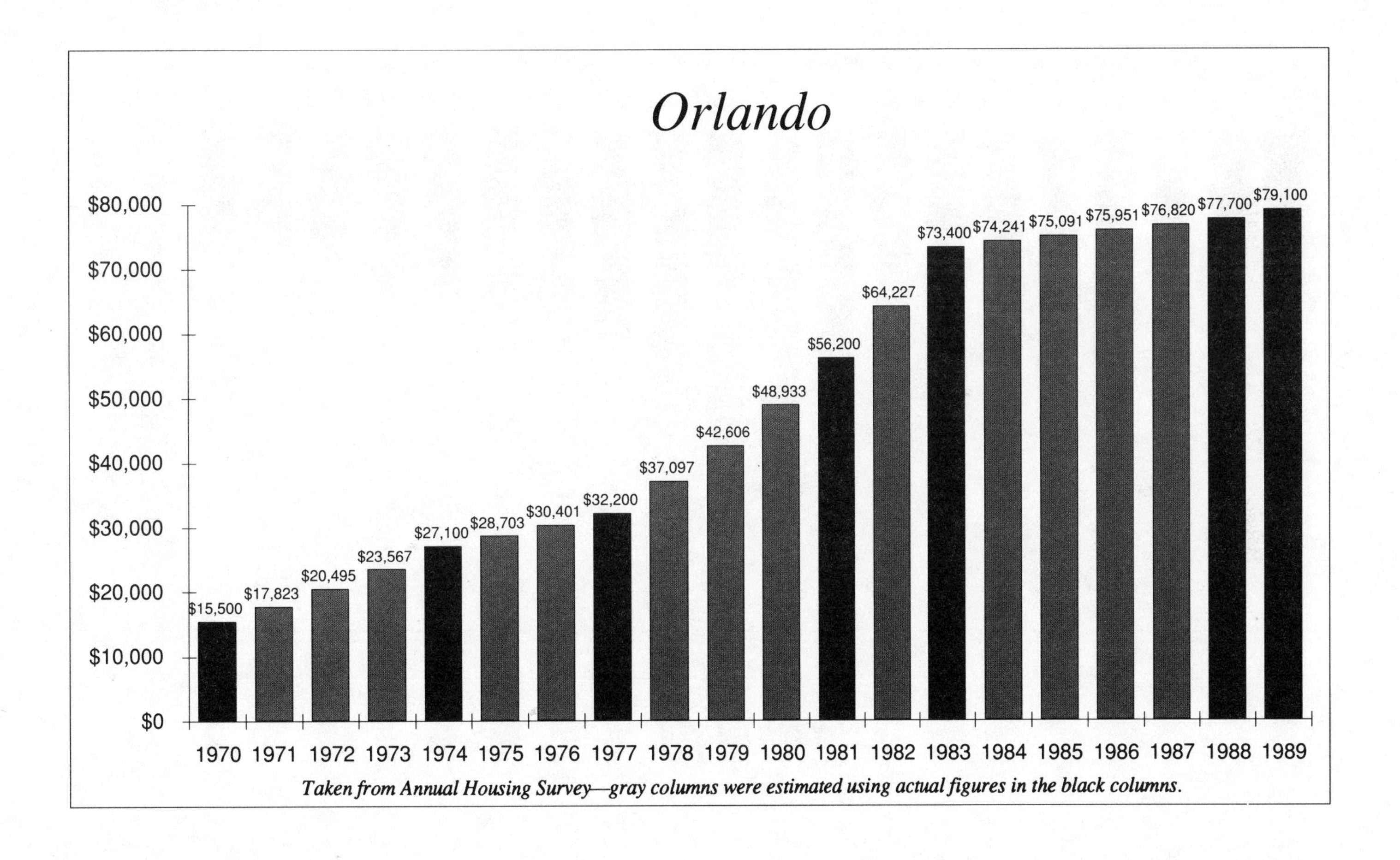

Taken from Annual Housing Survey—gray columns were estimated using actual figures in the black columns.

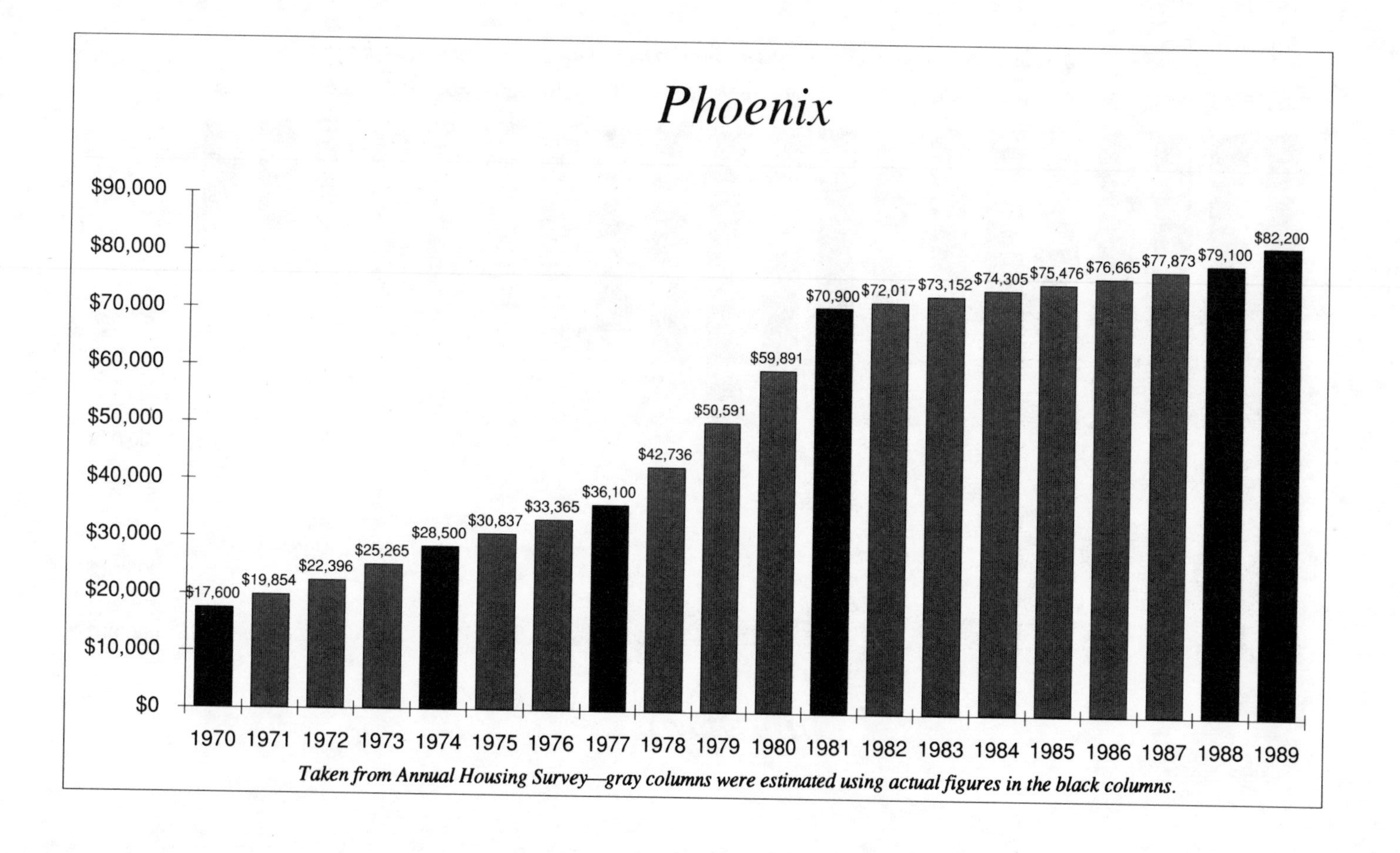

Taken from Annual Housing Survey—gray columns were estimated using actual figures in the black columns.

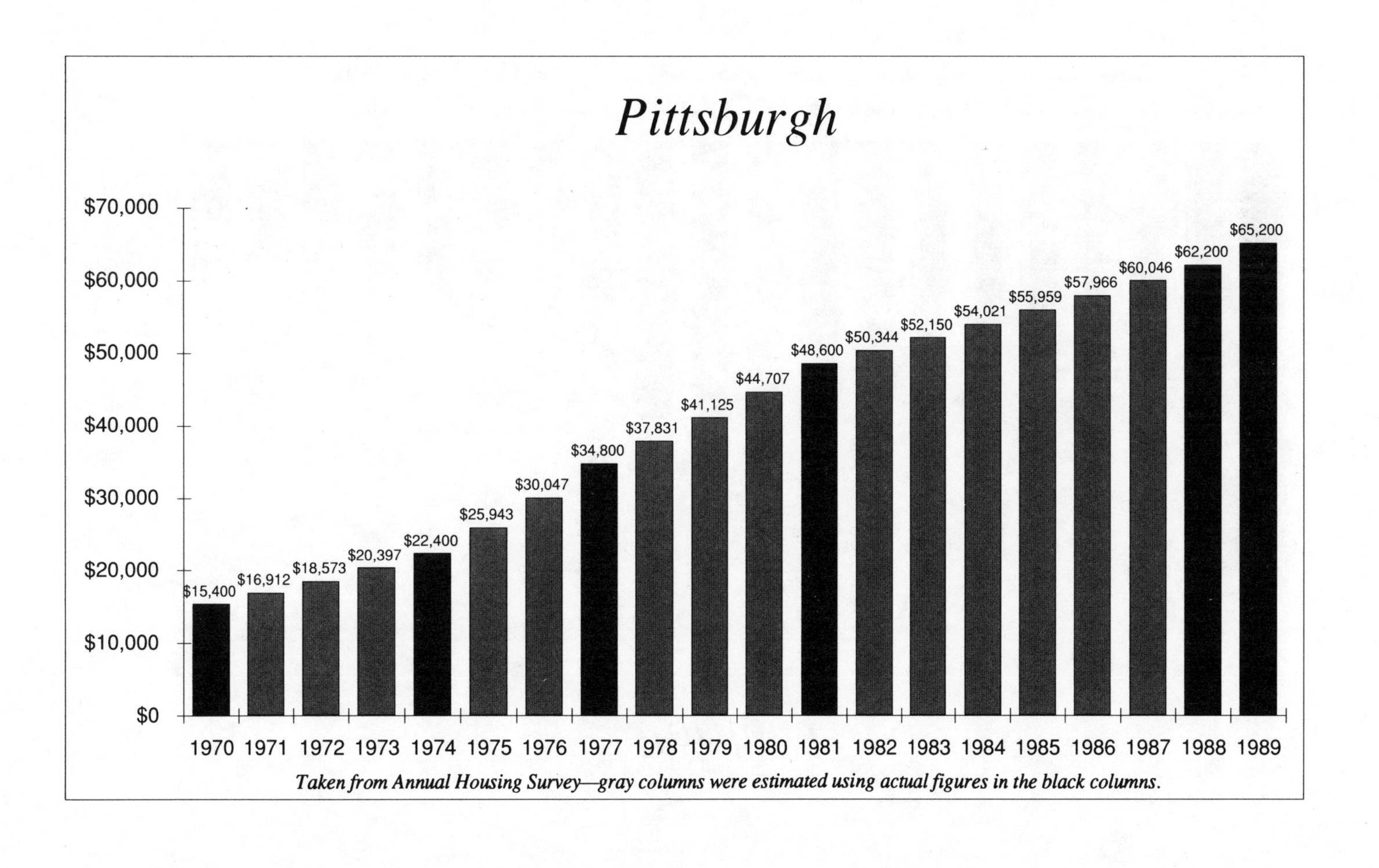

Taken from Annual Housing Survey—gray columns were estimated using actual figures in the black columns.

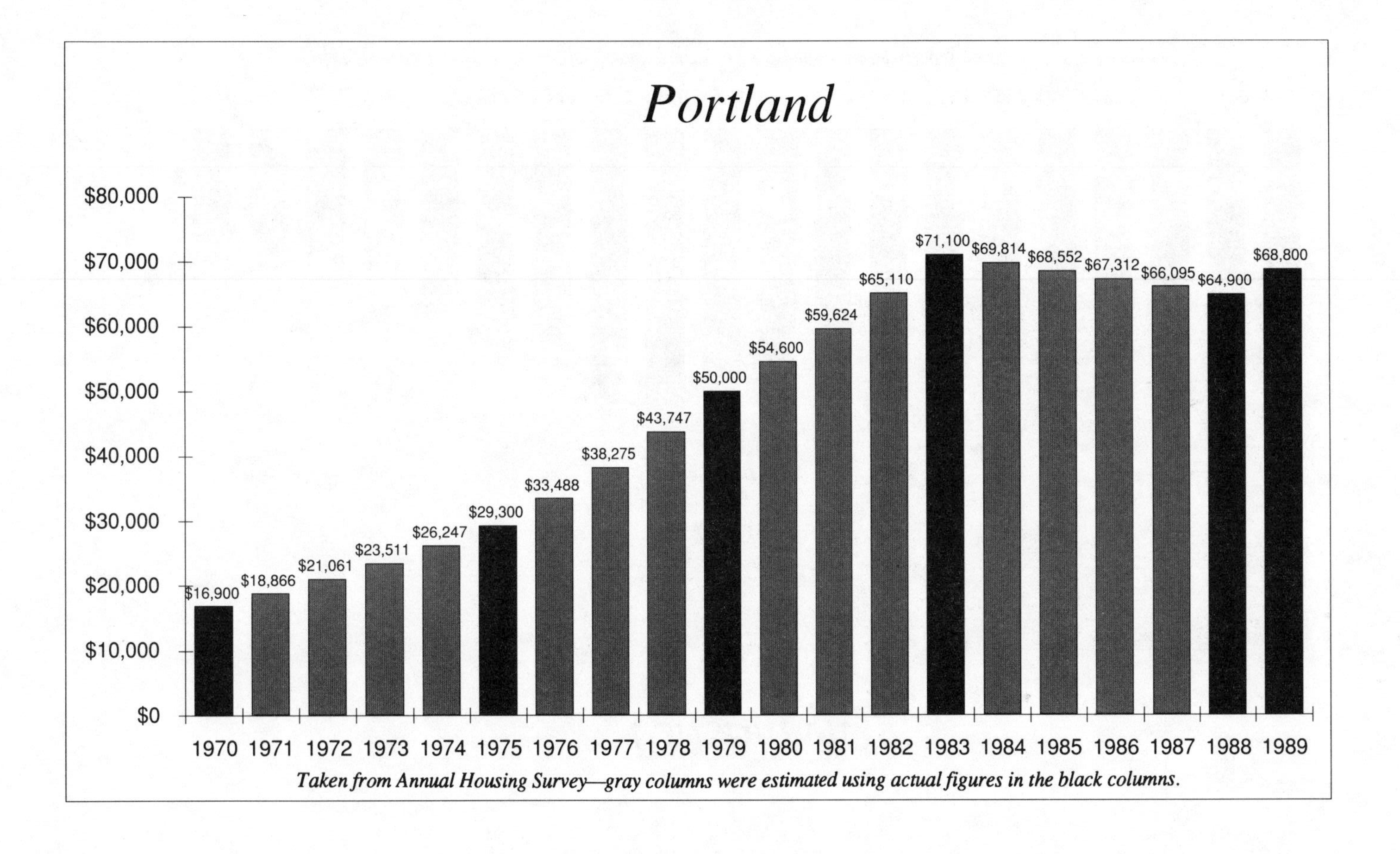

Taken from Annual Housing Survey—gray columns were estimated using actual figures in the black columns.

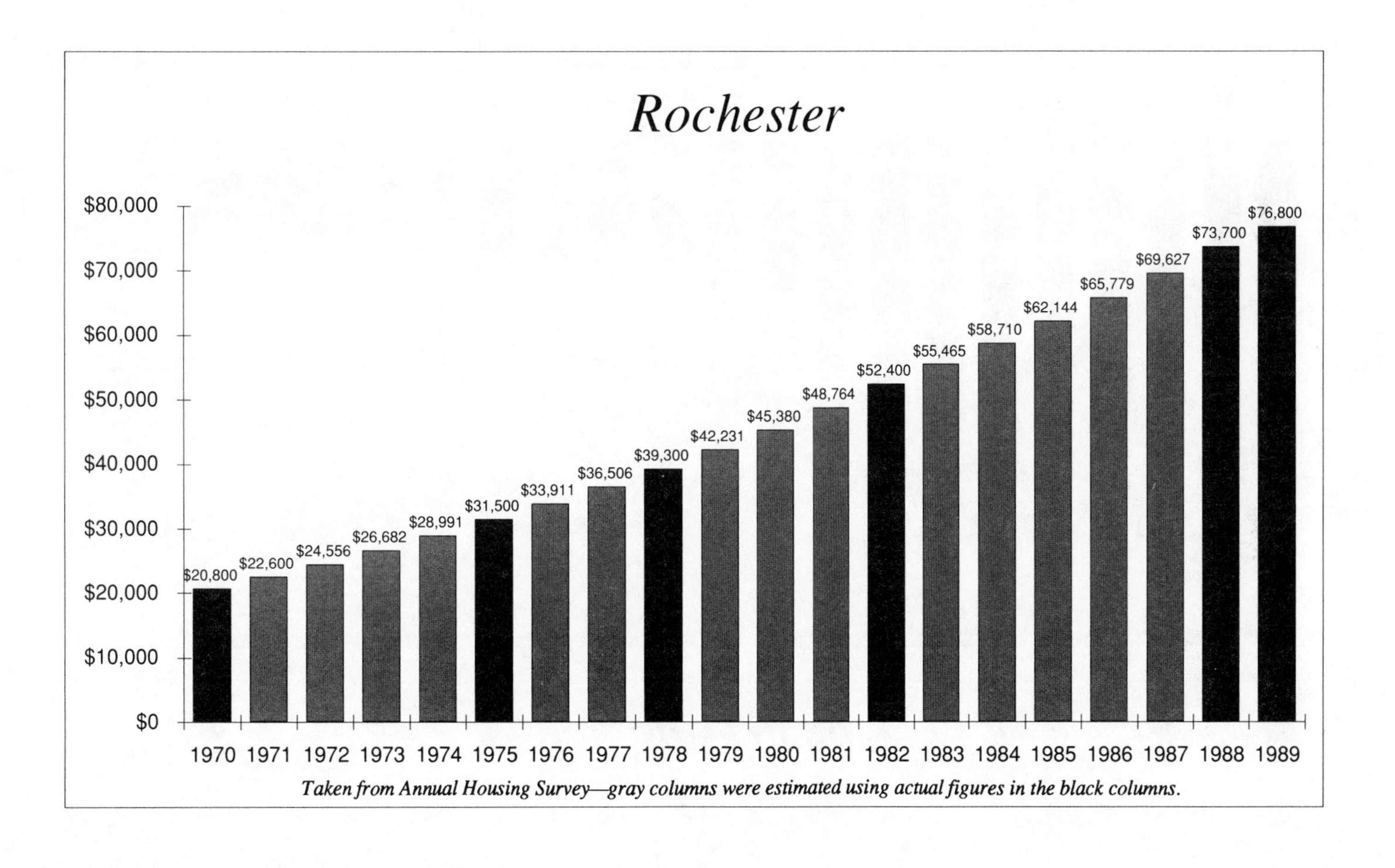

Taken from Annual Housing Survey—gray columns were estimated using actual figures in the black columns.

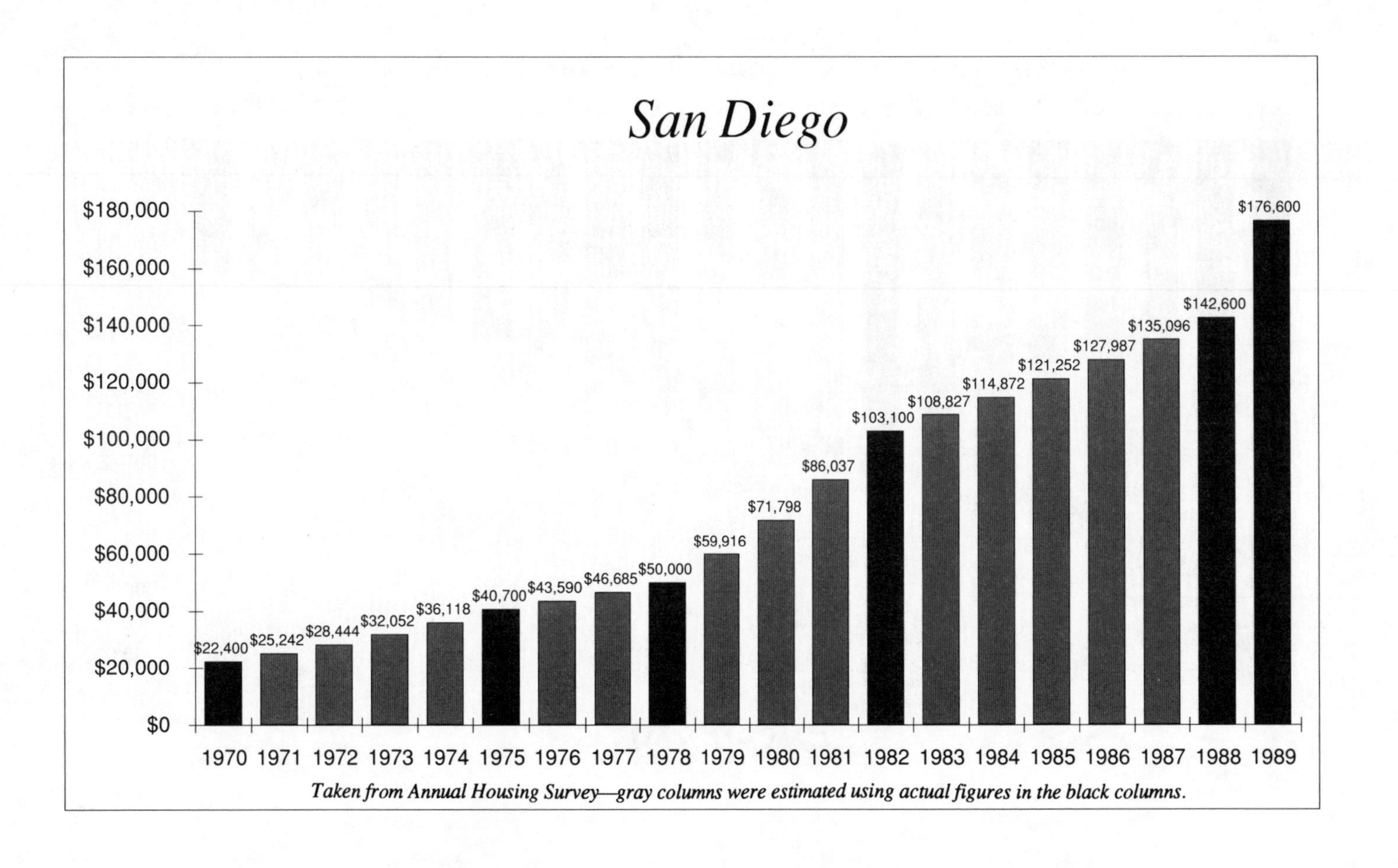

Taken from Annual Housing Survey—gray columns were estimated using actual figures in the black columns.

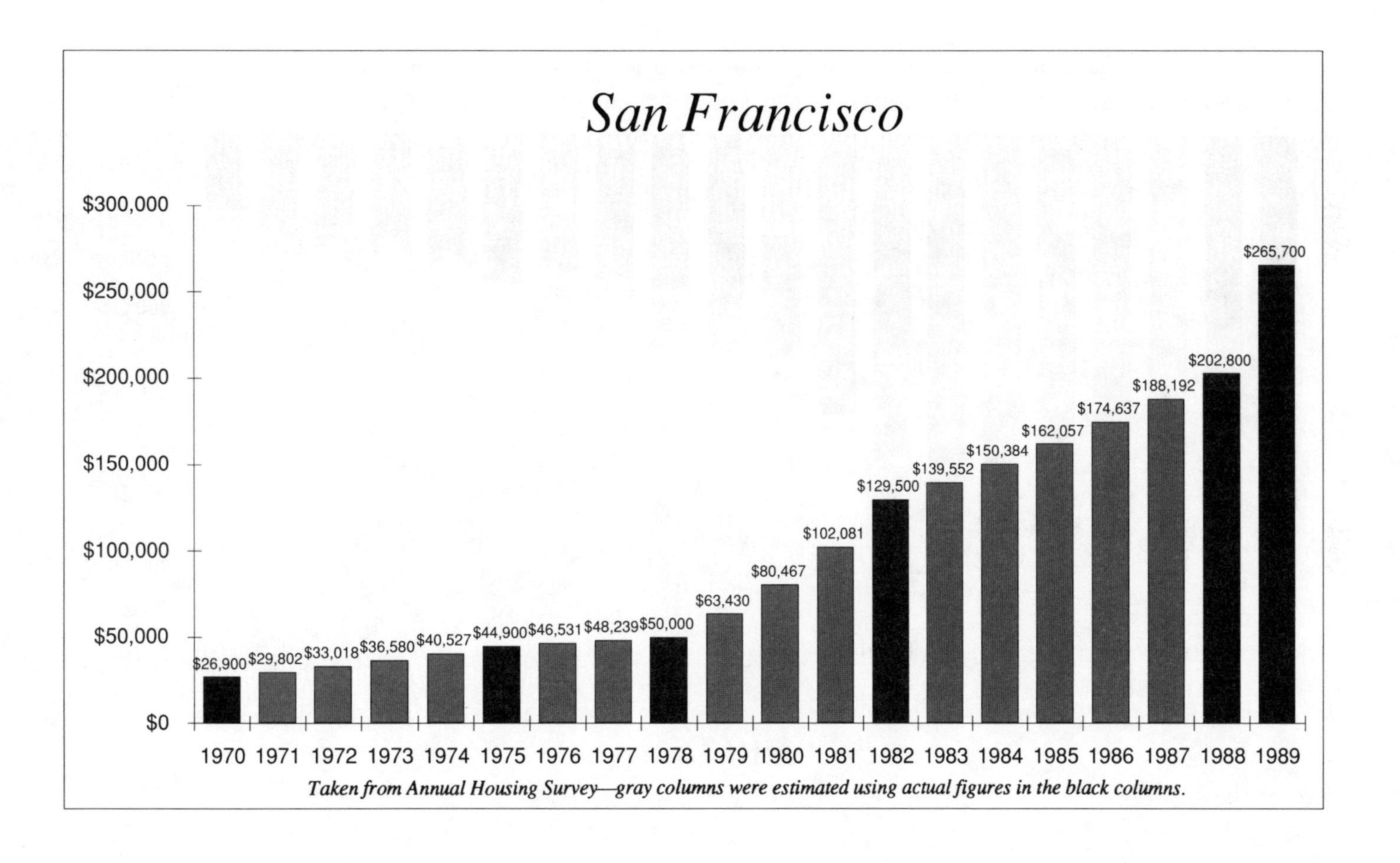

Taken from Annual Housing Survey—gray columns were estimated using actual figures in the black columns.

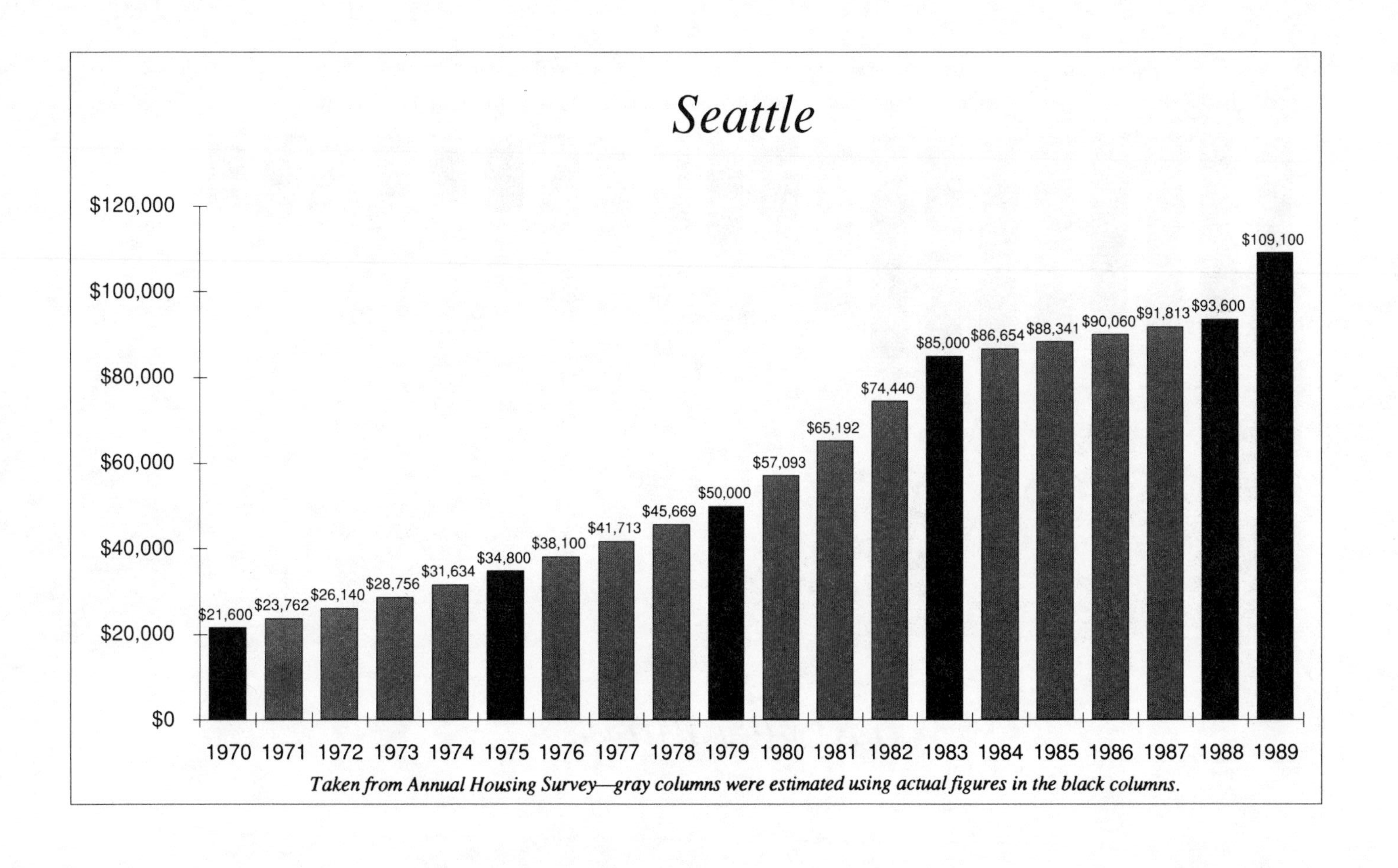

Taken from Annual Housing Survey—gray columns were estimated using actual figures in the black columns.

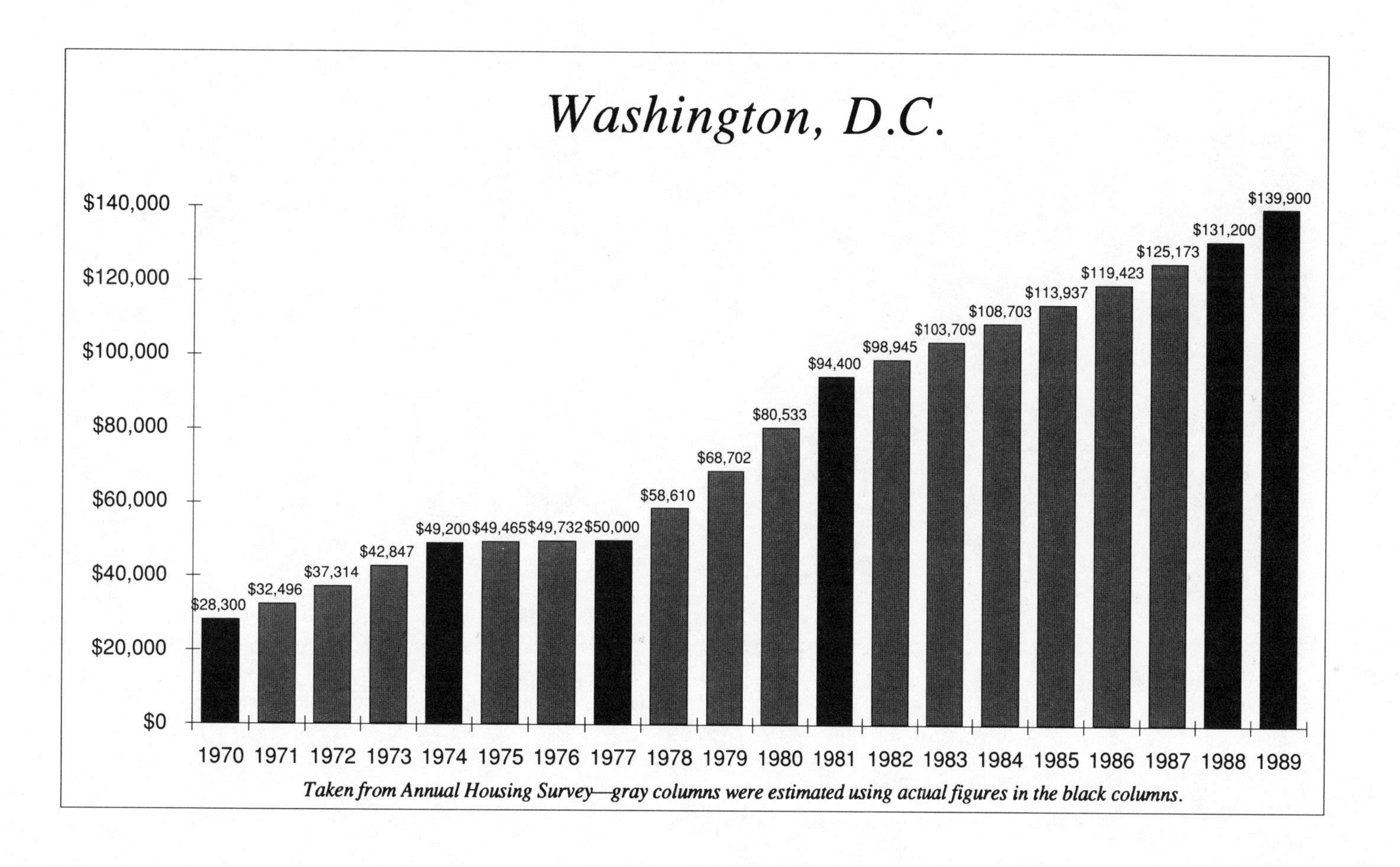

Taken from Annual Housing Survey—gray columns were estimated using actual figures in the black columns.

Index

Index

INDEX